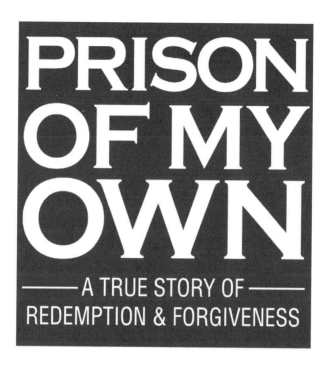

PRISON OF MY OWN

——A TRUE STORY OF——
REDEMPTION & FORGIVENESS

Diane Nichols

 LIFE JOURNEY®
Bringing Home the Message for Life

COOK COMMUNICATIONS MINISTRIES
Colorado Springs, Colorado • Paris, Ontario
KINGSWAY COMMUNICATIONS LTD
Eastbourne, England

Life Journey® is an imprint of
Cook Communications Ministries, Colorado Springs, CO 80918
Cook Communications, Paris, Ontario
Kingsway Communications, Eastbourne, England

PRISON OF MY OWN

This book is based on a true story. To protect identities and for ease of reading, some names have been changed, some characters are composites, and the chronology of some events has been adapted.

Cover design: Jeffrey P. Barnes

First printing, 2005
Printed in the United States of America
Printing/Year
11 10 9 8 7 6 5 4 3 2 / 05 06 07 08 09

Library of Congress Cataloging-in-Publication Data

Nichols, Diane, 1956-
  Prison of my own / by Diane Nichols.
     p. cm.
  ISBN 0-7814-4258-3 (pbk.)
  1. Nichols, Diane, 1956- 2. Christian biography--United States. 3. Prisoners' spouses--United States--Biography. 4. Murder--Religious aspects--Christianity. I. Title.
BR1725.N475A3 2005
277.3'0825'092--dc22

2004031109

To my family,
who loved me enough to make this journey with me
and never let me fall.

And to an awesome God,
who molds us and
shapes us into new creations so that we may
have the miracle of second chances.

Acknowledgments

I have many people to thank for offering their help to us during this difficult time.

First and foremost, my parents, for being our rock through this whole experience. I thank you with all of my heart for the endless love and support you have given us, taking us into your home, always being there with whatever we needed whether it was finances or just a simple hug. Without you, we never would have made it through this.

Sincere thanks to my sister, Denise, for her unwavering support and for being a constant source of inspiration. Your powerful prayers and belief in my family's healing meant more than you could ever know.

I thank my children for being two of the most courageous little women I know. You weathered a very powerful storm, and I'm so very proud of you for being strong enough to forgive so you could heal. Daddy and I love you both more than words can say.

Heartfelt thanks go to John, for his courage to face the monster within himself and dig deep to make a change. It takes a lot of strength to come out with hard truths even if it means losing the ones you love. You took that risk to be a better man, and I'm proud of you for making those changes. The children and I have found strength in your strength, and I know we'll all "go the distance."

To Bobby, I send a loving thank-you for being my dear friend through it all. You were there when we needed you during the roughest of times and helped us to smile and to have hope again. We may not have been the best of marriage partners, but I know in my heart that we'll always be the best of friends. I'll never forget you for all you did for my children and me. You'll be a part of us forever.

I'd like to thank our neighbors in Twinsburg for their help and caring in those early days after John's arrest. The food, hugs, and help with the children were more helpful than I could ever say.

Special thanks to Sergeant Deal of the Twinsburg Police Department, for his compassion and caring above and beyond the call of duty, which I'll remember all of my life.

Many thanks also to the guards in the visitation room at Mansfield Correctional Institution, for their warm hearts. I never expected people who work in a prison to care so much about the inmates or their families, but you have always been so friendly and helpful. You do the extras to make our visit more special like letting Mariah read a book on her daddy's lap and bending the rules to allow us to light a "candle" on John's birthday cupcake. Your compassion toward the prisoners and their families helps us to endure the hard years ahead.

I'd also like to thank Pastor Dwight Edwards and his wife, Mary, for welcoming my children and me into their church, where we found such compassion, warmth, and love from the people there. Your prayers and your caring will always be remembered and helped us tremendously in our healing process.

I couldn't possibly forget to acknowledge the very special woman from Angelique's Bridal and Formal who made my wedding day the fantasy I always dreamed of. Michelle, you are truly a special angel. I'll never forget you for your selfless gift so that I could marry my prince in my Cinderella gown. The world needs more people like you. I thank you with all of my heart.

Special thanks go to my agent, Les Stobbe, for having a heart for this story from the very beginning and believing in it as I did. Also, to Mary McNeil, my editor, for your enthusiasm and encouragement every step of the way as this book went from a manuscript to a prayer come true. In addition, many heartfelt thanks go to the entire staff at Cook Communications Ministries for all your hard work and support in making this happen.

From the bottom of my heart, I'd like to thank Lue Haring for going above and beyond the call of duty in being a good neighbor. You took us into your home when our world fell apart and protected us from the media. You hugged my children, dried our tears, and gave us huge doses of your wonderful positive spirit. You took us to the jail for those hard visits with John and held us together afterward. We'll never forget all you did to help us get through those tough days. We'll always remember you with gratitude and love.

Above all else, my deepest praise goes to God, who saved my life when I was about to give up. He showed me that the only way to break away from my prison of pain was to let go of the past and forgive. Because of him, I'm alive today, and my family has been joined back together. Despite the steel bars that still keep us apart, we are all finally free.

Contents

ONE

A Stranger on Trial

September 1997—Cleveland, Ohio

The double doors to Courtroom A on the fifth floor of the Cuyahoga County Courthouse opened. Mr. Garrett, my ex-husband's attorney, nodded toward me. I stood, smoothing the lines of my navy blue dress rumpled from hours of sitting, waiting, and wondering when I would ever awaken from this nightmare.

Garrett had met me that morning after I arrived in Cleveland from Florida. He took me to a hurried lunch in a café across from the courthouse to review what I was to say on the stand. With only minutes to spare before John's trial was to resume, Garrett gobbled a ham and Swiss on rye and explained my husband's chances. The odds were severely stacked against him. And I was the strength of his entire defense—me, the unsuspecting wife on the other end of Karen Romano's ill-fated phone call. He wanted emotion. It was a non-jury trial, so I only had to win over Judge Strickland, who was known for his compassion. I had to bare my pain, speak from the heart if my children's father was to be spared from a life behind bars. But I entered the hushed courtroom completely devoid of emotion. I took my place in the witness box, where I was sworn in with my left hand on the Bible.

"Do you swear to tell the truth and nothing but the truth, so help you God?"

Truth.... Did I even know the meaning of the word anymore? There had been none in my marriage since John's affair with this girl started two years ago. The man I loved and shared a bed with every night turned our life into a complete lie. My gaze shifted to John as he sat next to his other court-appointed attorney, Mr. Martinez. John had lost so much weight that he looked skeletal. I realized he was wearing the gray suit I'd bought him for Christmas, but it was baggy and hung on him as if he were a young boy in his daddy's clothes. The thirteen months in county jail waiting for trial had changed him. The man I married was handsome and athletic with stunning blue eyes, but in his place sat someone I barely recognized, a gaunt and broken soul who had orchestrated his own destruction. He slumped over, clutching a wadded tissue as he wept.

"Ma'am?" The bailiff waited for an answer.

"I do." All eyes were on me as I settled into the witness box. I could hear the judge writing on a legal pad. I wondered if anyone else had caught the irony of my last two words—the same words that began my marriage fourteen years ago to the man seated in front of me now began the testimony that could save him from life in prison.

Mr. Garrett approached me with a soft smile, trying to put me at ease. "Hello, Diane. Please tell the court your relationship to the defendant."

"I'm John's ex-wife." The words echoed through the microphone in front of me.

"How long were you married to the defendant?"

"Thirteen years."

"And do you have children from this marriage?"

"Yes, two daughters, ages four and eleven."

"What are their names?"

Girls, what I'm going to tell you is very hard to understand. Something terrible has happened, and Daddy won't be coming home. He's okay, though. You don't have to worry about him. But he got in a fight with someone and hurt that person very badly. He has to stay in jail for a very long time, and now it's going to be just the three of us.

I blinked back the memory of our children's bewildered tears. That August day was more than a year ago, yet the sounds, smells, and pictures still played in my head as if it were just yesterday.

"Vanessa is our eleven-year-old, and Mariah just turned four."

"Where did you reside with your husband and the two children?"

Our home was so perfect for us. The neighborhood was full of other young families and many playmates for the girls. We could look out our window and see a deer grazing or squirrels at play in the woods in back. The house was spacious, with a fireplace where John and I used to cuddle and savor our quiet time together. We had the life we'd always dreamed of. He always asked me how he got to be so lucky.

I cleared my throat, shifting in my seat. "Twinsburg, Ohio."

"And how long did you live there before this event took place?"

"A little over two years."

"Do you still live in Twinsburg, Mrs. Nichols?"

"No. After John's arrest, we moved to Florida to be with my family. We lived with my parents for a couple of months, and then they bought us a small house in their neighborhood. They've been a really big help to us."

He waited a beat. "Would you have described your marriage as a happy one, Mrs. Nichols? Can you give the court an idea of the sort of husband John was?"

The room fell silent. I didn't want to answer that question. How could I describe the perfect love we shared, when that same man was on trial for the murder of his mistress?

"He was all I ever wanted in a husband. He was my best friend. My soul mate. My lover. Our marriage grew better with every year instead of going stale like so many do. We had something very rare and special. We were as close as two people could be." I realized how pitiful I must have sounded and dropped my gaze to my lap.

"And was he a good father to your two daughters?"

I nodded. "He was their world. There was nothing he wouldn't do for them. He was the first to diaper both of our babies, he walked the floor with me during the early morning feedings, he played with them, took care of them whenever they got sick, went to school functions, and always made time to simply hug them and say he loved them. He was the best father I could have ever imagined."

Garrett paused to examine his notes. A clock ticked loudly from the far wall. I didn't know where to look, so I focused on the marble floor, wishing my testimony was over. He slowly walked back and impaled me with a dark, somber gaze. It was time to leave happy days behind.

"When did you first hear the name Karen Romano?"

I could still see the headline of *The Plain Dealer* on the morning after the shooting:

Wal-Mart Manager Murders His Secret Lover

A suffocating sensation made it hard to find my voice as I forced out my answer. "The newspaper story that came out the next day. That was the first time I ever knew her full name."

"Tell the court how the woman you came to know as Karen Romano devastated your life."

The prosecutor jumped to his feet as if he had suddenly been jabbed by a pin. "Objection, Your Honor! Leading the witness."

Garrett drew a breath of annoyance. "I'll rephrase it. Did you ever have any encounters with this young lady named Karen Romano?"

"Young" was an understatement. Her obituary said she was only nineteen. John was old enough to be the girl's father. How could he have had sex with her? I swallowed the acid taste in my mouth.

"Yes. She used to make prank phone calls to my home. She tormented me that way for many months."

"Describe these calls for us, if you can."

Who is this? Why do you keep calling me? Why don't you say anything? I know you're there … I can hear you breathing. What is it that you want with me?

My hands, hidden from sight, twisted nervously in my lap as I traveled back in time.

John had been hired as assistant manager of the Brooklyn Wal-Mart, where he had the promise of a bright career. It meant long hours and having him away from us most evenings and weekends, but in exchange for his hard work and dedication, he could climb the ladder and make district management level. It was the brass ring that he had always had his eye on.

Three months later, the calls began to come. Nothing was said, but I could sense someone on the other end—toying, breathing, listening. I'd hang up each time thinking the prankster would get bored and stop. Instead, the frequency of the calls increased, sometimes two or three times a day. I told John about them, but unfortunately, no calls ever came when he was at home. I would beg the caller to tell me what he or she wanted. We finally contacted the phone company and got a caller ID box.

"Hello?" The next call came the following afternoon. After listening to the same empty silence, I anxiously jotted down the number displayed on the ID box. Without waiting, I hung up and immediately dialed the number. The phone rang once. Twice. Finally, someone answered.

"Who is this?" I shouted. "Why have you been calling me?"

The baffled voice of a young man responded. "Calling you? I was just passing by and heard the pay phone ringing, so I picked it up."

"Pay phone? This is a pay phone?"

"Yeah."

"Where is it? Tell me where."

"Wal-Mart."

The room swayed as I caught my breath. "Wal-Mart? This is a pay phone inside a Wal-Mart store? Which one? Where is the store located?"

"Brooklyn. Just south of Cleveland on Ridge Road." He waited several seconds for a response, but I was too stunned to give one. "Lady? You still there?"

With a gulp, I nodded. "Yeah. Just one more question. Did

you see anyone using that phone before you happened to be walking past it?"

"Nobody was here. I was just passing by and heard it ringing, so I answered it. I really can't tell you anything more."

I thanked him and hung up, one step closer but still miserably lost. I had no clue as to who was making the calls or why, but at least now I knew where the last one had come from—the store where my husband worked.

"It's got to be one of my employees playing a dumb joke," John surmised that evening when I told him. "He must have somehow got my phone number from the office file and is getting his kicks out of driving you crazy."

"But why?" It didn't feel right. Not so many calls over such a long time. "What could someone possibly get out of it? And now we know that he went so far as to spend a quarter on the last call. Who spends money just to make a prank phone call?"

There were no answers, just two choices: change our number or continue with the ID box. I was a freelance writer for several magazines, in contact with editors and publishers. Changing my number and informing people of the new one would have been a hassle. It would be far easier to continue using the ID box and just nail the sicko who was doing this.

The calls began to feel more like a game of cat and mouse. The phone would ring; I'd answer to the silence, only to find the number of the same pay phone at Wal-Mart displayed on the box. Each time I'd call back, hoping to trap my tormentor, but I was always disappointed when no one picked up.

The game took a turn the day after Christmas. It was getting old now, and my patience had worn a bit thin. I wanted it to stop, and I decided to get aggressive.

"How nice to hear from you," I sarcastically said to the

silence on the other end. "Did you have a good Christmas?" The breathing was rhythmic as I waited for a response. As usual, the caller was too cowardly to give one. "You know, you must be a pathetic person to do something like this for kicks. Don't you have anything better to do with your time? Why not grow up and quit acting like such a psycho? Get a life and leave me alone!"

I slammed the phone down, hoping the children hadn't heard me as they played in the other room. I battled to calm myself, when the phone rang again. It was a sound that was beginning to drive me mad.

"Hello," I shouted, expecting silence in return. Instead, the caller spoke.

"Who are you calling a psycho?" The voice was female, small and childlike, with just a tinge of evil. Nothing like the monster I always pictured on the other end.

"So, you have a voice. How refreshing. Why don't you tell me what your problem is. Don't you have something better to do than call my house?"

She waited. Her breathing seemed to get louder. "I'm sleeping with your husband. We've been having an affair for a long time now."

I burst out laughing. This girl was trying, but batting zero. My husband and I had the kind of marriage most people only dreamed of. Leaving love notes for each other after thirteen years wasn't a sign of an unhappy union.

"Sure, honey," I spat in response. "Let's see … my husband works sixty hours a week. He seems a little busy to have all this time for an affair. Can't you do better than that?"

There was another pause. I could hear her moving, maybe switching the phone to her other hand. "Oh, he's busy all right." Her giggle oozed venom. "He's very, very busy."

The click severed our connection long before I was ready. Who was this girl? Why was she doing this? What did she get out of it anyway? I dialed the number back as my fingers began to tremble. *Pick up ... pick up ... please be there and just pick up the stupid phone....* I sank into the nearest chair in an exhausted heap as the ringing went on and on.

Mr. Garrett stood next to the witness box, facing the crowded courtroom. I found it hard to breathe. It seemed like an eternity since I'd left the hotel that morning. John's sobs had slowed, but he still kept his head down as if too humiliated to look up. I was relieved. I didn't want to see his eyes, since they were what made me fall in love with him in the first place. Never before had I seen such an awesome shade of blue.

"Did you believe her at this point?" Garrett asked. He shoved his hands into his trouser pockets and paced slowly.

"No. Not at all."

"Why not? Don't a lot of men cheat on their wives? Couldn't it have been something you would have at least considered?"

"No," I repeated. "Not as much in love as John and I were. It was an impossible notion."

"I see," he said, going back to his notes. John briefly lifted his head to swipe his nose with a tissue. "What was John's reaction when you told him of the garbage this girl was telling you? Did he deny having an affair with your caller?"

Again, the prosecution awakened and shouted an objection. Referring to what the girl said as "garbage" was misleading. Garrett stood corrected and politely changed his wording. He wanted nothing to destroy the delicate foundation he was laying.

I tried to appear calm and crossed my legs. Perspiration trickled down my sides. "John was angry when I told him. He said it was a cruel stunt to play, and he wanted to know which one of his employees was doing it. He swore to catch her and see that she was fired. He seemed as unsettled as I was."

"So, he gave no hint that he knew who it was? He was as baffled as you were?"

"That's right."

"And the kind of marriage you had with your husband was trusting, loving, and very sound? You had no reason to disbelieve him?"

"No ... no, I didn't."

"What happened then? Take us to the next call."

I remembered the night perfectly. I had just put the children to bed and was in my office working on a story. John wasn't due home until after midnight, so I thought it might be him. He often called once he knew the kids were in bed just to tell me he loved me.

Her voice startled me. "I'm having an affair with your husband."

I sat back from my computer, astonished that she'd call at this late hour. The house was dark and quiet except for the small light on my desk. Maybe it was the darkness that made her sound especially chilling, but I was frightened—almost as if I knew this was no longer a harmless joke.

"Look," I said in a steady tone, "just tell me what you want. I'm not buying your story, so give it a rest. John and I are very happy."

"I know."

"You do, huh?"

"I know a lot. He tells me everything."

I grew uneasy. It was too late at night. It felt like she and I were alone in the world. I wanted to see her. Have a face to put with the voice. Make myself believe that this madness was real.

"I still don't buy it. If all this is true, you'll have to give me some kind of proof. You should have something to back it up, but since you don't, I guess you're just some bored, jealous girl who has no love of her own, so you're trying to sabotage mine."

A stillness followed. I thought at first she would hang up since I had called her bluff and put the ball back in her court. She had no proof. All she had were empty words.

"I can get your proof," she finally replied, her tone edged with anger. "The next time I call, I'll tell you exactly where and when you can find us together. You'll see then that I'm telling the truth." The line suddenly clicked, and she was gone.

"And did she call back to let you know where you could find them together?"

Garrett took careful steps in front of the witness box. His expression was stiffly solemn.

"No. She didn't call back. The calls stopped for several weeks."

"And how did that make you feel?"

I shrugged. "Relieved somewhat, but still disturbed. I had the nagging feeling that I hadn't heard the last of her."

"And how did John feel about the way these calls were going? Did you tell him about the proof she claimed she would get? That she would let you know when and where to catch them together?"

"Yes, I told him. It boiled his blood that it had gotten that far. He kept vowing to find out who was behind it and make sure she lost her job."

"Did John go away on a business trip soon after that?"

"Yes. To Pittsburgh. It was a five-day seminar for Wal-Mart managers at their distribution center."

"And did you and the children join him on this trip?"

"No. It was just for the managers."

"And while he was gone on this business trip to Pittsburgh for five days, did you receive any calls from this young girl?"

"No. None at all. Things were very quiet."

He surveyed the room, letting my answer sink in. "Then there was a lull in the storm, so to speak. Now, take us to the next time you got a call. Wasn't it the call Karen Romano made to your home from Remington College on August thirteenth?"

A damp, clammy sensation feathered my skin. "Yes. She called me that day."

"Set it up for us. What time was it? What were you doing when she called? Tell us what happened from there."

The sweet summer air filled the house that afternoon. All the windows were open, and I could smell the fragrance of freshly mowed grass from the yard next door. It was close to five o'clock, and John was coming home for dinner. The girls and I had made all of his favorites since it had been so long since we had a family dinner together. Mariah stirred the batter for the lemon bars while Vanessa greased the pan. The phone rang, and I broke away from setting the table. I saw John's work number on the caller ID box.

"Hello, sweetheart," I answered. "Are you ready to leave for the day?"

"You bet," he said, sounding quite festive. "I can't wait to come home to my girls. I've just got a quick meeting with the guy from a McDonald's promotion we're doing, and then I'll hit the road. I love you and miss you. I can't wait to spend an evening relaxing with you guys."

The core of my heart melted. "I can't wait, either. Drive carefully, and we'll see you soon."

I hung up and saw Mariah licking both sets of her sticky fingers.

"Is Daddy coming home now?"

I smiled. "He's just about on his way."

Then the phone rang again. I figured it was John and that he had forgotten to tell me something. I didn't even bother to check the ID box. "Will you hurry up and get out of there?" I laughed as I answered. Then my eyes scanned the display screen. It was a number I didn't recognize.

"My name is Karen, and I'm having an affair with your husband."

Shock siphoned blood from my face. Now she had a name. I was too stunned to jot down the number, although I knew it wasn't the usual Wal-Mart pay phone.

"I told you I need proof. I don't believe you."

"Oh, I've got proof," she answered in a cocky tone. "I've got all the proof you can handle."

The list she gave me was endless. Things they did together. Places they went. Movies they saw. Gifts he had given her. But, like a snake preparing to strike, she saved the most lethal hit for last.

"And he took me on that business trip to Pittsburgh. I know everything he packed and even what time he called you from the hotel each evening."

My mouth grew dry as I struggled to swallow. "No ... you couldn't."

She laughed. "He called you and the kids at exactly 8:30 every night. I was right there waiting for him once he hung up."

My mind spiraled, trying to find some reason not to believe her, but to my horror, what she had just said was true. Still, there had to be some explanation. There was no way it could be real. She sensed my desperate skepticism and came back with both barrels loaded.

"He packed a pair of gray dress pants, a pair of brown dress pants, three ivory dress shirts, and silk ties. One he said was a gift from you. He says you have good taste in ties. He also brought his yellow sweats, his jogging shorts, a blue tank top, and his beat-up old Nikes. Should I go on, or are you finally getting the picture?"

By this time, I was crumbling. I felt a searing pain like I had never known before. The pain that comes from learning a truth too horrendous to bear.

"Do you have sex with him?" I already knew her answer.

Her laugh escaped again. "Of course. Lots and lots of sex."

"Where? How? He's always working, and then he comes home to me. How could this possibly be?"

"Oh, we go to my apartment or else get it on in the park across the street. His lunch breaks have been pretty steamy."

It all made sense. That was the one time during John's day that I could never reach him. He claimed his management job was so stressful that he used his lunch hour to walk in the park across the street from the store. That he turned off his pager and left his cell phone behind for that block of time so he could unwind. It fit. How convenient. An hour every day when we were completely out of touch. I felt the urge to vomit.

John squirmed in his chair and swiped more tears from the end of his nose. Mr. Garrett was now standing next to his client with one hand on his shoulder. "Did you wonder why she was telling you all this? Why expose the affair to you at all?"

"Yes. It didn't make sense to me. I asked her if she wanted him—if that was what this was all about. But she said no, she didn't."

"Did you ask her anything else?"

"Yes. I asked if he loved her."

"And what did she say?"

Tears slid from my eyes. "Her exact words were, 'No, he

doesn't love me, he loves you.' Then I asked what he was doing with her then. What kind of love was that? She never gave me an answer."

"What came next in the conversation?"

"I was absorbing so much. Even in my confusion and shock, I began to worry about whether they used condoms or if maybe she had AIDS. John and I made love often, and I was scared that he had put me at risk."

"So, did you ask her if they had used protection?"

"Yes, I did."

He faced the courtroom. "What was her reply?"

"She said no. That she couldn't have any more babies, so she didn't worry about protection."

"What was your response?"

"I told her with all the diseases out there that both she and my husband had played Russian roulette. She didn't know if he had anything any more than he knew if she did. I asked her if she even cared about that."

Mr. Garrett turned and stared straight at the prosecutor. "How did she respond?"

I broke down, not wanting to remember as the judge offered me a box of tissues. Karen's voice echoed so clearly in my mind. "She said the words that haunt me to this very day. She told me, 'I don't care what happens to me. *I deserve whatever I get.*'"

There was a murmur in the courtroom as I fought for composure. John sat hunched in his seat, his gaze fixed to the table, rocking back and forth with a Bible in his embrace. In that instant, I heard gunshots, saw the girl's body soaking in blood as she sat behind the wheel of her car. *I deserve whatever I get....*

"Did you feel that was a peculiar statement?"

"It hit me hard. She sounded very strange when she said it."

"Almost as if she were admitting guilt of some sort? Like she deserved something bad to happen to her?"

In a fury, the prosecutor objected. "Pure assumption. We don't know what the victim felt."

"Sustained," the judge ordered. "Strike the comment from the record."

Mr. Garrett didn't seem disturbed. His comment was heard by all. This trial wasn't a jury trial. All he had to do was win over the judge and prove that there was substantial provocation in this case. The calls and the cruelty showed that.

"And when did the conversation end?" He calmly straightened his tie as he went back to slowly pacing.

"She said she wanted to meet me somewhere and show me the cards and gifts John had given her. She said she even had one of his jackets."

"Did you agree to that? Did you arrange to meet her someplace?"

"No."

"Why not?"

"Because she frightened me. There was something about her. She seemed to want to destroy me while laughing in the process—almost like she got a kick out of watching me go down. I had no desire to be alone with her. I had the feeling she was capable of anything."

Garrett let those words linger. "So, you felt she was dangerous?"

"Yes. Very much so."

"You were so frightened by her that you refused to meet her?"

"That's right. Instead, I told her I had heard enough, and I hung up the phone."

"At that point, did you become aware of where your ten-year-old daughter had been during your conversation with Karen?"

Is it true, Mommy? Is what she said about Daddy true?

My chin quivered. "Yes. She saw how upset I was getting and grew protective and concerned, wondering who could have called and made me cry like that. She had gone into our bedroom and listened on the other phone. I had no idea until after the call that she'd heard everything."

Garrett pressed on, a bit softer. "That must have been very hard for her. What was her reaction to what she had just heard?"

"She was scared. Crying. I was falling apart. Then I had Mariah clinging tightly to my leg. At three years old, she certainly didn't understand what was going on. She just saw all the commotion around her and knew it meant something wasn't right."

John's muffled sobs drew my attention. Hearing about his children's pain must have struck a nerve.

"Then what, if anything, did you do?"

I hesitated. "I called my husband at work and went ballistic."

"Did you tell him about Karen's call?"

"Yes. I told him I knew her name and all the details of the affair. I was screaming and crying and asking how he could do this. I said I thought he loved me and our two girls. He was speechless until he finally said he'd be right home."

"And did he come home?"

"No."

"What did you do when your husband didn't come home?"

"When the children were calm enough, I put them to bed and then waited on the living-room couch. When morning came and he still hadn't come home, I felt very strongly that he had taken his own life. He kept a gun in his glove box for protection when he made nightly bank deposits. I just knew he had shot himself with it. I knew he'd rather die than face his family now that his secret was out."

"What made you think John would kill himself?"

You and the girls are my entire world. If anything ever happened to make me lose that, I'd die. I'd have nothing. There'd be no reason to live. That's how thankful I am for what we have and how very deeply I love you....

"Because he always told me how much our marriage and our children meant to him. That he'd have no reason to live if anything ever happened to that. I just knew. We'd been soul mates for so many years. I felt this cold black space of terror. I sensed very strongly the presence of death."

"What, if anything, did you do next?"

My heart ached as I thought back to the children waking that next morning, realizing their daddy still wasn't home. I wanted to hug them. To protect them. Make all the hurt go away, but at that point I had completely broken down. I couldn't function or even speak; all I could do was cry. I finally managed to get a few words out and told Vanessa to call 911.

"When the officers arrived at your home, did you tell them what had happened and that you thought your husband was dead?"

"Yes. They made me promise to pull myself together while they went to locate John. They were concerned for the children."

There was a pause. Someone coughed. Garrett went back to his mound of notes. "And did they contact you once they located him?"

We found your husband, Mrs. Nichols. He's safe. He's all right. But ... the girl is dead ... the girl is dead ... the girl is dead ... multiple gunshots ... multiple gunshots ... the girl is dead ... dead ... dead ...

The judge's voice drew me back to the present. He asked if I wanted a brief recess. I refused. It would only prolong the proceeding.

"Three squad cars pulled up in my driveway a couple of hours later. I knew they had found my husband's body."

"What were your children doing at this time?"

"They were outside playing. A female officer took them to our backyard while the other officers entered the house."

"And what did they tell you?"

"Sergeant Deal said they had found my husband and he was okay ... but ... that the girl was dead." I paused to hold back tears, then struggled to continue. "She died from multiple gunshots, and my husband was in the county jail charged with aggravated murder."

My words hung in the air as Garrett walked back to John's table. Reluctantly, I allowed my gaze to focus on the man I had married. It was so hard to comprehend that he was the murderer we were talking about. Through all of our years together, I knew him to be so wonderfully gentle and caring. For some stupid reason I momentarily remembered the cat he rescued from the middle of the road one morning. He stopped traffic to gather up this little fur ball and bring it back to the house. Because he saved her life, we named her Hope. I adored him for having such a big heart.

"After you were told about your husband, what happened next?"

"Sergeant Deal told me there was an ambulance waiting out front to take me to the hospital. The children were going to stay with a neighbor until I was able to come back."

This shot might prick a bit, Mrs. Nichols, but it's something to relax you.... Do you know where you are? Can you tell me who the President of the United States is? How about your birth date, Diane.... Can you remember your birth date?

"And why were you brought to the hospital while your children stayed at a neighbor's house?"

"For shock," I answered, my throat painfully dry. "I spent the day there being treated for shock. I was also coached by a child psychologist on how to tell my children what their father had done."

He set his notes down and walked over to where I was sitting. Garrett then leaned against the witness box. His eyes were so dark that they swallowed their own pupils. Like smoked glass, they held my stoic reflection.

"In your opinion, Mrs. Nichols, did John plan this killing the day before it happened as the prosecution will try and make us believe? Was this something he calculated, step by step in his mind, even before that fateful day?"

"No, sir. Absolutely not. I know he didn't plan to kill her. I have no doubt in my mind."

"How do you know? Can you tell the court how you can be so sure?"

Tears surfaced as I remembered the lemon bars the girls never had the chance to bake. *These are Daddy's favorites, right Mommy? He's going to be so happy!* I forced my gaze to square with my ex-husband's prosecutor. "Because he was about to leave work and come straight home to have dinner with his family."

Two

Closing the Door

The prosecutor stood, buttoned his suit jacket, then approached me on the stand. He wore a chipper smile, which I thoroughly resented since his job was to win this case and put my children's father away for life. He greeted me and introduced himself as Tom Dodson. I said nothing. I didn't want to give him an inch. He chuckled a bit, noting my prickly manner. "I certainly hope you and I get along a lot better than you and my assistant did when she called your home in Florida for discovery purposes. She mentioned you were a little hard to deal with."

"I found her highly offensive and didn't appreciate the mind games she was playing—wanting me to explode and say something she could use against my ex-husband."

A smirk spread on Dodson's lips. "Offensive? In what way? What kind of mind games are you claiming she played?"

"The woman who made the call and asked all your questions kept calling me Karen. She apologized each time, but kept doing it over and over. The more it bothered me, the more she liked it. I'm sure she was hoping I'd blow up and say something to help your case."

His tiny hazel eyes twinkled with false sincerity as he paced in front of the judge. The man was short, paunchy, and his double chins flopped over the starched collar of his shirt. He reminded me of a bulldog prepared to attack.

"That is unfortunate, and I do apologize for the error. I'm sure she didn't mean to cause you any problems. Hopefully, we can just put that aside and concentrate on the issues at hand today. Would you mind answering a few questions about the phone calls you received prior to the murder?"

"I wasn't aware I had a choice."

Again, a smile slid across his lips as if he enjoyed seeing me so agitated. That was probably the frame of mind he wanted me in for his cross-examination. He didn't want the distressed wife, tormented by her husband's mentally unstable mistress, to sway Judge Strickland to render a voluntary manslaughter conviction. It was his duty to nail my ex-husband to the wall so he'd never set foot outside prison again—to prove that John Nichols was a cold-blooded killer. All Dodson had to do was turn the tables slightly and cast the smallest doubt.

"You described the hang-up calls as bothersome and even went so far as to get a caller ID box."

I nodded. "That's right."

"Who requested the ID box? You or your husband?"

My memory was fuzzy. It seemed unimportant. "I don't know. I think John called the phone company about it."

"And did the fact that he was so willing to get an ID box help to put your mind at ease about his having an affair?"

"I was glad to see that he would do anything to catch the caller. We both wanted to know who it was."

Dodson smirked again. He had a habit of always looking as if he were amused by some private little joke. "But the number that ultimately came up on the ID box over and over again was that of a pay phone, isn't that right? A pay phone inside John's own Wal-Mart store?"

"Yes. That's right."

"A number John knew couldn't possibly lead you to the identity of the girl placing those calls. He could have known already who was making those calls and where they were coming from and had little to risk by playing the willing husband who would pacify his wife with a caller ID box … agreed?"

Garrett objected, shooting me a worried look. "Speculation, Your Honor."

Strickland glanced up over his glasses. "Sustained. Continue Mr. Dodson."

The exchange pleased Dodson. He fussed with his gaudy paisley tie to give plenty of time for all to observe my weak spots. According to Garrett, he was a master at bringing grieving witnesses to their knees if it meant winning a case.

"Let's move on," he said, casually shrugging off the objection. "You stated to my assistant during your phone conversation that you hated Karen Romano. That you thought she deserved to die and that, in fact, you would have killed her yourself, given the chance. Is this correct?"

"I said I thought she was evil. There was something about her voice and the way she kept taunting me and making a game of it that convinced me she was dangerous. I also said that I believed she pushed my husband to the brink after a year of threats and manipulation. He snapped the day he shot her. I told your assistant that if I were in his shoes, living in the hell she had put him through, I would have lost my senses and probably pulled the trigger, too."

"Evil?" he repeated incredulously. "Karen Romano was very well liked by her fellow students at Remington College. They described a friendly, quiet girl who got along with everyone."

"I knew a different side of her," I answered. "And that side was cold and evil. She took pleasure in the destruction of my family and my marriage. The phone calls were sick, proving how much she wanted to destroy John's world. I'll never forget her laugh each time I broke down sobbing. The same way she laughed in John's face seconds before he snapped and pulled the trigger."

His brows arched. "Is that the version he told you? That she laughed in his face and he shot her after that?"

I glanced over at John, who seemed lost in the process of determining his innocence or guilt. All he could do was sit between Garrett and Martinez with his Bible in hand, staring blankly at a spot on the table.

"I believe him," I retorted. "He told me he confronted her and asked why she made that call. She just laughed. It wasn't something he planned. His sanity just snapped. She pushed him too far, and he lost it."

"And you believe him? This man who has lied to you for so long, carrying on an affair behind your back? The man you divorced for reasons of adultery?"

"Yes," I blurted out. As foolish as it seemed, I believed what John told me. The letter he wrote to me after his arrest was so raw. He had nothing more to hide. He had lost everything and was reduced to nothing. What point would there be to play games anymore?

"She was like that," I continued. "She laughed at me when I

was breaking apart on the phone after what she had told me. Why wouldn't she do the same thing to John?"

"But you weren't there, were you Mrs. Nichols? You didn't see her laugh at your husband, did you?"

My palms were sweating. I pressed them together as I kept my hands in my lap. "I still believe him. She was sick like that. I'm sure it happened that way."

Dodson was getting angry now. He didn't like feeling that his grip on the presentation was slipping. "Then, you believe a liar."

"I believe my husband … my ex-husband."

"But you weren't there, were you? You can't testify to what happened when John pulled that trigger. You don't know because you weren't there."

I narrowed my eyes, piercing the distance between us. "No sir, that's true. But then again, neither were you."

The courtroom broke into a hum of conversation as John looked up for the first time. His dazed blue eyes made contact with mine for one brief second. Then Dodson began ranting about how he was the prosecutor in this case. How he had all the facts from a professional investigation and I had only lies from a cheating husband. Garrett jumped in, shouting that Dodson was badgering the witness. Judge Strickland thumped his gavel until the frenzy finally died down. John went back to staring at the table.

Dodson approached me with new fire in his gaze. I thought he was moving in for the kill and hardened myself in preparation. Instead, he waved his hand and told the judge he had no further questions. The bulldog was sick of this feisty adversary and was releasing me from his jaws.

I was dismissed from the stand and passed John's table. He couldn't make himself look up at me again and kept his focus safely low. Tears were rolling off the end of his nose and dripping onto his lap. Garrett patted John on the shoulder and then turned to me and smiled. He gave a thumbs-up as if I had just scored the winning touchdown. I walked out of the courtroom and through the double doors, rushing for the nearest rest room. I cranked on the faucet in the first sink I came to, hoping the noise would drown out the wrenching sound of the sobs I couldn't hold back anymore.

When I arrived at the courthouse for the second day of the trial, Garrett's and Martinez's moods were far from the optimism they displayed after my testimony. I was immediately brought into a small, private room with just a table and several chairs. They stood while I nervously sat. I didn't like their paled expressions.

"A piece of new evidence has surfaced, and the prosecution plans to use it," Martinez explained. "It isn't good. It will make it impossible to get a voluntary manslaughter charge out of Strickland."

"I don't understand." I felt like someone had yanked the rug out from under me. "How can there be any new evidence? I know John didn't plan to do this."

Garrett moved closer and leaned against the table. I wished he would sit, make it more casual. Meet me eye to eye. With him towering over me, I felt so small and helpless. Maybe because of this new evidence, he was convinced that I was.

"Karen left a letter behind," he stated as carefully as he could without losing his professional edge. "It was found in her purse. It was dated the day before she was killed. She points the finger at your husband if anything ever happened to her. She claims he put a gun to her head that afternoon and threatened to kill her. He promised to bring her down if she ever told you about their affair. Diane, this kind of evidence is a major advantage for the prosecution."

I sprang to my feet. "That's ridiculous. It has to be a bunch of lies. How can the court believe anything this wicked girl says, when she was obviously out to ruin my family? She told me about the affair the next day, so how scared could she have been?"

"There's more," Garrett disclosed. "A new witness has been added to the list. Someone John worked with at Wal-Mart who heard him say that he would kill Karen if he found out she was making the phone calls."

I felt sucker punched. "He didn't plan it. I know he didn't."

Martinez shook his head. "We don't have the proof on our side. With these two new developments, the prosecution is going to skin John alive in that courtroom. He's hanging by a thread as it is. You saw him yesterday. He's crying most of the time. He can hardly keep his words from slurring when he talks to us. I think they've got him on something to help him cope with the stress of the trial. His blood pressure is also dangerously high. He's not holding up well at all. I think it would be in his best interest at this point if we considered another route. Karen's family has agreed to a plea bargain of fifteen years to life. I think that would be a fair solution. He'd be better off to go with that and not put his life on the line."

"You mean you're giving up? I thought my husband had a chance at winning a voluntary manslaughter conviction because of all the provocation in this case. He shot with his left hand when he's right handed, for God's sake. Doesn't that prove he didn't plan to pull the trigger?"

Garrett sat down in the chair next to mine and compassionately touched my arm. I knew it was a gesture of comfort, but instead it made me uneasy. I knew Garrett had to be getting desperate.

"We've been trying cases like this one for many years, Mrs. Nichols. We know this girl was a wacko, and we know she put you and your family through hell, but the fact is that the letter she left behind will be admitted into evidence and will seal John's fate. If we don't consider a plea bargain, he'll most likely get a first-degree murder conviction and be sentenced to twenty-five years to life. With the plea, it will be considerably less than that. He'll have more of a chance going that way."

Tears rolled down my face. I didn't bother to wipe them away. Nothing mattered anymore. There was nothing left to fight for. I could almost hear Karen laughing again from some distant plain as our lives went from hell to beyond.

"I want to see him," I insisted. "I need to talk this over with him before he makes a decision."

"We can't arrange that right now," Garrett answered. "The trial is starting in five minutes. We can go ahead and try the case today, and you can visit John this evening. But he needs to agree to the plea right away if we're going to have time to submit it. I'll meet with him first thing tomorrow morning. He'll have to give us an answer then."

As I sat in the courtroom, I kept thinking about the gamble we were taking. The coroner testified about Karen's gunshot wounds, and the receptionist at Remington College testified she heard the argument in the parking lot prior to the shooting and had dialed 911. A college friend of Karen's gave a glowing depiction of the deceased. The letter from Karen saying John would most certainly be her killer if she were ever murdered made me realize it was a gamble not worth the risk. No matter how deeply John had hurt me—and even though he had destroyed our marriage—he was still my children's father. They needed him in their lives. Fifteen years was far better than twenty-five to life. Vanessa would be twenty-six, out of college, and fresh into a career, possibly with a husband and children of her own—children who would need their grandfather. Mariah would be nineteen and probably just starting college. John could be out in time to share in that and do things only a father could do, like walk her down the aisle. With the plea bargain was the hope he would be back again. If we gambled and lost, the girls might never see him outside of gloomy prison walls.

I waited nervously for the guard to escort John into the visitation room that evening. We had only fifteen minutes, which didn't seem long enough to talk him into a plea. I knew he intended to fight until he couldn't fight anymore. White as chalk against the neon orange of his prison jumpsuit, he took a seat across from me. His inmate number was stamped in black ink on his pocket. It felt strange not to embrace once he was within arm's length. We were awkward with each other. Like strangers.

"How are you?" My question sounded stupid.

He swept my face with his troubled gaze before looking down at the table between us. "Wanting all of this to be over. I just want to come home."

I couldn't believe it. There was no home anymore. *I think they've got him on something to help him cope with the stress of the trial … his blood pressure is also dangerously high … he's not holding up well at all.…* Garrett's words echoed in my mind as I stared at John's trembling hands. They were folded together between us as if he were praying. His breathing was ragged and loud.

I dared touch his arm. It was cold as if he had no life left inside of him. "Are you doing all right? I mean, really, I need to know if you're okay."

"I'm not okay," he shot back in a choked voice, tears streaming from his eyes. "I've lost my wife, my kids … over one stupid mistake. I need to find a way to get out of here and come back home. I can't lose the three of you. I can't. You're all I ever loved in this world. Just tell me I haven't lost you."

I felt sick inside. I had no idea what to say in response. How could he ask this of me when we were divorced and he'd shattered everything our love was based on? The clock on the wall behind him drew my attention.

Our time was down to twelve minutes.

"If you love us that much, then you have to listen to me. Karen's family has agreed to a plea bargain. They are offering fifteen years to life and I want you to take it. The way it looks now, there's no way to escape a murder one conviction if you go all the way."

"It's that letter, isn't it?" His chin quivered. "That's a load of crap, Baby. She framed me. She knew what she was doing."

"You never threatened her with a gun to her head?"

"God, no," he answered. "She knew I had a gun in my car. She saw it once and asked me about it. The only thing in that letter I really said was that I'd take her down if she ever cost me my family. I didn't mean I'd kill her. Honestly, Baby. I never meant that. If I intended to do that, I wouldn't have done it in broad daylight in a parking lot filled with witnesses. I would have held the gun in my right hand instead of my left and aimed at her head or her heart instead of just shooting randomly all over. The coroner said her wounds were in her hip and down her leg. I swear, I just went nuts. I don't even remember what I was doing. All I remember is her laughing at me after our argument as I turned and walked away. I didn't even look where I was shooting."

I watched as he put his head in his hands and wept openly. Never in our thirteen years together had I heard such gut-wrenching sounds come out of him. The guards at the table behind us just sipped coffee and continued discussing last weekend's Browns game.

"You've got to take the plea," I said, now taking both his hands in mine. "Do it for the girls. They need their daddy back again. If you gamble and lose, you may never get out of prison."

"Why?" he said, a world of pain on his face. "Why can't I just prove that it wasn't something I planned? I swear to God, something snapped inside of me when she laughed. She didn't even care what that phone call did to my life. I didn't know what I was doing. That's the absolute truth."

Tears streamed from my eyes. "I believe you. I know you aren't capable of plotting to kill someone, but the letter she wrote and this witness from Wal-Mart are going to nail you to the wall."

"I said that like everybody says it. Like you saying you're going to kill the kids if they don't clean their room. People say stuff like that every day. It doesn't mean they're really going to commit murder! I said it out of anger and fear of being exposed."

"John, even so, once the testimony is presented along with that letter, I don't see how you can win. I'm asking you, from the bottom of my heart, to take this plea and not risk a murder one." His hands squeezed mine back. They were large as catcher's mitts and perspiring heavily. They used to touch me and melt me to my soul whether he was swiping my hair away from my face, making love to me, or clasping hands as we walked together.

Now, his touch was disturbing and chilling. Those hands had actually killed someone.

"I have to beat this. I can't give up. I know I should get voluntary manslaughter instead of murder. How can I take a plea when I know what happened that day? I know I just snapped. Under the Ohio law, Judge Strickland has to consider a voluntary manslaughter verdict if there was provocation and the crime was done in the heat of passion with mitigating circumstances."

Quickly, I checked the clock again and saw that only three minutes of our visit remained. Panic jumped my pulse up a notch. "Do you love your daughters?"

His expression softened. "Of course I do. I love you and our girls more than anything in this world."

"Then take the plea for them. Don't risk doing any more time than you have to. They need a dad in their lives. You could be back in fifteen years. Just take the plea bargain for them."

One of the guards took a last gulp of coffee from a Styrofoam cup before rising and looking our way. "Nichols … time. Inmate stay seated while the visitor exits the room."

Our eyes didn't leave each other as I stood and pushed in my chair. No more words came to mind for me to say. "I love you" didn't fit anymore. I didn't even like the man he was. "Take care" seemed senseless since he was stuck in a jail cell. Finally, I just brushed the tears from my face and turned to walk away.

"I love you," he called out. "No matter what, I always will."

My steps slowed for a moment but then quickened as I headed for the door. Deep down, I knew if I turned around and looked at him, I'd never be able to let go. I'd be as disillusioned as he was, believing this whole mess would go away and we'd go home together, arm in arm, and live happily ever after. The last thing I needed was to get lost in the blue of his eyes and let myself get swept away by his words. The guards smiled politely as I stopped at the table to drop off my visitor's pass and ID.

John stood in front of Judge Strickland the next morning and accepted the plea of fifteen years to life. It was over. He gave up the fight just as I begged him to do. I wept openly as he was led from the courtroom. Garrett walked me out with his arm on my shoulders, assuring me that my ex-husband got a good deal. He shook my hand and wished me well before walking off. It was on to the next case for him. Another defense to piece together over a ham and Swiss on rye while I headed back to Florida to face a life of raising two children alone.

I tried to feel relieved as I rode the elevator down to the main floor. There would be no more testimonies to listen to, no more grim meetings with lawyers. I didn't have to see John broken and weeping at the defense table. I could close the door on it now. I had done what I came to do and had to concentrate on building a new life with my children. The thought overwhelmed me and left me paralyzed. I had nothing to give them either financially or emotionally. I felt completely drained, yet I was all they had left. *John got a good deal. He did the right thing.…* My heart ached as I reflected on Garrett's parting words. How could it be a good deal when two innocent children have to grow up without their father?

I waited two hours to see John. As a special request visit, it took time to receive final clearance. While waiting, I stood outside the courthouse, leaning on the railing as a cool September wind caressed my face. I listened to the sounds of the traffic, the bustling of the people, admired the birds soaring in the sky overhead. I drank it in like never before, experiencing it for John because he could no longer enjoy those things for himself. His world had no color. Nothing but a claustrophobic cell for the next fifteen years or more. I couldn't imagine what impact that would have on the human spirit. Time must feel so different when it ticks away behind prison bars. Tears clouded my eyes as I flipped up the collar of my jacket. I suddenly felt cold despite the warmth of the sun.

John entered the visitation room, weeping. He didn't look like a man who had just gotten a prison sentence. He looked like a little boy, afraid of the dark, needing the shelter of loving arms around him.

I rocked him back and forth, my eyes closed as I felt his heartbeat slamming against me like a thumping fist. I kept expecting the guards to tell us to break it up, but I was thankful they allowed us that time to simply hold each other.

"You're okay," I whispered to him. "You're going to make this. You just have to stay strong."

"I can't," he wept, squeezing me even tighter. "I can't do this. I won't make this. I'll never survive in here."

An icy fear flowed through me. In an odd way, I understood. I felt the same hopelessness about my life on the outside. It didn't matter if there was grass under my feet and a brilliant sky overhead. It didn't matter that I was still out in the world. It was now a horrible place with no joy or hope. I dreaded the morning sun bringing another day. We had both been sentenced to a prison we didn't have the strength to face.

We sat with the table between us. Already I missed the comfort of his body pressed against mine. It always felt like two halves making a whole. Even now, after all of this, he was still a part of me. I didn't know how to accept the horrid things he did or how to carry on without him in my life. How would I tell the children that Daddy will be gone for fifteen years to life? His hands were drenched in sweat. Mine hungrily held on to his. Soon, the visit would end and we would have to say good-bye, and a simple touch between us would be as impossible as turning back time. As if my heart was protecting me from getting too carried away, I had a vision of him pulling the trigger. I heard popping noises in my head. I withdrew my hands from his and folded them in my lap. He stared at me as if wanting to still feel that precious contact between us, but then relaxed against his chair.

"Thank you for what you did today." My voice echoed in the near-empty room. A guard sat at a corner table, looking through paperwork, stealing glances at us, then going back to his papers again. "Now, there's closure. The girls will know you'll be back again one day. They will most likely be grown and out on their own, but you'll still be there to share in their lives and to hold your grandchildren. They'll need you then as much as they need you now. Because of this plea, you can be there."

He focused on me with sorrowful eyes, his breathing still labored. "But what about you? Will you still be there?"

I hesitated. "What do you mean?"

"Locked up, waiting for trial, I've had nothing but time to search inside of myself and have sessions with the psychiatrist. I wanted answers to why I did all this when I had a family I really loved. It helped. I see how sick I've been for so long. I'm beginning to see where it all came from. Maybe, if I could share it with you, make you understand, there could be a chance for us somewhere down the road. I know it's not fair to expect you to wait for me, but I just want some hope. Anything at all. Tell me I won't lose you forever."

My body went numb. I couldn't comprehend what he was asking. Not only was he facing over a decade of prison time, if the parole board ever let him out at all, but our relationship had been shattered by his betrayals. "I can't," I whispered. "It's over. I've got to concentrate on our girls and building a new life. We're divorced now. There's nothing left between us to try and hold on to."

"I never meant to hurt you."

"Did you think sleeping with that girl would make me happy?"

His gaze dipped with a remorse I hated. "No … it's just … I never meant for all of this to happen."

"You mean, you never meant to get caught."

"I never wanted any of it to happen."

"So, she forced you into the whole thing? Come on, John. Take responsibility. You had an affair with a girl young enough to be your own daughter and you ended up killing her for blowing the whistle on you. That's not something that 'just happens.' You had a relationship with her behind my back for a whole year, for God's sake. Don't pretend this was all something you didn't have control over. You could have stopped it. You could have gotten professional help if you were sick, as you call it. But you kept on seeing her, sleeping with her and playing me for a fool. Now she's dead, and you're facing hard time in prison. I'm left to raise our two daughters alone, and you want us to sit here and talk about hope? Talk about a new beginning together one day? Damn you, John. I don't know how in the world you could even think that way."

"Because if I don't, I'll die in here. I need something to hold on to. I can't make it in here if I know I've lost my family. You and the girls are all I have. You mean the world to me."

"You will make it." I said, angrily. "Because if you don't, your children will never get over it. They keep hoping that you'll come home one day. Are you going to let them down again? Are you going to show them how weak you still are? Don't do that to them, John. I can't keep picking up the pieces. You're going to have to make it through this just as the girls and I have to."

He fumbled for my hands again. His palms were damp, yet he felt ice cold. I wanted to pull back so we couldn't touch. I didn't want to fall apart, but I gave no resistance.

"Were there others?" I asked, needing to know. "Was she the only affair you had?"

"Just her," he answered in a tone laced with loathing. I wasn't sure if that was for the man he'd become or for Karen Romano, who was the apple in the Garden of Eden.

I wanted to crawl inside of him and try to understand the monster that he was. How do you take someone as your lover for an entire year and then pump bullets into her as she sits defenseless? My stomach pitched as I pulled back from his grasp.

I was thankful, the guard signaled it was time to go.

John and I stood, then shared an embrace. "I'll always love you, Diane Nichols," he whispered into my ear. The heat of his breath stirred something in me that I wanted so much to die. "For the rest of my life, I'll love you with all my heart. That will never change no matter what. I'll always be here for you."

It sounded so good, but stabbed at my heart. Where was this eternal love when he was having sex with Karen? Where was this dedication when the children and I really needed it? I grew frightened, knowing how good John was at lying. He did it so flawlessly when we were together. Making love to her, coming home to me, telling me how much he missed me and loved me. He was doing it again, and I had to get out of there. Back to Florida, my parents, my children. I had to get out of the tempting clutches of his fantasy world and go back to the misery of reality.

Something inside of me clicked off. I was somehow still functioning, but I didn't feel a thing. It was my body's way of protecting me from what I was about to do. This hug would be our last. These words would be our last. Once I walked from this room and out of this building, I wasn't going to ever look back.

"You stay strong," I told him steadily. "For the girls. Promise me. They're depending on you to make it. As long as you're doing okay, I know they'll do okay, and one day you will be free to see them again."

"I promise," he answered, his voice choked with tears. "I won't let them down."

It was meaningless to hear. He had let them down enough for the next twenty lifetimes, but I wanted to believe he could keep this one promise. I closed my eyes as his arms enveloped me, so strong and warm, just as I always knew them to be. I could feel him shaking, hear his stifled crying as he buried his face against me. I couldn't share his tears. I had none left. My shock and sorrow were my suit of armor, preventing the pain from getting through. It was what I needed. The only way I could bring myself to finally walk away. It felt strange, but I was deeply thankful for it.

"I love you," he said, squeezing me tight. "That will never change."

I nodded as if I understood, but in truth, I was miserably lost. "I love you, too. I just wish that were enough. Take care of yourself, okay?"

We pulled apart, searched each other's eyes, and then I turned and walked away. John's stare bore into me, acting like a magnet to pull me back, but I signed out at the guard's table and waited for the steel door to slide open. When it did, I quickly walked through.

The echo of it slamming behind me was like the door closing on my past. I just kept walking. Every step I took felt like the longest mile until I got outside the building. Karen Romano was dead, but my heart was still pumping. John was behind bars, but I was still free. But, in that instant, as I stood on the sidewalk looking up at the narrow windows on the top five floors of the justice building where inmates were waving from their cells to pedestrians below, I didn't feel any difference between us at all. Because of John's double life and the murder of his secret lover, I was sentenced to a prison of my own.

THREE

Starting Over

I met Bobby that October. He stood talking to our neighbor Dorothy as the girls and I drove to the store. I slowed the car to say hello, then locked eyes with the silver-haired man who stared back at me intently. We exchanged introductions, but even after saying good-bye, his soulful brown gaze and gentle smile haunted me. I had the distinct feeling that the two of us were destined to meet.

Since returning from John's trial in September, I had fallen into a despair like I had never known before. I thought how lucky Karen was not to have to feel anything anymore. I wanted to end my life. Suicidal thoughts rolled around in my head, growing more and more serious.

So, why be so aroused by the sight of this stranger? Why was it so electric when I looked in his eyes? All I knew was that I had a distinct impression something would develop between us.

I later learned he lived several houses down the street. At times he would be outside when I drove by, smiling and waving while I stared back in my rearview mirror. The sight of him jarred me with a sense of feeling powerfully drawn to him.

I thought I was losing my mind. It wasn't a romantic feeling. John had killed any chance my heart had for ever loving anyone that way again. But, for some reason, this simple, quiet man who looked years older than me with his thick crop of shaggy gray hair made me feel fluttery when I saw him. Nervous. Excited. The brief waves we had come to exchange kept my heart pounding long after he was out of view. What it was, I had no clue. What it wasn't, however, was something that fit into my plans. A suicidal woman didn't need a new man.

Bobby and I came face to face again on Halloween night. It was a difficult holiday to get through. John had thoroughly enjoyed the ritual of shopping for pumpkins at a farm near Twinsburg. He helped the girls choose just the right ones and then carved the pumpkins with such amazing detail that we always had the best jack-o'-lanterns on the block. He also took the girls trick-or-treating while I stayed at home to hand out candy. Afterward, he'd sit on the floor with the kids and go through their mounds of candy, stealing a few for himself. Facing Halloween without him in a new neighborhood was hard, but we had to try. I suggested to the girls that they ring Bobby's doorbell.

He handed out some candy and complimented them on their costumes before looking over at me. That same reaction exploded inside me as we nodded hello.

I wanted to say more. I wanted to tell him that I was going through a really rough time and could use a friend to open up to and talk to. *Talk about what? How I've been destroyed by a marriage I treasured and believed in? That everything feels so hopeless now? What good would that do? He can't change the hell I'm living any more than I can.* I smiled politely and gathered the children, thanking him before walking away.

The girls lacked their usual excitement and only half-heartedly snacked on a few pieces of candy before going to bed. I knew they felt the wide, gaping hole in our lives where happiness used to be. Where their daddy used to be. I tried to pat myself on the back about still doing the costumes and the trick-or-treating thing, even though it hurt more than it helped. We didn't buy a pumpkin, though. That was just too hard. None of us wanted to take John's place.

I drifted off into a fitful sleep, even though I had taken pre-scription sleeping pills. The hollow in my heart was torturing me to the point where there was no turning it off. There was no finding a comfortable place. It was like slowly bleeding to death from an open chest wound and wishing each breath was my last. Fuzzy dreams began drifting through my mind. Images of John and the girls, laughing. Vanessa was on a swing, begging him to push her, while he had Mariah hiked up on his shoulders. *Push me, Daddy ... higher and higher until my toes can touch the sky ...* their laughter swelled. *More, Daddy, more ... higher and higher ... make me go as high as the clouds....* He laughed again and said something about her getting bigger now. That if she wanted to touch the clouds, he'd need some help pushing her. He turned and called out to someone, but I didn't know who. A sick feeling swept over me as a dark-haired girl approached the swing set. She and my husband shared a long, lingering kiss before she dotted Mariah's pug nose with her finger and then helped to push Vanessa higher on the swing. But, as she moved, I saw numerous holes in her jeans and shirt where blood started leak-ing out, oozing from blackened gunshot wounds all over her body, soaking through her clothing, trickling down the length of her arms, and splattering on my children. I wanted to scream, but I had no voice. I was nonexistent. My terror kept building until I thought I would explode. I awakened, kicking my legs as if trying to break free from invisible shackles. Sitting up, I gulped air and blinked in the darkness until the familiar sounds of the night crickets outside my window reminded me where I was. My nightgown was plastered to my skin with perspiration, my heart slamming like a hammer in my chest. *Just a dream … just a dream … it's okay … it was just a dream …* But the nausea didn't go away as my eyes adjusted to the night shadows in my bedroom. Instead, it rolled like an ocean wave getting stronger and stronger until I abruptly ran to the bathroom. Closing the door so the children couldn't hear me, I sank to the tile floor in front of the toilet and retched through my tears.

I began attending a weekly divorce support group in a church. Up until those meetings, I had avoided people, shunning family and friends who only wanted to help. The group looked like a good way to be around others in pain. I needed to share what I was carrying and feel as if someone really understood. Walking into that room full of strangers was difficult, but once we began exchanging stories and leaning on each other, I realized it was the right place to be. So many others had gone through painful break-ups, most dealing with issues of infidelity and the struggle to make it through each day with broken hearts. When it was time for me to tell my story, I wasn't sure I could. It was my choice. I didn't have to, but it felt like a caged animal needing to be set free. I couldn't hold it in. It had to come out, if only so that I could hear myself tell it in an effort to somehow deal with it. Maybe even digest it.

So far, I had walked around in a fog of denial. I knew it was over and John was in prison. I knew a girl was dead because of him. I knew I was alone to care for my two children. I knew, but I didn't accept it. It still felt surreal. Sharing it with the divorce group that evening was like baring my most private wounds, but once I started, I couldn't stop. The room was so silent that I could hear my own breathing. When I finished, I dissolved into sobs, and everyone gathered around me to offer a giant embrace. I remember what an awesome sensation that was—to be surrounded by others who cried with me because they knew what it felt like to be broken inside. They all knew the sting of betrayal and lies, struggling to survive both financially and emotionally after losing a life that was good. Most of them were also single mothers who knew my panic when it came to raising children alone. For the first time since that tragic day, I didn't feel so isolated and misunderstood. It felt so good that I was tempted to go on and share my thoughts of committing suicide, but it was too private. So I kept it buried deep inside where no one else could see. I had exposed enough truths for one night.

"You ought to get together with Bobby. You both have a lot in common." Dorothy and I shared a cup of coffee one morning as she filled me in on the man with the silver hair. She obviously had been close friends with him and was concerned about his problems. "He's been going through a lot. His thirteen-year marriage ended in a bitter divorce, and now his ex-wife won't allow him to see their little girl. It's killing him. I've been really worried, as a matter of fact. He makes comments like he doesn't care if he lives or dies. I just hope he doesn't try anything stupid. Maybe the two of you could kind of give each other some support since you're both going through a tough time."

That thought stuck with me for several days. I would drive by his house hoping to see him outside so that I might casually strike up a conversation, but either his pickup truck wasn't there or I didn't have the nerve. What good could I possibly do for the man? I was barely surviving through my own pain. I had no room to take on anyone else's suffering. And if he was planning on doing something stupid, as Dorothy so bluntly put it, what a pitiful couple we would make. Two suicidal people headed absolutely nowhere except to separate graves. Yet it intrigued me. Was that the reason we locked eyes the day we met? Was that why this man was so hard to shake from my mind? I began to feel that we needed something from each other.

I was writing a magazine article in my home office one night. My wages as a freelance writer barely got us by, but it was the only way I knew to earn money while still being at home to take care of the girls. In their tender frame of mind, I couldn't bear to leave them for forty hours a week. When the doorbell rang after ten o'clock, I was curious as to who would be out at this time of night. The girls, who had been watching a video, rushed to open the door. Just as I was about to scold them for it, I saw a bulky silhouette in the open doorway. There was no mistaking who it was. The moonlight made his silvery hair turn to platinum.

"Hi," he said awkwardly, smiling at the children and then gazing beyond them at me.

"I was wondering if you're going to use that lamp in your carport. My brother and I have been stumbling around in the darkness since ours went on the blink. I'd pay you for it. That is, if you weren't going to use it."

My mind whirled trying to figure out what lamp he was talking about. I had completely forgotten about it because it was big and cumbersome. I had planned to donate it to the Salvation Army, but never quite got around to it.

"That's fine," I answered, self-conscious about my appearance. Baggy silk pajamas, no makeup, sporting fuzzy gorilla slippers.

He eyed me up and down with a look of amusement. It only made me want to run and hide.

"You gave us a lot of candy," Mariah said, gaping up at him standing tall as a redwood over her. "For Halloween. I was the witch, in case you didn't know."

He laughed and stooped down to be at her level. "I knew, but you're just too pretty to be a witch. Those big blue eyes and long blonde hair kind of gave you away. You probably should have been an angel. Maybe next year you could give that a try."

"You think?" she asked, wrinkling up her nose. "I kind of like scary things."

Vanessa rolled her eyes, then shoved her little sister in a playful way. "You cry over thunderstorms. Don't pretend you're big and brave."

Bobby laughed again. His expression literally beamed with an obvious love for children. It was as if he couldn't soak up enough of their presence to replace the absence of his own little girl.

"Take the lamp," I said, eager to close the door. There was no sense inviting him in like a friendly neighbor. Not when we were both hanging on by a thread. "I'm not going to use it. I was donating it to the thrift store, so don't worry about paying me for it."

He stood up and met my gaze with the most compelling brown eyes I have ever experienced. They were small, yet intense, twinkling with the most unsettling mixture of warmth, compassion, and need. He didn't look at me, he looked into me—like he could read my feelings and thoughts. They smiled; they explored; they invited me to explore him, too; but I wasn't ready. I didn't want to. I quickly closed the door.

"Good-bye," he said, trying to get it in before it was too late. "Thanks."

I dared to breathe only after the door was shut with him safely on the other side. Vanessa gawked at me as if I had sprouted three heads.

"What did you do that for?" she asked. "You practically slammed the door in his face."

"Yeah," Mariah added. "He's really nice. I wanted him to stay."

I didn't want him to be nice, and even more, I didn't want my children to like him hanging around. It was bad enough that he soaked them up like a sponge. And the way he looked at me … I couldn't quite decide what it was that rattled me so. His eyes made me feel vulnerable and weak.

"You like him, don't you?" Vanessa asked, squinting and cocking her head.

It knocked the breath out of me. "What? Of course not. I'm not interested in him or anyone."

"Then why do you always get all funny when you're around him? You act like he makes you nervous or something."

"I'm not nervous."

Mariah giggled and joined in. "No, you just turn funny colors."

My hands flew to my face. "I do not."

Vanessa grinned and nodded. "Do so. Every time you see him."

"Do not." I started laughing, for lack of something better to do.

Vanessa started laughing, too. "Do so. You're as red as an apple right now."

We broke into a crazy fit of giggles while Bobby carried the lamp off down the street. Maybe it was because it was late and we were all tired. Or maybe it was because it had been so horribly long since that sound filled the air, but that silly, wonderful laughter was as welcome as summer rain.

Thoughts of Bobby began nudging John out of my mind. It felt so good to have someone else to think about. I thought of Bobby's quiet way, his gentle smile, and that mane of sterling silver hair. He responded so well to my children. He was so nice even while I completely brushed him off. Vanessa was right. I did slam the door in his face. I knew he had dropped by for reasons that had nothing to do with an ugly old lamp. He most likely thought my children would have been asleep at that hour, so he and I would have a chance to get to know each other. He felt the same pull I had been wrestling with. Every time we were within a few feet of each other, the air became electric.

Instead of being scared by it, it began to fascinate me. I knew it was my turn to make the next move if I was ever going to figure out this attraction. With my divorce group meeting that evening, it gave me the perfect reason to slip a note into his mailbox.

"Thanks for inviting me," he said as I drove us to the meeting. "I was really glad you told me about this divorce group. I think it might help me to unload some of this baggage that's been so hard to deal with. It's never easy when a marriage comes to an end, as you well know."

I glanced over at him, wondering how he would react if he knew the details of my story. It wasn't every day that a man went for a ride with a lady who was once married to a murderer. John did the act, but it still made me feel dirty. I always felt as if we were literally connected to each other. Soul mates in every sense of the word.

Even now, knowing everything John and I had together was

nothing more than lies, I felt shame as if my hand was molded to his hand and we had both blindly pulled the trigger. As if I'd taken every step with him. Every breath with him.

What God has joined together, let no man put asunder … I now present to you Mr. and Mrs. John Nichols.

"You okay?" Bobby eyed me with worry.

My hands grew clammy on the steering wheel. I didn't even remember driving for the past several minutes. "Yeah, I'm fine," I lied. "I'm just thinking."

Then his hand reached out and touched my arm. I flinched. "I know about what you and your children have been through. Dorothy told me that day we first met. My heart went out to you, and quite frankly, I haven't been able to get you out of my mind. I've wanted to come over and talk with you. Maybe see if there is anything I can do to help. I've been worrying about how you're coping with all of this pain and how it's affecting your children."

Tears trickled down my face as I pulled back from his touch. I didn't want to. It felt so good that I could have melted like April snow, but it had been fourteen years since a man other than John had touched me. I didn't know how to react. As desperate as I was for comfort, it scared me to the point of panic.

"We're hanging in there," I said with fake optimism. "We have family who help, and I'm working hard on my writing career. It's bound to get better in time."

He didn't answer, but as he drew his hand back, his lips wore a slight curve of understanding. I wasn't ready. It wasn't time to share and trust, yet he seemed patient and willing to let things move in their own time. I already liked that about him.

The group welcomed Bobby and listened intently as he shared his testimony. His marriage was never a sound one, which he attributed to marrying a woman he didn't truly love. He described Denise as a younger woman, lost and frail, always in crisis and needing his rescue since they met in a diner. He felt sorry for her and saw their marriage as a way of protecting her from an abusive family. It was amazing that they had a child together since they slept in separate bedrooms, but Mandy was conceived on one of the rare nights when Denise came to Bobby's bed. According to him, those moments were few and far between. When Mandy was born, she became Bobby's everything. She had his brown eyes and cleft chin. She was small and helpless in his arms, filling his lonely heart with someone to love who would actually love him back.

He claimed that Denise didn't love him any more than he loved her. Mandy filled that void with hugs, kisses, and love. That was why it hurt so much when, after the divorce, Denise refused him parental visits.

"I guess I have my own self to thank for that," he admitted. "Those years with Denise were so lonely that I started drinking and depend on the stuff now. That's her crutch in court. That I'm an alcoholic so I'm not allowed to see my daughter. And no matter how many times I've tried to get the court to overturn its decision, it always sides with Mandy's mother. The bottom line is that Denise doesn't want me to see my little girl. We're divorced and she wants me out of their lives. I have to accept that unless I find a financial windfall somewhere and can hire a top-notch attorney, I've lost my daughter."

His voice choked with emotion, and I gently touched him. It was amazingly easy to comfort him. I didn't think I would know how or even have anything inside of me to give, but as I rested my hand in his, he squeezed it and gave me a smile through his despair.

My dad was baby-sitting and expected me back in a few minutes, yet I hated to have this night come to an end. I was more and more drawn to Bobby and his gentle soul. He wasn't afraid to share, even to cry in front of people. He was as genuine as anyone I'd ever known. It was a safe feeling. Bobby was like a warm, inviting haven after catching the brunt of a storm, and I wanted to let myself enjoy it.

We ended up sitting in my car and talking a while more before leaving the parking lot that night. Dad would wonder why I was getting home later than usual, but I reasoned it wouldn't be that late. A few minutes wouldn't make that much difference. Those few minutes turned into over an hour. Even then, I wished I didn't have to go home.

"This was nice," Bobby said as I pulled up in his driveway. "Thanks for taking me, and maybe next time I'll do the driving."

"I'm glad you came. I hope it helped."

"Talking about what hurts always helps," he answered. "That's why I hope you'll open up to me one day. I want to be helpful in getting you through all you're dealing with. My problems are nothing compared to the nightmare that you and those young ones are living with. All I want is to be a friend and help in any way that I can."

I was so raw inside that my tears spilled down my face before I had a chance to hold them back. The beauty of it was I didn't feel the need to hide them. Not with Bobby. Whatever was building between us was based on real truth and honesty. Something I hadn't had in a long time. Then he surprised me and asked if he could kiss me. To my amazement, I said that he could.

It wasn't anything like I expected. He didn't come on fast and hard, overwhelming me with urgency that most of the men in my past had demonstrated. There was no heavy breathing or tongues swirling in a frenzy. Instead, he cupped my face with the warmth of his hands before lightly kissing the tracks of my tears, never even placing his mouth on my lips. I relaxed into it, closing my eyes as his kisses trailed down my cheeks. It was as if he were tasting my tears, making them his own, showing me I wasn't alone. By the time he softly smiled, said good-bye, and got out of the car, I was practically too limp to drive home.

Bobby started coming over every evening after that. He'd play with the girls, sometimes have dinner with us, and treat us to the zoo or a movie on the weekends. It seemed like a good friendship and a wonderful distraction from our problems. He didn't have to deal with his sorrow over losing Mandy because now he could play a father role with Vanessa and Mariah. I didn't have to fear being alone anymore and even had something to look forward to each day. I had companionship again. He was someone to talk to, go places with, cook for, and joke with. I started paying attention to my appearance. In truth, I wanted him to find me attractive. I needed to feel desired.

I may have been distracted from dwelling on my heartache over John, but my insecurities from his betrayals still gnawed at me. Whenever I noticed Bobby was staring at me a little longer than usual or watching me cross the room with an appreciative gaze, it would feed that place inside of me that craved attention and validation. Having another man find me attractive was wonderful ammunition against the monster I still fought since learning of John's affair. The one that constantly told me I wasn't sexy enough or good enough because my husband strayed with another woman. What man would ever find me appealing when my own husband preferred somebody else? Well, Bobby did.

Bobby started filling the empty spaces that John had caused. I had a friend again. It wasn't as good as the life I loved and lost, but it was something to cling to. I didn't even contemplate suicide anymore—at least, until one Saturday when the mail came.

John's handwriting caught my eye as I gathered my bills from the mailbox. It was an envelope addressed to me and stamped in red ink with *Inmate at Mansfield Correctional*. I didn't have to do any more than hold it in my hand. That was enough to start the tears flowing. I wasn't sure if I should open it or just throw it away. Nothing he could say would make any difference. I walked toward the garbage can by the side of our house intending to throw it out, but when I got there, it was as if my hand couldn't let it go. I finally tore it open and read it.

> *Hi, Baby,*
>
> *I'm sorry if getting this letter upsets you. I know you probably don't want me to write since you made it clear you were going to move on. I wasn't going to, but it's just so hard in here. I don't think I can take another day. I miss you and my girls so much and hate myself for all the pain I've put you through. After everything I've done, telling you how much I love you probably sounds empty, but I do and I always have. It was never because of you that I messed up so bad. I don't even know why I did. You and our girls were my world and my everything, but something kept making me turn into this other person every time I was away from you guys. I hated who I was. I hated the things I did, but I couldn't stop. No matter how hard I tried, I kept going back to that dark side that eventually destroyed us all. Being in prison gives a person a lot of time to think. I remember the happy times we had, the thirteen years of memories that nothing can ever take away from me. I play them in my head like movies over and over until my heart aches to go home so badly that I think I'm going to die in here. I know I have no claim to you anymore. I know you won't*

wait for me, but please know that my love for you is real. My love for my family was the only thing that was really meaning-ful to me. I only pray that one day you'll understand. I know God forgives me, but the trick from now on is learning to for-give myself.

With forever love,
John

Everything disappeared around me. I was no longer aware that I was standing over the garbage can or that my children were in the house patiently waiting for me to fix them lunch. All I could do was clutch the page with my husband's handwriting on it, shaking and struggling to breathe as my eyes blurred with tears. The wound I carried deep inside was now oozing again. John's words of love, remorse, and saying that God forgave him were so totally ridiculous that I wanted to laugh. Since when did he care what God thought of him? Certainly not when he was committing adultery with a teenage girl.

"Mom? Are you alright?" Vanessa appeared out of nowhere, gaping at me with deep concern as I stood weeping next to the garbage. *"What's going on? Tell me what happened."*

Her voice sounded far away. It didn't even register that she was actually next to me or that I was scaring her with my bizarre behavior. All I could do was grip the letter tightly in my hand, feeling my hurts surfacing again. On some level, perhaps John intended this reaction. To make sure I didn't heal. To prevent me from being free. Why else would he still write words of love when he knew I wouldn't believe them anymore?

My sadness turned to anger, making me sob uncontrollably and start kicking the garbage can with all of my might, over and over again. Now Mariah was outside, just as frightened and upset as her sister. I could feel their eyes on me. I knew they were terrified, but I was in a cocoon with my anger. I rushed inside the house, where a cartoon blared on the television. My tantrum led me to my bedroom, where I continued unleashing my fury. I kicked the wooden sliding doors to the closet, leaving a gaping, splintering hole that matched the hole in my heart. From there, I went to my dresser, knocked the lamp over, sent papers, letters, and photos flying, and smashed the clock radio with my fist. Everything in my path took the form of John and his filthy lies. I wanted to destroy him the way he destroyed me. I wanted him to hurt. To suffer. To end up in little pieces that could never be put back together.

The girls stood in my bedroom doorway, their faces pale with fright.

"I'm going to call Bobby," Vanessa declared and ran to the kitchen. My tears kept falling, and the punch of John's letter kept aching in my gut. Was he that deranged? Did he really think he could just drop me a line after all that we've been through? It was unfathomable how he could even think I would care what he had to say—but I did. Too much. If I didn't, I would have thrown out the letter, unopened and unread. I hated him for always hurting me. I hated myself for letting him. Wait until I ended it all. Then he'd know how his affair destroyed the woman he claimed to love. Then I'd be in peace, never to be devastated by him again.

"He's coming." Vanessa rushed back to my room, the cordless phone still in her hand. "I told Bobby you were really upset, and he's coming right over to make sure you're okay."

When did we stop depending on my parents who lived right around the corner? Hadn't they always been there from the beginning of this nightmare to open their home to us when we had nowhere to live, buy us our house with their retirement savings, and tell us that whatever we needed, to just come to them? Didn't they always have open arms for hugs, shoulders to lean on, and loving hearts that shared our pain? It used to be them that we turned to when things got tough, but now the first person Vanessa thought of when she was scared was Bobby. He'd make it all right. He'd know what to do. He'd drop everything and save the day just like her daddy used to do when she fell off her bike or wiggled out her first baby tooth with a blood-soaked tissue. Had she gotten over him already? Was it now Bobby's job? I wasn't sure if that was a good sign or a red flag.

It had been over a year since we'd left Ohio and moved to Florida. She had received a handful of letters from her father since then, mostly saying he was sorry over and over, then telling her to be brave, to help Mommy with her little sister, and to work hard in school. She wouldn't talk too much about how she felt. She'd just share them with me and then tuck them away in a box she kept under her bed. I knew her stomachaches and sliding grades in school resulted from her grief. Mariah dealt with hers by clinging to me and having bad dreams. So much was bottled up inside each one of us that we didn't know what to do with it. Sometimes I thought all three of us were walking time bombs just waiting to explode.

My flurry of destruction finally started to wind down. I was tired. So horribly fatigued that I wondered where all that energy had come from to sustain such craziness. I looked around at my damaged room, then to the worried faces of my helpless little girls. I didn't like feeling out of control, especially in front of my children. Tears pooled in my eyes as I tried to regain my sanity. I mumbled something about being really sorry and then hurried back outside where there was air to breathe, space to calm down, no worried gazes pinning me to the wall.

That was when I looked up and saw Bobby coming. All I could think to do was run into his arms.

"It's okay, Baby," he whispered, rocking me back and forth as I sobbed against him. "I've got you. You're okay. I promise, from now on, I'm not going to let anything ever hurt you again."

And as we stood in the middle of the road, blocking out everything around us, I believed him. The one who swore to herself that she would never trust anything a man ever said again was actually letting her guard down. God knows I needed something to stop the hurt. We needed a rock to lean on, and Bobby seemed as solid as anything I had seen in a long time. I found myself clinging to him, right or wrong, not really knowing what it meant. I wasn't in love with him, yet I loved how safe he made me feel at a time when I had so many fears.

For the first time since opening that letter, I closed my eyes and relaxed inside the blissful calm of Bobby's embrace, relishing the shelter from the storm.

Four

Broken Pieces

I didn't think we'd have a Christmas tree that year. Not only could I not afford one, but the thought of holiday music, festive decorations, and packages wrapped and tied with ribbon would only be like salt in our wounds. I wanted the holidays to simply pass us by.

We had managed to get through Thanksgiving by explaining to my parents and my sister's family that we weren't up to it. While most families were gathered around a traditional turkey dinner giving thanks for all of their blessings, I took Vanessa and Mariah to the movie theater to see *101 Dalmatians*.

Sitting in the dark, swallowed up by a giant screen—the perfect way to escape reality. For an hour and a half, we lived in a world of lovable spotted puppies. But Christmas was much harder to face. John wasn't here to bring in the usual fresh-cut tree that was so tall and spectacular that it would graze the ceiling. He didn't teeter on the ladder outside, stringing lights on the house in his bright red Santa hat or come through the door after doing his Christmas shopping, grinning like a kid with a mountain of secrets that none of our begging would coax him into exposing. No happy, magical feel to the air. No sense of anticipation, excitement, or wonder. Just a quiet dread.

"Remember when Daddy used to do that?" Vanessa said one night as we were watching a commercial for batteries. The father in the ad put batteries in a train set on Christmas Eve to supposedly test it out and ended up playing with it so long that he fell asleep on the floor. "He'd always play with the stuff Santa brought me. He acted more like a kid than like my dad."

Mariah twirled her hair and yawned. "I don't remember that. I hardly remember anything about Daddy at all."

"You were too small," I explained, putting my arms around her. "You were only three when your daddy went away."

"Tell me about him," she begged. "Tell me funny stuff he did."

I couldn't believe it, but Vanessa and I smiled at each other. So many wonderful memories crossed our minds at once, bringing back happier times when our family was healthy and whole.

"There are the photo albums," Vanessa said. "Would you like me to get them?"

I was hesitant to put us through reliving the past again. Even though our photo collection held only fond memories, it still hurt to go back. Still, I actually hungered to look back and remember, just like the girls seemed to be doing. Vanessa was already off the couch and getting the albums before I could decide whether or not I was really ready to join in.

Mariah listened intently as Vanessa and I flipped through the albums, pointing out favorite photographs that brought to mind funny stories. Halloween Daddy dressed up like a punk rocker wearing an orange Mohawk wig and tons of chains around his neck. Next was the photo in which he sported a cast after breaking his hand at work demonstrating some exercise equipment. Wedding pictures, pictures in the hospital after Vanessa was born, and photos of newborn Mariah cradled in the crook of his arm as he spoke on the telephone and bragged to friends and family about the second perfect daughter we had been blessed with. Then we found some Christmas pictures of decorating the tree, baking cookies, opening packages on Christmas morning. It was then I lost my composure. Mariah noticed my falling tears first.

"I think it would make us happier to have a tree," she said in her best grown-up voice, sliding an arm around me. "We're sad and everything, but the pretty lights and presents will make us feel better."

Vanessa hovered protectively, worried that I was headed for a tantrum again. "No. Mom isn't up to it this year. We don't have to do it so soon. Just leave her alone, and don't make her feel guilty because Daddy ruined our Christmas."

I was stunned. It was the first time Vanessa acknowledged that her father had ruined anything. So far, she had kept it all hidden inside, only letting her pain show if she was frustrated over something. Then she would blow. I had started her in counseling, but even in her weekly sessions she didn't reveal how she really felt about her dad.

The next day after Vanessa went to school, I told Mariah we had a mission. We would get an inexpensive artificial tree and have it up and decorated by the time her sister came home.

"I thought you didn't want to because of Daddy," she said, unsure how to react. "I don't want it to make you sad."

I could have promised her that it wouldn't, but I wasn't going to lie. Instead, I sat on the couch and drew her onto my lap, locking my arms around her as she snuggled up against me. She was so small and sweet, smelling of fresh air and bubble gum. As I relished her, I couldn't help hurting for John. He'd never experience the joy of holding her like this while she was still little and precious. Even Vanessa had gotten so much taller and grown up since the last time he had seen her. Would he even recognize her with her wild nail polish and pierced ears? So many years of his children's lives were going to slip by like sand through his fingers. I couldn't fathom missing out on seeing them change and grow, as he would have to.

I stroked Mariah's silky golden hair. "I think a tree will be just what we need around here. We're not going to miss out on Christmas."

A knock at the door Christmas Eve startled me. I had just put the children to bed. After enjoying eggnog at my parents' house, we had walked around the neighborhood admiring everyone's outdoor lights before coming home to put out stockings and a plate of cookies for Santa. I was so glad. That was one joy their father hadn't stolen from them.

"I wanted to drop these off," Bobby said as I opened the door. He had several presents wrapped in fancy red paper. "I hope I'm not coming over too late. I tried earlier, but you weren't at home."

"No, it's not too late. In fact, your timing is just perfect. I was going to call and invite you over. I know tonight is going to be hard for both of us to get through."

He gave a sad smile. "Mandy used to ask to open one present on Christmas Eve, but it always turned into two or three. Then we'd put her to bed, but she got up off and on all night long, saying that she heard footsteps on the roof or sleigh bells in the sky." He cleared his throat and shrugged, chasing away the onset of tears. "It's hard not having her here to do that anymore."

We ended up sitting in the kitchen for several hours, talking about Christmases past and sharing eggnog. He was so honest with his pain that I had to ask if he thought it would ever go away.

"No," he said frankly. "I don't see it going away. Maybe it will get easier. Maybe it will fade with time, but the void of not having my little girl in my life will always be there."

I remembered what Dorothy said about him not caring if he lived or died. "Do you ever think about not going on?" My question sounded foolish. I regretted asking it the moment it escaped.

He cocked his head and looked at me. "Why? Do you?"

"I'm asking you that question. Can't you just answer me?"

"You already know."

"I don't know."

He squinted at me, as if peering through my outer shell to the inner core of my thoughts. "Yes, you do. We both know what's going on with each other. I think we knew it from the day we met. I decided there was nothing to live for soon after I realized Denise was going to make it impossible for Mandy to be a part of my life. You decided the same after John's betrayals shattered your world. It's in your eyes whether you realize it or not. I see it every time I look at you. The funny thing is, wanting to save you from dying is saving me from dying myself."

I traced the rim of my empty glass with a nervous finger. Knowing how easily he uncovered my deepest secrets made me hesitant to look at him or speak. What he claimed to be so obvious, no one else seemed to notice at all. My own parents who saw me on a daily basis and went through every step of this nightmare with me didn't see it.

My own children had no idea. The people in my divorce group didn't know. It rattled me how Bobby could so easily walk into the picture and become aware of my desire to commit suicide as if my plan was flashing in neon lights across my sweater: *I'm going to kill myself because I can't take it anymore!*

I was tempted to get up and refill our glasses for distraction, but the way he was staring left me no room to move. He wasn't about to let me out of this conversation so easily.

"Maybe if I help you, you can help me," he continued. "I think we'll both feel better if we have a friend to lean on. Deep down, I think we both want to make it."

"I've thought about it a great deal," I reasoned, keeping my voice hushed in case the girls were listening for Santa. "It isn't something I would do just because I was hurting. Yes, I want an end to this and truly believe I'll never heal, but if I end it, my girls will have a better life. That's the bottom line. They'll have my sister and her husband to raise them, a gorgeous house in Orlando to grow up in, and money for their future from my life insurance policy. I'm not ever going to be able to offer them anything, Bobby. Look at me. I'm not a career person or anything. I've been a stay-at-home mom for nearly nine years and earn less than ten thousand a year with my writing. We're on food stamps because I can't even afford to feed my children myself. I can't send them to college. I won't be able to afford braces if they need them. I'm so messed up that I pitch temper tantrums and scare them half to death. I'm broken inside and won't ever be okay again, so what's the use in trying to be super mom? It will be hard for them at first, but I believe they would have a better life in the long run. Is that so wrong? I'd be free of the horrendous pain I live with every second of every day. If you're my friend, you'll understand. That's what I need from you right now."

"I understand," he answered. "I know what it is to lose hope, but in answer to your question about it being wrong … yes, it would be. What those babies need far more than a fancy house or life insurance money is their mom to love them and take care of them. They've already lost one parent. Their hearts can't take losing another."

"They've lost me already," I argued. "The night their daddy shot and killed his secret lover, I died right along with that girl."

There was a brittle silence as I huddled in my chair. It wasn't good that I had shared so much. I thought Bobby could relate since he was also torn apart by loss, but it was clear that he didn't. I was getting no understanding at all. That made me angry and disappointed at the same time. It would have been such a help to have a friend who knew what having your soul ripped apart felt like and could appreciate the lure of killing yourself as a way to recapture peace. I wanted him to nod and agree with all the far-fetched things I was saying. As selfish as it was, I wanted his blessings for my suicide plans.

"Don't you believe in love anymore?" His question was simple, yet it was the hardest thing I ever had to answer.

"Do you?"

His grin flashed briefly. "Now, you're the one answering a question with a question. Just tell me … do you or don't you?"

Love existed. I knew that. My mom and dad certainly had the real thing, sticking together through thick and thin since they were childhood sweethearts. My sister seemed to have found it with her husband of ten years. But I knew he was asking if I still believed that my own heart could love. Flashes of John's smile teased my mind; my lips tingled with the memory of his kiss.

What we had together felt about as real as true love could get, but I was blind, deaf, and dumb. Thirteen years—all for nothing. How could I ever trust my own judgment again?

"No," I answered, an edge of bitterness hardening my voice. "I could never love another man again."

He remained still, watching me as I got up to pour us more eggnog. In a way I was hoping he'd leave. It was getting far too intense, and I didn't enjoy digging deep down into my gut to produce answers to his personal questions. Yet, wasn't that what I admired so much about Bobby's character? That he didn't play the games most people played?

I returned to the table with two more rounds of holiday cheer. As I looked out the window, I could see the pitch black of night giving way to the pale gray of dawn. I did it. I survived Christmas Eve without my husband. There were still stockings to fill and a dollhouse to put together, but I wasn't tired anymore. I'd have plenty of energy to get started on those projects shortly. The thrill of my victory over loneliness gave me a second wind. Thanks to Bobby, the night wasn't so long, and John's ghost barely had the chance to haunt me. I smiled at Bobby, forcing the shadows from my heart, and raised my glass for a toast.

"Merry Christmas," I said. "Here's to making it through the night."

His eyes sparkled as he clinked his glass to mine. "It just goes to show that we can both do things we thought were impossible. We just need to give ourselves a chance."

I thought of his words long after he left. As I filled stockings, nibbled on Santa's cookies, and set up Mariah's dollhouse, I thought about all the baby steps I had taken and the progress I had made. Progress I never thought would happen. I made it through John's trial. I held him up and even gave him hope for the future by telling him his daughters would always need him. We made it through Halloween, Thanksgiving, and now Christmas Eve without him. The world was still intact and turning. I sat back and admired our small artificial tree, twinkling with white lights and decorated with strung popcorn and ornaments. It wasn't the magnificent nine-foot spruce we used to enjoy, but it was ours. It stood like a symbol of sweet accomplishment, leaning slightly to the right with branches crooked and bent. It was beautiful. We three girls had managed to carry on despite the ache in our hearts.

We just need to give ourselves a chance.… We can do things we thought were impossible.… Bobby's words filtered through me as I gave a tearful smile. I realized that he gave me what I needed more than anything for Christmas—a ray of hope.

The more time I spent with Bobby, the less I thought about my suicide plans. Gradually, I experienced more smiles than tears, more happy days than hard days. The children grew very close to him. He helped with their homework, taught Mariah how to ride her bike without training wheels, and even lectured Vanessa on the boyfriend she bragged about having at school. We started feeling more and more like a family with a daily rhythm, doing all the things a family would do except at the end of the evening, Bobby would say good-bye and head back to his own house. It was a comfortable arrangement that worked well for both of us. We were close but didn't cross over any boundaries.

"It's a full moon," he commented one night as I walked him down the driveway.

I gazed at the perfect silver circle reflecting in the black of his eyes. "It's beautiful, very romantic, actually."

It had been building for some time—moments when Bobby had taken my hand as we strolled through the supermarket, brushed my hair from my eyes, slid my shoes off and rubbed my tired feet. We were pressed up against each other when I taught him how to dance the box step, and I always massaged suntan lotion on his shoulders whenever he mowed the lawn. I began to look forward to any excuse to touch or be touched. It astounded me that any man could awaken my desire again, even though it scared me enough to keep those desires in check. But it was getting harder and harder for us to keep our relationship on a platonic level.

"It is romantic," he answered, looking up into the star-filled sky as the breeze riffled through his hair. "It makes it hard not to do what I'd really like to do. What's been on my mind all night."

I swallowed hard. "And what is it that you'd really like to do?"

He looked at me and hesitated. He looked like he was going to speak, but then he bypassed words and pulled me into his arms. As good as it felt, I immediately drew back.

"I'm not going to hurt you," he whispered. "I know you're scared, but I would never do anything to make things worse. I care about you and the children. I want to be here for you and show you there is such a thing as a safe place to give your heart. If you'll let me, I'd like to be the one to teach you how to love again."

He tilted my chin with his finger, kissing the tip of my nose, my eyes, my cheek. Finally, he kissed me softly on my mouth. It was tender at first, soon building to something more urgent and demanding. Fear flowed through me, chilling my blood, making me want to turn and run as far from this man as I could get, but my physical need for the closeness of someone was stronger than I had realized. I was shocked by my own eager and willing response to the touch of his lips. I leaned into him, trying to relax and enjoy the pleasure—until a siren sounded in the distance. He kept on moving the velvety softness of his heated mouth over mine, but as the siren got nearer, passing our street and wailing louder and louder, I was no longer there. I was no longer under the full moon in Bobby's arms, letting myself be kissed. I was inside Karen's car, seeing her body jerk as John towered over her, squeezing the trigger with a crazed expression on his face.

"No!" My voice pierced the air as I shoved Bobby away. My breathing was ragged, and I staggered as if unable to keep my footing. I was so afraid the images would return that I started sobbing and covering my eyes.

"What is it?" Bobby's tone was desperate and concerned. "What happened? Tell me what's wrong."

"He killed her," I cried. "He just kept shooting and shooting. I hear it. The shots, the sirens. It's like I was there and I can see it all."

He forced me back into the haven of his arms, holding me so tightly that there was no room to tremble. I wondered if I was going mad. Wasn't it insanity when someone calmly kissed a man under the light of the moon one minute and then screamed hysterically over imaginary gunshots the next? I had no reason to flip out like that. I had actually been doing much better. Spending every evening with Bobby had been wonderful therapy for the girls and me. The void John left us with had become less monumental. Now all that progress went straight down the drain all because I heard a siren.

"It's going to be okay," Bobby assured me. "It's going to take time. Probably lots of it, but you will get over this, and I'll be right there to make sure you do. That's a promise."

I blinked at him, wanting to tell him how I hated that word. How any man who promised me anything filled me with fear. Bobby meant to soothe and encourage me, but no matter how I wanted him to be the answer to the nightmares I still suffered, he couldn't protect me from myself. He could kiss me and hold me and tell me everything would be okay, but it was all a lie. Just like the years I shared with John. Nothing but a convincing, poisonous lie that I couldn't let myself believe. Believing makes you helpless. It puts your life in someone else's hands, and once they have you there, they have the power to destroy you. I'd never let myself be that stupid again.

"I've got to go," I said, looking back at the house. "I've left the children alone for too long."

"Are you going to be all right?"

I shrugged, feeling very uncertain. "If hearing gunshots is normal, I guess I'm perfectly fine."

"It's part of the process you obviously have to go through. Just give yourself time."

Time didn't appeal to me. I didn't want any more time. Time meant more hurting, suffering, and struggling. I was growing so weary. I just wanted it to end so I could live a normal life again. I really just wanted to die.

"If you need me, I'm right down the street. Call me. Any time, day or night, and I'll be right here to hold you and help you through. I promise. You and the children are going to make it through this. I know you don't believe that now, but I do. Truly, I do."

Do you take this woman to be your wife, to have and to hold from this day forward, in sickness and health, for richer or poorer, for better or worse until death do you part?

I do … I do … I promise … I do … I'll always be there … I do, I do, I do….

Tears slid from my eyes as I absorbed his words, so sickeningly familiar. "I'm sorry, but I've got to go," I uttered. He stood motionless as I ran back inside the house, slamming the door behind me.

Just as I began questioning my own mental state, Vanessa also started going downhill. Trying to concentrate in school was difficult. She often became tearful and scared to talk to other kids because they might ask questions about where she moved from, why we left Ohio, and where her daddy was. The shame she felt weighed heavy on her heart, yet she rarely expressed it, except when a letter would come for her from her father. Then I'd see her eyes well up and her chin quiver, but only until she had finished reading it. After that, she'd boldly dry her tears and place it in the box under her bed. Nothing I said broke through to her. She wouldn't share her feelings with me. All I could do was hope she would share with her therapist.

"Mrs. Nichols? Would you mind stepping into my office?" Peggy smiled at me as I entered the room where my daughter had just had a thirty-minute counseling session. It was Vanessa's fifth week in treatment, and I was hoping for some kind of miracle.

I took a seat on the leather couch next to my daughter. Within the walls of this room a world of problems had been shared, but the atmosphere was still cheery, with a play table and Legos, stuffed animals and puzzles, along with scads of drawings taped to the wall. I focused on one that depicted a boy frowning in his bed with a caption that read *I hate my bad dreams.*

Peggy assumed her chair across from us. "I think it's time to talk about where we go from here. Vanessa is obviously having a hard time attending school and making friends, which is no surprise after all she's been through. I'd like to put her on an antidepressant as a way to help her cope."

I was horrified. My doctor had already prescribed an antidepressant for me, which I took faithfully, but Vanessa was just a child. She was only twelve. It broke my heart to think of her needing a pill in order to function.

"Is it really necessary?" I asked. "I was hoping these sessions would get her out of this depression without medication."

Peggy looked at Vanessa, who still hadn't lifted her gaze from her tissues. "For those who are deeply troubled, both medication and therapy are key. They work well together. She will be carefully monitored by our staff physician, so you don't have to worry about her safety or any side effects. I think it will help her greatly and give her the edge she needs to start working on things."

"Like what?" I looked hopefully at Vanessa, but she looked the other way.

"I've recommended a few things for her to do on her own time," Peggy said. "One is for her to open up to you more about things on her mind. She has talked a great deal about Bobby and how she feels about your relationship. I think she needs to feel safe to express herself to you on that subject without worrying that you'll get angry at her or not understand."

My jaw dropped. "You love Bobby. I didn't think you had a problem with him coming around."

She shrugged her shoulders. "He's nice and everything. I like him, but...."

The silence was awkward. Peggy leaned forward and leveled a gaze at her young patient. "Tell your mother exactly what you told me. She has a right to know how this relationship makes you feel."

I didn't want to get angry, but the longer Vanessa sat saying nothing, the more agitated I became. We had always been able to talk to each other about anything and everything. We were more than mother and daughter. We were the very best of friends. Since when did she fear baring her soul to me?

"I saw the two of you," she finally said, a shadow of annoyance crossing her face. "When you walked him out the other night before he went home. I saw him kissing you and running his hands all up and down your back. I saw you kissing him right back. It made me sick. I don't see how you could do that when I thought you loved Daddy so much."

"My God," I blurted, feeling the need to defend myself. "It's been over a year, and it's my business anyway. I guess since your father disappeared on us, you want me to grow old alone?"

Peggy lightly touched the back of my hand. "If we can listen to what Vanessa is saying, she's just telling you how your kissing Bobby made her feel. It isn't about who is right or wrong. It is simply how she feels."

I clenched my teeth in an effort to tame my outbursts. I was supposed to be helping her through this mountain of misery that she had to deal with, not making it more difficult for her.

"I'm sorry," I said, reaching over to take her hand. I flinched at the tears rolling down her face. "I don't want you to be afraid to talk to me about how you feel. I'll try to be a better listener. It's just very hard for me, too. I've got a lot bottled up inside."

Peggy watched our interaction. "And I've asked Vanessa to do one more thing between this session and our next. It has to do with the letters she's been receiving from her father. He is sharing his feelings with her and trying to explain himself and redeem himself. He is telling her the things he needs to express. I think Vanessa needs to do the same in return. If she isn't ready to write back to her father, then I told her to get a journal and write her thoughts in there. I want her to talk to her journal as if she is talking to her dad, telling him how angry she is, how hurt she feels, and how hard her life is now that he has turned her world upside down. Every night before she goes to bed, I want her to take a few quiet minutes to talk to her dad like she would if he were here. I think that could free up a lot of this hurt she is holding inside."

Just picturing her able to talk with her dad again rocked my composure. They used to be so close and loved doing things together. With his silly jokes and pranks, he could make her laugh until her stomach would hurt. I knew that losing her daddy was like having a beloved friend die. She must miss talking to him and having him there just as much as I did.

"I think that's a good idea," I said to Vanessa. "We can stop at the store and get a journal on the way home. Would you like that?"

"That would be okay," she replied. "Do you want one, too? Don't you want to talk to Daddy?"

God help me, I did, more than I wanted to admit, but it was senseless. What could I possibly have to say to him except I hated him for destroying our lives? Besides, I had Bobby now. He was my friend, my companion, the person I could talk to about anything. I didn't need to turn to John for anything anymore.

"I don't think so," I said softly, hoping it wouldn't upset her. "I think your father and I have said all we need to say to each other."

But even as I heard my voice make that statement, my soul felt restless as if something important remained incomplete. The door to my past wasn't quite closed. I hated feeling that way because there was nothing more for John and me to talk about. Mentally I had severed all ties between us a long time ago. I had to do everything in my power to make sure it stayed that way. Vanessa's therapy may be to open up to her father, write her feelings about him in a journal, and share her pain, but I knew mine was the exact opposite. I had to let go. I had to forget, and I knew that was exactly what Bobby was there for. As long as his arms were around me, John's shadow couldn't follow me anymore.

FIVE

Private Battles

Each month I swallowed my pride and stood in the food-stamp line for our coupon book. No matter how many times I did it, I never got used to it. It was a place I never imagined myself being. I have always had a comfortable life, was raised in a loving home by both parents, never wanting for anything. We weren't wealthy, but my father earned a good living while my mother stayed at home and raised my sister and me.

Waiting in line for food stamps was terribly hard, especially while holding Mariah's hand. Although she couldn't comprehend what needing government assistance meant, I wondered if she sensed from me how frightened I was about our situation. Every dollar mattered. We usually made our money stretch as far as possible by eating macaroni and cheese most nights and diluting the laundry detergent. If anything extra came up like wanting to go to the movies or eat out, I said no. I knew it wasn't something I could help, yet it made me feel like such a failure. Despite my parents always offering to help financially, I kept insisting on trying to make it on my writer's salary, even if it meant literally scraping the bottom.

I'd watch the other people waiting in line for their stamp books, looking weary and dismal. Many braved the long and tedious wait with fussy, crying babies and young children. I would scan each woman's face, wondering what her story was. In my heart I knew they had to be similar to mine. Lost dreams and failed relationships, leaving a single mother to raise children without a father. I wondered if they had gotten the rug yanked out from under them as I had or if it was something gradual that they could see coming. I wondered if they were taking sleeping pills and antidepressants. If they cried themselves to sleep. All I knew for sure was that we had one thing in common: we didn't have enough money to feed our own children.

"I hate to think of you in a place like that," Bobby told me one night as we relaxed on the porch, sharing a beer from the six-pack he brought over. "It tears me up to know you have to rely on food stamps."

"I have no choice right now," I answered. "I'm barely making ten thousand per year with my writing, and that's just not enough. It takes two people to support a family. I have to use food stamps because it's impossible for me to do it alone. I refuse to take any more from my parents."

His face softened. "Maybe you don't have to."

I took a swig from my beer and let it pool in my stomach. It was beginning to ease the tension in my muscles. Bobby loved his beer and had at least three every evening. Now I was beginning to depend on them myself at the end of the day. Anything that helped me unwind and relax was fine with me. "What do you mean?" I asked. "Do you know the winning lottery numbers or something?"

"No, I just thought that maybe I could help you out. I make pretty good money as a welding foreman and live rent free since it's my mom's property. All I really have is food and child support, plus the electric bill, which my brother and I split. I have enough left over after each paycheck to give a weekly amount to you. That way perhaps you could get off the food stamps and not have to go through that degrading ordeal. I'd really like to be able to do that for you."

"I don't need that," I snapped, taking another swallow from my beer and shifting in my chair. "That's not your responsibility. It's mine. I don't want to depend on a man for anything, Bobby. I got burned doing that with John and it left me defenseless. I can't repeat that mistake by depending on you."

"I'm not John," he replied. "I'm not the past. I'm someone who cares very deeply about you and your children. All I want to do is help you in any way I can. Getting you off government assistance would be a good place to start."

"And I'm not your past either."

His brows furrowed. "What does that mean?"

"That I'm not Denise. You don't have to see me as a frail, forlorn person who needs rescuing."

"I know that."

"Do you?"

"This has nothing to do with Denise. I just want to help you until you are able to get on your feet."

My blood boiled. I wasn't sure if it was because Bobby was offering a lifeline or because I was drowning in the first place.

The more I struggled to survive what John had inflicted on us, the more I hated him. I thought of him in his cell, getting three square meals a day, having no responsibilities, no bills to worry about, with free medical and dental if he needed it. Prison wasn't a punishment. It was a cowardly escape.

I shook my head and stared at the brown glass bottle in my hands. "I know you're only trying to be a friend, but I need to face this on my own. I need to find my own way."

Sighing with defeat, he chugged the rest of his beer and headed to the kitchen for another. All I could do was hold back the tears that I was so tired of shedding and hope he'd bring me one, too.

I didn't really consider suicide anymore. I wasn't sure if it was because I had Bobby as a daily distraction from my pain or because I didn't have the nerve to do that to my children. But the urge to just slip off into eternal sleep was gradually being replaced by a vow to myself not to let John crush me. I hated him too much to let him win. My rage was so much more comfortable than wallowing in hopelessness and seeing my life as nothing without him in it.

Still, Vanessa and Mariah handled their grief in the opposite way. Instead of their growing stronger with time, Mariah had become more insecure and clingy, needing to stay close and be with me all the time, while Vanessa continued with stomach problems and poor school attendance. Even though she was writing in her journal every night and taking her antidepressant, she remained so hurt that she was unable to function. I finally had to go to her school and speak to the principal. It was agreed that Vanessa needed to drop out for a while and do her assignments from home. Being around other kids was too much for her to cope with. My children were dysfunctional, and I was living each day held up only by my rage. I wondered if we'd ever fit in with the rest of the world again.

"I want her to start writing to her father," Peggy said to me privately at Vanessa's next counseling session. "The journal isn't enough. She needs to communicate with her dad and get some things resolved. I think once she faces that hurdle, a lot of these symptoms she has will go away and she'll be able to get her life back."

I gaped at this woman in amazement. "You've got to be kidding. I don't think that is going to help her at all. She cries when she reads his letters. It tears her apart inside. After all he's done to ruin her life, I really don't think she wants to be pen pals with him."

"She may not," Peggy said. "But I would like to at least ask her how she would feel doing it. No matter what your husband has done, Mrs. Nichols, he is still your children's father, and they will be connected to him forever. This process of loss and grieving and anger directly involves him. I think Vanessa is suffering so badly because she hasn't been able to share any of it with him. It may be hard for you to understand, but sometimes the ones who hurt us the most are the ones who can help us to heal."

"And what about Mariah? I wonder if she'll be able to start kindergarten in the fall because she is so afraid when she's away from me. She cries unless I'm right there with her. Is her problem related to hearing from her father, too?"

"Since she is so young, I think the impact of what happened in Ohio won't hit her for quite a while. All she knows is that Daddy disappeared awfully fast, and now she worries that Mommy will, too. Everything that was familiar was taken away when you moved to Florida. All the sudden changes, along with seeing you and her sister crying, have really disrupted her world. Give her time. Keeping her close to you is the right thing to do. She just needs reassurance right now. She needs to feel safe and loved and know that you're not going anywhere. This insecure phase will pass once she lets go of that fear."

"I hope so," I replied. "All I want is for my children to be okay again. I'll do anything it takes to make that happen."

Peggy peered at me. "And what about you? Are you willing to do anything you have to do to be okay again?"

"I'm okay. I'm doing much better, actually."

She cocked her head. "Are you?"

Was I really doing much better or just operating in a mode of denial, letting my hatred and rage toward the man I once loved fill me with a false sense of strength and energy? I didn't know, nor did I care to dissect it.

"Yes. I am better. I feel stronger every day. At first, I didn't think I'd ever make it on my own. I thought it would be easier to give up and die. But I'm going to make it because I refuse to let John ruin us. I'd say that I've come a long way."

"But have you been on your own? Vanessa describes your friendship with Bobby as being so close that he's over at your house on a daily basis. I just wonder if you've had a real chance to go through your own grieving process or if Bobby has been a conven- ient way for you to avoid that. You've suffered severe trauma. It may take years for you to go through all the growing, healing, and changing that need to take place. A lot of times, if we take short- cuts in that process, we end up making mistakes."

"He's just a friend," I insisted. "And I am on my own. He offered to help me with finances to get me off government assis- tance, but I told him I had to do this myself. Believe me, I'm not turning to another man for anything."

I wanted her to pat me on the back and tell me that was good, but instead she wrote something in a manila file, then excused herself to get Vanessa.

The communication between Vanessa and her father made me very uncomfortable. She would get a pen and pad of paper, close the door to her bedroom, and stay in there for hours. Once she did emerge, she'd have an envelope addressed to her dad in her hand and a drained, sober look to her face. Her eyes would be swollen and red from crying, but I could tell she didn't want to talk about it with me. When she got letters from her dad in response, the same routine would happen all over again. She'd go into her bedroom, close the door, stay there for hours, and then eventually come out looking horrible. I wanted so badly to ask her what they were saying to each other but knew it was meant to be personal between them. Several weeks later, after reading another letter from her dad, she finally approached me with it in her hands.

"He wants to call me and Mariah," she informed me uneasily. "He told me to ask you if that would be okay and then write the answer in my next letter. You don't have to talk to him or anything. It would just be for me and Mariah."

Her request caught me off guard. The letter writing between them had been tough enough to handle, but now they wanted to kick it up a notch to communicating by telephone? I had managed to stomach his handwriting popping up in our mailbox, but to think of him calling the children nauseated me. And what if I was the one who answered the phone? Hearing his voice again would be unbearable after all the emotional distance I had finally put between us. I wanted to say no; however, the look on Vanessa's face took away my ability to do so. "You can read the letter," she said, handing it to me. "He talks about you in there. How much he misses you and stuff. He says that he's changing and is working hard on himself. I think he really is sorry."

I hesitated, swimming through a haze of feelings I didn't understand. It shouldn't have mattered to me what he felt, what he thought, if he's changing or sorry at all. It didn't change the fact that he had destroyed our world and that the marriage was finished. And he missed me? Was that some kind of lame joke?

Without wanting to, I took the letter. Vanessa watched intently while I read his words, my posture rigid as the paper quivered in my hands. The two of them had obviously become more civil in their exchanges through the mail. He spoke of her last letter, thanking her for letting him know how Mariah and I were doing. He commented on a drawing she sent and encouraged her flair for art. He told her how much he hoped she'd feel better enough to return to school soon. When I read the part about the phone calls, I was astonished to learn it was Vanessa's idea.

He assured her that he would love to call, if only to hear both her and Mariah's voices again, but that he wasn't sure how I would feel. He didn't want to do anything that would make things harder on me, so he wanted her to ask first and let him know. I was thankful he at least had that much sense. He went on to say how much he loved her and that he was so sorry for all he had put us through. He told her he was learning how sick he really was by taking Bible classes and having long, heartfelt talks with the prison chaplain. He said he only hoped that one day we'd be able to forgive and understand.

My breath caught as he spoke of me in the next line. He said that he loved me deeply and missed me so much that it hurt every minute of every day. There was no way to take back the wrongs he had done or to make me understand what happened, but he hoped that one day we could at least be friends.

The letter ended by telling her to pray for our family and to give Mariah a hug.

"Can he call, Mom?" Vanessa stared at me, tears glistening on her pale face.

I tried to swallow something that refused to go down—my pride, my anger, my determination to keep him out of our lives. Whatever it was, it lodged in my throat like a dry wad of bread. All I managed to do was hand the letter back to her and give her a feeble nod.

I don't think it was a coincidence that I was so aggressive with Bobby that night. The evening was spent as it usually was, playing board games with the kids and watching videos before tucking them into bed. But after they fell asleep and he and I were finally alone, the passionate kisses, combined with a couple of cold beers, led the way to something more. The first time he even got as far as to unbutton my blouse was several weeks earlier, on New Year's Eve. We had lots of champagne, making us giggle as we huddled in my darkened bedroom once the girls fell asleep. I made him sit with me on the floor because even in my drunken state, I couldn't bear to have someone other than John in my bed. But while Bobby's hands were on me, it wasn't pleasure from his touch I was feeling. It was revenge. Even though I knew it was wrong, I was angry, and I hoped that John could in some way feel what was happening from prison. He wasn't the only one who could get it on with someone else.

Bobby wants me, you ungrateful bastard. He finds me hot and sexy and can't keep his hands off me. You obviously didn't appreciate it, but now I have someone who does! Those voices chanted in my head, prodding me to close my eyes and give myself to Bobby. Once it was over I curled up into a fetal position, feeling sick and gulping back tears.

Making love with my husband was always so beautiful, but that first time with Bobby, it left me feeling saddened and dirty. It was as if I was betraying something I held very dear. He wasn't sure what made me react that way, but he didn't press me to explain. He held me and rocked me until I calmed down, and then we agreed not to attempt that again until I was ready.

"Are you sure?" he asked that night as I tugged on his belt. "Last time you found out that it was too soon. I don't want you to feel pressured."

My hungry kisses trailed down his throat to the indent in his collarbone. I could feel his pulse pounding like a jackhammer. "I'm ready now. I want you."

He willingly followed me to my room, where I closed and locked the door. He stood awkwardly, not knowing if we were taking to the floor again, but this time I lay back on the bed and pulled him down on top of me. This time, there were no voices chanting in my head, no sadness or shedding of tears once we were finished. Making love was what I longed for because if I got close enough to Bobby, as close as I could get, then things like John writing and John calling wouldn't rattle me so much. I'd be in love with someone else, and my heart would be immune to him. It was working already. I felt a wonderful contentment holding Bobby in my arms, as he whispered something about how great it was and then drifted off to sleep.

Whenever John's calls came, I went outside to give the girls privacy. At least that's what I told them, but I really left the house because the thought of him so close, on the other end of the phone, made my hand ache to take the receiver. It had been nearly two years since I walked away from him in the Cuyahoga County Jail, and I had grown in many ways. I wasn't suicidal anymore. But having John call our home was like having him walk through the front door. I longed to just wrap my arms around him.

The call that changed everything came in June. It was Father's Day, and John had phoned the children late that Sunday afternoon after we returned from my parents' house. Bobby had just come over, since it was a particularly hard day for him, and he was outside barbecuing chicken. Neither one of us spent much time talking about our feelings that day. Though his heart was longing for Mandy—and mine hurt to see my children without their father—we laughed and drank several beers. Perhaps the buzz from the beer was what gave me the courage to stay in the house when John's call came. Instead of distancing myself, I got another bottle of beer from the fridge and paced in the background as the girls took turns talking to him.

Mariah seemed animated as she told her daddy about the cake we just had at her grandpa's house and how we gave him a new shirt for Father's Day. She told him about the lizard the cat caught on the porch, how she tried lima beans but didn't like them, and that she didn't have any girl playmates on our street—just boys who were mostly mean to her. Then she told him she loved him, wished him a happy Father's Day, and gave the phone to her sister.

"I miss you, Daddy," Vanessa said, trying to smile as tears welled in her eyes. "Did you get the card me and Mariah made for you?"

She paused, listening. I took several chugs from my beer.

"Yeah, I got your letter. You made me laugh when you told me that you fell asleep during the football game on TV last weekend. You always used to do that at home."

I pictured the way he looked stretched out on the sofa in front of the wide screen. His eyes would fall closed long before halftime, and he'd end up with his mouth wide open, snoring louder than the roar of the crowd at the game. He used to get so angry at himself for missing all the action. I couldn't help but break into a grin as I remembered.

"It's been a hard day, Daddy," Vanessa said. "I've missed you so much and felt like crying a lot. It doesn't feel right not to be with you for Father's Day."

I edged closer to Vanessa, touching her arm. The pain was so raw on her face. She gave me a sad look and then held the phone slightly away from her ear so that I could also hear what he was saying.

"I miss you guys so much," he told her. "I keep your pictures near my bunk, and I look at them a thousand times a day. That's the only thing that keeps me going in here."

His voice crumbled me. I took another quick gulp from my beer and let my gaze wander outside the kitchen window to where Bobby was jabbing the grilled chicken with a fork and Mariah hunted lizards in the grass. I hoped the chicken wasn't done. I wanted to stay and listen to John. It was so rare to be this close to him, hearing his words and knowing he was right there. All I had to do was reach for him. As if my heart took over my mind, my hand gently took the phone.

"Hi," I said. Vanessa stared wide eyed.

John paused, as if trying to figure out what happened to the conversation he was having with his daughter. Once it registered with him that it was my voice he was hearing, he gave me a surprised "Hi" right back.

"Happy Father's Day."

"Thank you." His voice sounded wonderful.

"We missed you today." Shock flowed through me. Where did that come from? I saw a broad smile spread across Vanessa's face.

His response was hesitant, as if he were too taken aback to say a word. When he finally did, his tone was filled with total elation. "I miss you, too, Baby. More than I can tell you. I keep praying somehow that you guys will be okay. I know how much I've hurt you, and I'm so very sorry. I'm hoping you and the girls learn about God and how powerful his love is. He can make a way when there seems to be no way. I rely on that promise every day."

He sounded so different. I couldn't quite identify what it was, but I had a sense that something had changed. He was strong, almost peaceful. Not desperate or pleading or pushing for anything, but merely telling me of a God who can make all things happen, and he wanted the girls and me to know him. It didn't make me want to laugh this time when he mentioned his newfound faith. It didn't seem like a slap in the face anymore after all the wrongs he had done. Whatever he had discovered, it was something that made a real difference for him. I held my bottle of beer, knowing that later that night I'd most likely have a hangover. I actually envied John for having faith while I had nothing but my futile attempts to escape. I watched Bobby reach out and take a swig of his own beer. The two of us were masters at escape. We found it in booze and each other.

"I want to thank you for letting me call the girls," John said. "It has meant so much to be able to hear their voices and let them tell me about what they're doing and how things are going."

"It's done a lot for them, too. They have had a hard time without you."

His breathing was loud. I wondered if he was fighting tears as I was. "I'm ripped in half without them. Without you. All I ever think about is holding you guys again, even though it would take a miracle."

I saw Bobby piling the chicken on the platter while Mariah ran ahead of him toward the house. She had her hands cupped as if she finally had caught a lizard. Panic pulsed through me as I pressed the phone to my ear.

"It sounds like you believe in miracles," I said, wishing there were time to say so much more. I wanted to know how, after so much despair, he could believe in anything.

"I do. Because I believe in God, and when you believe, he blesses you with miracles."

Bobby was almost at the back door now. I told John to take care and quickly handed the phone back to Vanessa. She beamed as she finished her conversation with him.

My premonition about a hangover that night was right on. I drank more than a six-pack by myself trying to recover from my brief conversation with John. Bobby had no idea that I had spoken to him. My drunken behavior didn't make him suspicious at all. He matched it with his own before going home. It wasn't anything offensive or outlandish. Bobby was a quiet, sleepy drunk. I always knew when he had more than his limit because he'd just pass out cold somewhere. The kids were getting used to seeing the two of us drink. They'd dismiss my slurring words and step over Bobby as he slept on the floor as naturally as bypassing a log in their path. I kept telling myself that it was going to stop one day. I just wondered how long we could keep up the charade.

Two letters came from John the following week. One addressed to Vanessa and one for me. After we spoke on Father's Day, it was as if the ice had been broken. I didn't wince at his handwriting anymore or resent his correspondence. It actually excited me to see one of the letters with my name on it, and I read it eagerly. Most of it thanked me over and over for talking to him that day and told how it lifted his heart. It made him believe that God was answering prayers.

> *I know I hurt you and I don't deserve anything from you, but I just hope you hear me out. I'm so sorry for the evil things I did. More than you could know. I was an empty man, despite the loving family I had, because of things in my past that I never realized were left unresolved. Chaplain Smith helped me to understand that we are products of our upbringing. We've spent many hours talking about my past and how I ended up destroying everyone I cared about. God is what I've always needed in my life, but it took this tragedy for me to finally learn that. I didn't have loving parents, but now I have my faith as a foundation to stand on. It's given me the strength to change.*
>
> *That empty space that drove me to do such unthinkable things is now filled for the first time since I was a small child. Now, all I want is for you and the girls to find the wonderful things I've found. I know you guys are hurting and struggling. I know the girls have had a lot of problems, unable to go to school and Vanessa having to take medication. I know I'm to blame for that, and it's hard to take. I'll never forgive myself, but there is a way to help them, Baby. There is a way to start healing. Take them to church. Learn what God's love is all about and I promise you, the hurting will be comforted. Nothing else can heal us when we're wounded this deeply in our souls. Will you do that for our children? Will you do it for yourself? If I never hear from you again, at least tell me that you'll do that, so I'll know that you're going to be okay.*
>
> *I love you, Mrs. Nichols. I always have and always will.*
> *John*

I read the letter repeatedly before tucking it away in my dresser drawer. It confused me that I didn't want to throw it out. I had a million reasons why I shouldn't believe anything he said, but what he wrote was like a piece of his heart on paper. Perhaps he had betrayed me before, but I believed he was honest with me now. He wasn't making excuses or trying to win me back. He wasn't even asking me to wait for him. He was showing me the way to heal so the girls and I would be okay, and it sounded far better than the way I was going.

That began my own double life. I'd spend my evenings with Bobby, do things with him and the girls every weekend, anesthetize myself with beer, make love on occasion when the kids were asleep, and watch him return to his house every night before I went to bed alone.

When he wasn't around and my time was my own, I'd write to John. Long, soul-baring letters about the pain I was trapped in and how hard each day was to face. I realized that my relationship with Bobby was a treasured friendship, but in honesty, my heart was still with John. I begged him to help me understand why he had done what he did. His answers came in the next letter. They were hard to read, but they were exactly what I had asked for.

Karen had worked at Wal-Mart as a clerk in the health and beauty department. He described her as very fragile and troubled. As the store manager, John was involved in a dispute she had with a customer one day. After calling her into his office to discuss the incident, John said she began to cry, terrified that she'd lose her job since she had a son to support and needed her weekly paycheck. John found himself comforting her and taking time to listen to her problems, which she was more than willing to share. A bond between them grew, combined with a mutual attraction.

By the time he realized how wrong it was and tried to cut it off, she told him she would make sure his family knew about their affair and that he'd lose his job since it was against Wal-Mart policy for employees to date other employees. She would make sure his life came crashing down if he tried to sever the relationship. That explained the phone calls. She was making sure he knew she meant exactly what she threatened.

He described much of what he went through with her as a sick game of blackmail. He'd try to stay away from her, but she'd manipulate him with her threats until they were involved again. Even the business trip to Pittsburgh, he explained, was her entire doing. She knew he was going, so she came up with this elaborate scheme to get him to take her with him. She showed him bruises on her arms and claimed that her baby's father had been beating her. If John took her on this trip, she'd be able to give this guy space to cool down and she'd be safer. John said he refused, but then she did what she usually did and threatened to call me with the truth if he didn't do what she said. He ended up taking her. It sickened me to read in his own words the intimate details of what transpired between them. I couldn't understand how he could have fallen for her stunts and let things get so far out of control. At the same time, his newfound honesty was refreshing. It was like he had nothing to hide anymore, and I'd never again be seduced by lies.

Whatever I wanted to know, he would tell me—and that helped. I could let my guard down when we communicated with each other. All those questions I carried of why and how were finally being answered. It didn't make the ugly past disappear, but it opened the door to John and me being friends again. I never got used to us being enemies, and it helped me to be honest with him in return.

Hi,

It seems so unreal to read all these things that were going on during our last year of marriage. I didn't know I could be so close to someone and not even know him at all. You were such a loving husband and wonderful father. You seemed as happy as the children and I were, but to find out you were such a different person with a double life is hard to comprehend. I get angry with myself for not seeing the signs. I keep wondering how differently this whole mess might have turned out had I known. Perhaps you could have gotten some counseling, or we could have gone together. Anything, other than losing our marriage and our family with you sitting behind prison walls.

I want to feel sorry for her, too. I have a hard time with that. I wonder why she had to be so vengeful. I'm not sure that this God you speak of would forgive me for what I'm about to say, but I hate her. I think of her phone calls and how she toyed with our lives as if we were pawns on a chessboard. I'm not saying that I'm glad she's dead. I don't understand how you could have done such a thing ... but, I hate her for her part in all this. It was as if she enjoyed our family's destruction.

I felt so safe all of those years. It never dawned on me that our vows could be broken and I wouldn't be the only one you made love to.

This is amazing. I can't believe how easily I can tell you my feelings now. I never thought I'd be able to talk to you ever again, but communicating with you has helped so much. I feel happier than I did before when we had no connection and I had lost you forever. I know I have Bobby now and I should probably make this work. He's always there for us and wants a family so very much. I just haven't been able to let go of our past. I haven't let Bobby become a part of our lives as much as he would like to be. Maybe now that you and I are getting things cleared between us, I'll have an easier time moving forward. I wish it could be different. I'd give anything to have my life back with you, but I can't raise our children on tears and daydreams.

Bobby is a good man, and I think the girls need a father figure in their lives. As hard as it is to say this to you, I hope you can give this relationship your blessing. For some dumb reason, I feel like I'm betraying you, and I've yet to figure out where that comes from. It's totally stupid under these circumstances. I'll never get used to any other man in my life or the children's lives besides you. No matter what happens, I know you will always be in my heart. I've learned the hard way that although some things change without warning, other things never will.

Take care in there …
Diane

Six

The Visit

With things going so well between the children and their father, they began wanting to see him. It had been two years, and with his birthday coming up in September, I considered taking them to Mansfield for a visit. They would be so happy to have time with him and to finally get to hug him, but I also worried how seeing their daddy in prison would affect them. It was hard enough for me to handle when I went to his trial.

Prison is not a lovely place. The dismal atmosphere; the colorless walls; the solemn guards with guns on their belts watching your every move; and, more than anything, the echo of the steel security doors opening and closing was impossible to shake from my mind. How would the girls be able to deal with that? But then I had to consider how they would deal with it if we didn't go and they didn't get to see their father at all.

I made the choice to take them after consulting with Peggy, who thought it would be a very positive step. Even Bobby encouraged it, helping fund the trip. After a three-day drive, we arrived in Mansfield. The night before we were to see John again, it was hard for any of us to fall asleep.

"What will Daddy look like?" Mariah asked. She lay snuggled under the covers in the double bed she shared with her sister. I pondered her question from my bed next to theirs. The last time I saw John, he didn't look at all like the man I knew. I hoped somehow *that* much had changed.

"He'll certainly look happy to see you," I replied in the darkness. "He'll be wearing prison clothes instead of regular clothes, and there will be guards in uniforms all around to watch us during the visit."

"Why?"

"Because it's a prison, sweetie. They have to watch the inmates all the time."

"To make sure they don't get away?"

My heart weighed heavy as I nodded. "Yes, that's right. To make sure they don't get away."

"I bet Daddy would run away from there if he could. I had a dream once that he did and he was back home again so we could play together."

Vanessa shifted under the blankets. "I dream about that all the time. It's always this big surprise where the doorbell rings and we answer it and he's standing there with a great big smile. We all hug him and cry. It's so real that when I wake up and realize it was only a dream, I'm really depressed for the rest of the day."

"Do you dream about him, Mommy?" Mariah asked.

I did. Very often, but they were dreams I would never share with the girls. They were hurtful dreams of John with that girl, lying to me and betraying me while laughing at my tears. Sometimes I would dream of the shooting, waking up in a cold sweat and muffling the urge to scream, but I never had a wonderful dream about him happily coming home. Even my subconscious couldn't stretch that far.

"Sure, I do," I answered truthfully. "I dream of him a lot."

It grew quiet, and I thought that perhaps the girls had fallen asleep, but then Mariah came up with one final question. One I wasn't prepared to answer.

"Why did Daddy hurt that person he was fighting with?"

I stared wordlessly at the ceiling, my heart pounding. That was all Mariah knew. That was what the child psychologist who counseled me in the emergency room that day told me to say to the children. Daddy had gotten angry during an argument with someone and hurt her so badly that he had to be punished and spend time in prison. Mariah was only six and still too young to absorb the notion of murder, but Vanessa knew the truth before we left Twinsburg. It was in all the newspapers and on the evening news. She understood that it was something we would keep from Mariah until she was old enough to comprehend it. I was forty-two and still couldn't comprehend it at all.

"He got very angry," I cautiously replied, noting the tension from where Vanessa lay next to her sister in stillness. "Too angry to really know what he was doing. He's very sorry; I know that for sure."

That must have satisfied her. Finally, the talking stopped, replaced by the breathy rhythm of children sleeping, but I remained awake for hours, anticipating what tomorrow would bring. I knew I had done the right thing in bringing them to see their father, but I wrestled with the exact same questions Mariah asked earlier: *How will he look? Why did he hurt someone and have to go to prison?* All I knew was that there was no turning back, and tomorrow we'd be behind prison walls, too.

Mansfield Correctional didn't look at all like what I expected. If it wasn't for the massive electrical fence topped with coiled razor wire surrounding the building, it could have passed for a college campus. There were even flower gardens along the walkway offering a cheerful array of colorful blossoms as we walked up to the front doors. As soon as we stepped inside, however, all pleasantries were left behind. We first stopped at the check-in counter, where a uniformed guard behind a glass window took my picture ID and the children's birth certificates through an opening with just enough room for my hand to slide through.

"What's his inmate number?" he asked, writing our names on a visitation slip.

I cleared my throat before nervously reciting it.

"He's death row, isn't he?"

My heart hit the floor for a moment. I had no idea where he got that impression, but noticed two filing cabinets behind him. One was marked "General Population" and the other "Death Row." I didn't dare look at the children's faces and only hoped they hadn't heard the question.

"No. He's general population."

The man shrugged at his mistake and retrieved John's file from the cabinet. After filling out a few forms, he returned my ID and gave me a pass for the visitation room. We then went to the security area. Two guards watched intently as we emptied everything from our pockets into little plastic baskets. All we were allowed to take in with us were car keys, ID, a hair comb, and money for the vending machines to be carried in a clear zippered bag. Then we had to walk through a metal detector one by one. Mariah and I went through without any problem, but Vanessa set it off with her belt buckle. Once we were cleared, the backs of our hands were stamped with invisible ink only an ultraviolet light could detect.

We stood by the steel door until security buzzed it open. I glanced at the girls, who had become very quiet. Mariah gripped my hand tightly.

"Door one!" the security guard called out.

A shiver ran through me as the door was electronically unlocked with a loud clanging sound. I pushed it open, hustling the girls through. It was a short walk through an outdoor courtyard to the building that housed the visitation area. This time the cheery flowerbeds and lush green landscaping didn't fool me. I was more focused on the rows of cement buildings I could see in the distance with slots for windows, barely big enough to let through the light of day. Heavy iron bars encased each one, giving it the appearance of an animal kennel.

Inside, two female guards checked ID again, initialed our pass, and logged us in on a visitor's sheet. We chose a table to one side of the cafeteria-sized room. Numerous vending machines and four microwaves lined the back wall.

Other visitors arrived. Soon, families with small children settled at the tables around us. Some weary-looking young women held tiny babies in their arms. My heart ached for them. It was hard enough raising children without their daddy, but to be on your own with a new baby who never had its father at home in the first place must be horribly overwhelming.

One such mother locked eyes with me momentarily, but I quickly looked away. I wanted to give her a smile of hope or a nod of understanding, but instead I couldn't bear to make that connection. I wanted it all to just go away.

I looked back at the young mother, who switched her baby to her other arm while catching a falling pacifier. I wondered if she needed to laugh about something, soak up the sun, walk, breathe, and forget, if only for a little while. It didn't matter which side of the wall we were on. We were all paying the price together.

A door in the front of the room opened, and a lanky guard ushered a few prisoners to the check-in table where the two uniformed women sat. They quickly signed in and then turned to find where their visitors were sitting. The girls and I remained motionless in our seats as we watched the smiling, laughing, and hugging of inmates all around us joining their families.

"Where's Daddy?" Mariah sat up tall in her chair, keeping her eyes on that door up front.

"He should be coming any minute," I assured her. "He's probably all excited about seeing you two." With a quick smile, I looked at Vanessa. She was still watching the other inmates getting their welcome hugs.

Soon, the door opened again and more prisoners in blue emerged. This time John was in the group, briefly looking our way before walking to the sign-in desk. I wasn't even sure if he saw us. I didn't know if I should stand up and wave. As he turned and made eye contact, my heart felt like an elevator with a severed cable, plunging down the shaft. He could always do that to me, since the very first day we met. Just one look—knowing he was near—everything inside of me went crazy. "He walks the same," Vanessa said softly as he approached us.

A knot formed in my throat as I swallowed. My spine felt stiff, and I didn't know how to move. Should we stand? Do we hug him? Should we just stay in our chairs?

Vanessa must have made her own decision because she suddenly rose up from her seat as her father came to our table. His face was pale from too little sun and his eyes glassed with tears. He seemed just as awkward as we felt, not knowing how much he could do without breaking the eggshells he walked on. Finally, he gave a weak smile and looked directly at his oldest daughter.

"Spunky," he said, letting tears fall. He reached out and she walked into his arms.

Mariah got up then, seeing as her sister didn't disintegrate at her daddy's touch. He looked down at her and enveloped her in a giant embrace, too. For several moments, he just held them both and relished the feel of his children. My arms crossed tightly at my waist as I stayed seated. I wasn't ready to touch him no matter how close we had gotten in our letters. Just looking at him was challenge enough.

Once the hug broke up and the girls settled into their chairs, his focus turned to me. He took his own seat across the table and gave me a soft, shy smile. The same kind he gave me when he first asked me out to lunch fifteen years ago. Tinged with nervous, hopeful expectations, clumsiness, and charm, not knowing if he was welcome to make a move or if he was going to get rejected. "Hi," he said. "Thanks so much for bringing the girls to see me. You just don't know how much this means to me."

True. I didn't. Did any of us mean anything to him at all? If we did, how in the world did we end up in this God-forsaken visitation room? I glanced down at the inmate badge pinned on the pocket of his blue shirt. Every breath was uncomfortable.

"They really wanted to come." I shifted in my chair. It felt strange talking face to face. Mailing letters was far better. I didn't have to see his expression or have him examine mine. I didn't have to worry that he could see the pain I was feeling.

Vanessa reached out and took his hand. "Daddy, I just started volunteering at the Humane Society back home. Sometimes on Saturdays I go and clean out the dog kennels and help people choose a pet for adoption."

Tell him why, Vanessa. That it was a suggestion from your counselor because it would help you to feel good about yourself and maybe help you to get back into school. It would be something to chase away the guilt you carry that maybe your daddy did this because you weren't loved enough or good enough or wanted enough.

"That's great," he exclaimed. "Do you still want to be a veterinarian when you grow up? This would be good training for you."

To my utter amazement, they chatted happily back and forth for several minutes. I wasn't sure what I expected to happen when we all got together, but I found myself getting agitated. Should it be this breezy? Should the children he crushed with his unforgivable actions be so ready to just let it blow over?

I felt totally lost as I watched them interact. Periodically, as they told him more things about their lives back in Florida, he would look over at me with a pleading pull to his eyes, wanting and hoping to share with me, too. I could only dodge his gaze and go back to watching the inmates walking circles in the outside courtyard. I wanted to get up and join them. To be out in the fresh open air, talking and laughing about something unrelated to the here and now. I craved a reprieve from my emotional bondage. It had been days since I even had a beer.

"I want to live in here with you, Daddy," Mariah said, going to sit on his lap. She leaned her head against his chest and gave a big yawn.

He smoothed her golden hair and swallowed a lump in his

throat. "No ... you don't, sweetheart. It's not a good place to be. Daddy wants to live outside these walls with you."

Mariah looked up at him and began tracing his cheek with her finger and then tugged on his earlobe. "When are you coming home? I want to play with you. I never had a daddy to play with."

There was no answer he could give her. All he could do was cradle her tighter, dipping his face into the sweet silkiness of her hair as silent tears fell. This was what I needed. For him to see in person what he had done to the children. How hard it was for me to handle all of their pain, their questions, and needs and how frustrating it was to feel so damned helpless when there was nothing that could take it away. It was supposed to feel good to see him suffer and to see him experience the trauma he had inflicted on our daughters, but instead I was breaking apart inside. In a way, I felt he and I were still one. That whatever hurt him, hurt me. There was nothing there to separate us even though our marriage had been destroyed. He wasn't on the bad team with us girls being on the good team. As outlandish as it seemed, we were still a family circle, all hurting and struggling to survive. He may have done the wrongs that landed us all here, but seeing him choking with the same heartache and crying the same tears made me realize we were all in a common place of pain and recovery.

Vanessa darted her watery gaze at me, not comfortable with seeing her father breaking down. It had a domino effect on the rest of us, and she didn't want to lose her composure, let alone see me lose mine. She quickly took her sister's hand.

"Mariah, let's go to the vending machines and see what they have. Maybe we can get a candy bar or something."

John watched our daughters walk off with quarters in hand, a world of remorse and love shining in his eyes.

"I can't believe I've done this," he uttered. "I love you so much. I love my girls. Losing what we had is killing me."

His hand reached out for mine, and I gave it to him. They still fit together so naturally.

It felt wonderful to simply touch like that again. We had shared so much through our letters and phone calls, describing our hurts, our fears, what we were each going through, but it wasn't the same as feeling the warmth of his hand, seeing the want in his eyes, watching the tracks of his tears. To be able to cry with him and let our pain blend was the most healing thing I had found.

"It's killing us to be without you," I finally answered. "Bobby is very good to us. He's been there through a lot and really loves the girls as if they were his own. I know that is a blessing, and I'm thankful. But it hurts. He's not the man my heart belongs to. No matter what has happened and no matter how much the children and I hurt, we feel such a void in our lives without you. It just doesn't go away. I'm trying to love Bobby and move on like I know I should, but you're still a part of me. It makes no sense after all that's been done, but you are. Just touching now feels so right."

He squeezed my hand inside of his. "We've got to survive this, Baby. I can't lose you or our girls. I've been meeting with the chaplain and working hard on myself. I was sick. Sick for a very long time and never said anything to anyone. I never meant for it to end up like this. I've hurt so many people and destroyed all the things that meant the most to me. I just want a second chance to be the man God intended for me to be. I'm learning a great deal through my Bible studies and our church services in here. I know that giant hole inside my soul that I always tried to fill with the wrong things was my need for God. Now that I've given my heart to Jesus Christ and turned my entire life over to him, I'm not empty anymore. For the first time, I'm at peace inside. I'll never be that twisted person who was capable of such horrible things again. That man died on the same day Karen did. The old John Nichols is gone."

I felt a tear roll down my cheek and stared at our hands folded together on the table between us. "It sounds like you're saying that being sent to prison actually set you free. Like if this didn't happen, you would have never changed."

He leaned forward and looked at me with his cool blue gaze. "As much as I loved you and the children, I know I wouldn't have stopped what I was doing. It took losing it all, tragically killing someone, and sitting on suicide watch for two weeks with nothing but a paper gown, a bunk, and a Bible to rescue me. I had to hit rock bottom before I could be healed."

"You could have just told me," I said, wanting desperately to turn back time. "It would have been hurtful to admit you were having an affair, but at least none of this would have happened. She wouldn't be dead, and you wouldn't be in prison."

He looked down at something, nodding, before his troubled gaze met mine. "I know. I should have done that, but I wasn't strong enough. I hated who I was, but I couldn't bear to be exposed. I wanted to be the husband you loved. The one who kept his promises to you. I had the family I had always dreamed of, but it just never felt like enough. Since my mom left me when I was a kid, that empty hole inside never went away, no matter what. I could never feel satisfied or like I was good enough, and I wanted to chase that feeling away even if it meant breaking our marriage vows. I knew it wasn't right and I hated myself for it, but having an affair made me feel like I could escape reality for a while. I could be somebody else, feel special and wanted. It sounds dumb, I know … but it's the truth."

Mariah came back with a Snickers bar in her hand. "Here, Daddy. Vanessa says this is your favorite."

The interruption was timed perfectly. Hearing John actually explain what drove him to have sex with another woman made me clench my fists when what I wanted to do was scream. The pain felt like a knife had slit me down the middle and everything inside me was about to pour out on to the floor. John thanked Mariah, giving her a kiss, and tore into his candy bar, glancing at me with a worried expression. Vanessa joined us with a bag of chips and a Coke, tensing up once she saw the condition I was in. She edged her chair closer to mine and patted me on the leg.

I stared back at my ex-husband, who now bounced our little girl on his knee. My heart and soul were absolutely numb. I couldn't comprehend the things he had just described to me. I wanted to ask a million more questions so that it would somehow all make sense. Instead, only one made it to the surface.

"Didn't the girls and I make you feel loved and wanted and special every day of our life together? I don't understand what you needed her for."

He stopped chewing his Snickers bar long enough to look at me. "Yes … you did, Baby. It just wasn't enough."

Somehow, we got through the rest of the day, and when the girls and I finally left the visitation room at three o'clock that afternoon, I felt thoroughly drained. It was an effort just driving back to the hotel. I knew we had four more days of visits before we had to go back to Florida, but already I dreaded the end of our time together. There was a happiness in my heart just knowing I'd see John again tomorrow. I'd touch him, talk with him, and share more tears and smiles. I'd watch our children as they bought him more candy bars and got their hugs and kisses.

Being together still felt right even if my logical mind told me it was horribly wrong. I didn't even know why it felt right. There was nothing left. No trust. Holding on to something that had already slipped through my fingers was useless, but the thought of going back to Florida to a home that didn't feel like home and to a man I was trying to fall in love with depressed me. Was I so completely messed up that being with John under any circumstances was better than any other life without him? I felt as if I were going crazy.

I hated my own thoughts and feelings. Bobby was a good man, very loyal and family oriented. He took such good care of us and was always there no matter what. If he knew how bonded I still felt to John, it would hurt him, and he didn't deserve that. Bobby was our future. What was I going to do? Fool myself into thinking John and I still had a marriage and deny the girls that?

"Hi, Baby. How'd it go?" Bobby asked that evening when I called.

"It was good," I answered, watching the girls bouncing on their bed and laughing. "I think it went well, and the children enjoyed seeing their father. It's hard, but it was what they needed."

"Are you talking about the girls or yourself?"

I hesitated. "The girls. You know that's why I brought them here."

"I'm not trying to start anything here. I just sense you needed to see John as much as the children did. For closure, more than anything. I know you and I are together now, and I hope we always will be, but I can tell you haven't let go all the way. I'm hoping this trip helps you to do that because when you get home,

I want to talk about us and where we go from here. I love you. I love the children, and I think we could be a family. I want to take care of you and help make a better life for the girls. I love you with all of my heart. I didn't mean to lay all of this on you over the phone like this … but I miss you. I just can't wait until you all come home."

Tears rolled down my cheeks as I struggled for an answer. *Family … home …* those were words I knew so well and held so dear, but they didn't include Bobby. Family was John and me with our two beautiful girls, and home was right here in Ohio.

"Don't worry about it now," Bobby added after a long silence. "You and the girls just get through this week. I know it's hard on you, and you don't need any more to deal with. Do you mind if I talk to them? Are they close by?"

I sat on the edge of my bed and watched as both Vanessa and Mariah took their turns talking to Bobby. They seemed so happy and told him all about our trip, how it was cool today, the leaves were changing color, and that they bought their daddy a Snickers bar. At the end of each of their conversations, they said that they missed him and loved him. A part of me melted as they handed me the phone. Bobby had become an important part of their lives. My dismay started transforming into thankfulness.

"We'll be home on Monday," I told him. "I'm glad you're doing okay. I'm sorry if I sounded a little out of it tonight, but I'm just really tired. We'll talk when I get home, okay?"

"I know you're tired, Baby. Just get your rest, and don't worry about a thing. I miss you and love you and will be waiting right here for my girls to come back safe and sound. Hug the babies for me, okay?"

I looked at the girls, now watching cartoons on TV. "I will. We love you, too."

That night I slept fitfully, unable to let myself relax completely. Dreams swirled in my subconscious, broken and confused with no real meaning. Dreams of getting lost in a huge parking lot, the children playing with a puppy, and of Bobby teaching the girls how to swim in a beautiful, tranquil lake. When the alarm clock sounded at five, shaking all the scattered visions from my mind, I shut if off and lay in the darkness, staring up at the ceiling.

I love you ... I love the children ... I think we could be a family. I thought back to the dream I just had where I was scared and lost, but the one with Bobby in it, doing what fathers do, and teaching the kids how to swim, was happy. Joyous. Peaceful, even. I closed my eyes and willed it to come back.

"Mommy?" Mariah called over in a groggy voice from her bed. "Is it time to go back and see Daddy?"

SEVEN

A Bond Unbroken

Chaplain Smith came into the visitation room that afternoon. When he came over to our table, he gave John a friendly pat on the shoulder and then smiled down at the children and me.

"This must be the beautiful family John talks so much about," he said. "I'm so glad you were able to make it so you could have this time together. I would like to pray with you today."

John eagerly agreed, and we all joined hands. It wasn't comfortable. Praying wasn't something I did or taught my children to do. It was never a part of our marriage. We bowed heads, and Vanessa started giggling with Mariah. Obviously, they both felt silly and couldn't wait to get it over with. John paid them no mind and tightly closed his eyes, squeezing my hand in his. Chaplain Smith held on to my other one.

"Heavenly Father, we thank you for the blessing of this visit for this family. Time is so precious now, especially with them being so far apart. I pray for healing in these hurting hearts, Lord. For your light to shine in the darkness. May you take the trials they have already faced and are going to face in the long years ahead and turn them into blessings, all for your glory. Help them to make peace with the past and to know that you truly forgive, just as we all must forgive. Welcome John as a new life, Lord, reborn in your love. Cast away the man he used to be. I pray that his wife and children will also find comfort and the will to forgive with you guiding them day by day. Help them to see that all things are possible if you only have faith. Amen."

I didn't want to raise my head. I was a mess. The prayer touched something hidden deep inside and made me weep as I listened to Chaplain Smith's words. He saw my reaction and stooped down to touch my hand. I was embarrassed by my tears and dabbed them with my sleeve.

"You've got a good man in John," he said, burning me with a truth that blazed in his eyes. "Evil can find weaknesses and use them to destroy loving families. I'll pray for you, for John, and for your children. I'll pray that you won't let evil win."

"It already has, hasn't it?" I asked, seeing nothing left in the ruins to pray for.

His smile was knowing. Strong. His gaze shining with faith. "Oh, not by a long shot, Mrs. Nichols. This story is far from over." He then patted my arm before bidding good-bye to John and the girls. I watched as he made his way to other families in the room.

"He's great, isn't he?" John seemed pleased that I had such a strong reaction. "He's been there for me through some pretty hard times."

"You want a Snickers bar, Daddy?" Mariah chimed, already gathering the quarters in her hand.

"Sure. I'd like that. Thanks a lot, sweetheart."

Vanessa went to the vending machines with her as John leaned across the table and grasped my hands. He wanted to make good use of our few moments alone. As alone as we could be with three guards at the front desk and a ceiling dotted with security cameras.

"I'm not giving up on our family," he said sternly. "I know I can't ask you to wait for me. That wouldn't be fair, but I just can't let go of the dream that we're going to make it through this. I love you and my girls so very much. I've just got to have faith that, somehow, one day we're going to be together again."

"How?" I shot back. "How can you even hope for such a thing when we've lost everything? How could I ever trust you after what you did? How could we ever be together with this sentence hanging over your head? It's impossible. I can't get caught up in believing in dreams, John. I've got two children to raise and reality to deal with. I've got a man waiting at home who wants to marry me."

I expected a fight. I wanted to hurt him. Instead, he gave himself a few moments to digest it and then turned his gaze to our children at the food machines before looking back at me.

"No matter what happens, I'm not going to give up. I know you need someone to help you, Baby. I know it's hard to raise our girls and afford everything all on your own. I put you in this situation, so I have no right to tell you what to do. I just won't give up on us one day being together, no matter what you decide."

I looked down at his hands, at the finger that pulled the trigger, wondering how many times he had caressed her, pleased her with his touch over that entire year before he finally killed her.

"Where was this burning desire to put family first back when it would have counted?" I asked. "Why do you love us so much now that it's too late?"

"I always loved you. That was never the reason I did the things I did."

"I can't believe that. I don't see how you could sleep with someone else and lie to me and the children if you loved us, John. I just don't see it."

"I was sick," he answered through clenched teeth. "It was because of me, not you. Not the girls."

Quiet settled between us as I looked at the other inmates and their families sitting all around us. We seemed to be the only ones engrossed in a serious, heartrending conversation. The other families were enjoying their visits by playing cards, reading the Bible, or sharing food. All smiles. Plenty of laughter. No one crying, shaking, needing answers so badly that his or her gut ached.

"If you were sick, why didn't I see it? I lived with you every day and night for thirteen years. You seemed fine to me."

He shook his head in disgust. "I wasn't fine. My life got to be one lie after another until I dreaded getting up each day. I loved you and our girls, but I didn't know how to stop feeling like I was never good enough. It was like an addiction I couldn't control. It had control of me. No matter how I hated it or how I wanted to change, it was always stronger than I was."

"Were there others? If you were sick all this time, she couldn't have been the only one."

"No. She was the only one. I've never cheated on you before."

"Why just her? Why not others if you had this problem?"

"Because I knew it was wrong. When I was with her, she came on so strong and threatened to tell you things if I didn't go places with her or do what she wanted. She was blackmailing me from the time our friendship began. I got caught up in her threats and lost my ability to resist. I knew she'd expose me if I tried to cut things off."

The children came back, laying candy bars, soda, and crackers on the table. I wanted to discuss it further, but it wasn't something I wanted the girls to hear. Instead, I sat back in my chair and drew a deep breath. My insides were balled up in knots.

"I love you," John said point blank, probing my eyes for something to cling to. "I am not that man anymore. The dark side is gone for good. You'll understand more if you start reading the Bible. I'm sure your hotel has one in the dresser drawer. Try to read a little tonight before you go to bed if you can. That's how it starts. A little at a time. If you do only that much, I promise you, it will change your life."

Promises. That was the last thing I needed from John, but I believed him. I didn't know why. Maybe it was because of his deep sincerity, his tearful eyes, and the fact that we all just had prayer with the chaplain, but I believed him. By the end of the day, we had actually squeezed in some laughter and reminisced about good times. It was refreshing and inspiring to me that we could leave our space of hopelessness for a little while and find some happy thoughts. It was almost like it used to be. All of us together, joking, talking, laughing, and enjoying. How I missed that. I thirsted to have it all back again even more than I had realized.

When we stood up to say good-bye, he kissed me. I didn't expect it and sure didn't know how to react, but after he finished hugging his daughters and telling them he looked forward to their visit again tomorrow, he took me in his arms and kissed me. Nothing long or deep or passionate, but a brief, beautiful kiss that nearly knocked me to my knees.

"I love you," he said, his voice a husky whisper. "I hope I didn't overstep my boundaries."

"That's just the problem when it comes to you," I managed to answer, my legs a bit weak. "There don't seem to be any boundaries."

He gave me a gentle smile as I gathered the girls and walked away. I was wearing one also, which felt pretty good. The wounds stung, my heart was still broken, but by some miracle I was still capable of feeling pleasure.

My mind was clearer that night since I didn't have to call Bobby. I was able to relax on the bed after my shower, watch TV with the kids, and sort through the events of the day. Chaplain Smith's visit and the prayer he shared with our family stood out. It reached my hurting places where nothing else had been able to touch. No beer, no antidepressant, not even making love with another man—nothing but those powerful words to God soothed my pain and calmed my fears. I began to think about the change in John since he had turned toward God—all he had learned about himself and his dark side, and how he had cast away that old part of himself and become a new person. I even thought about how determined he was not to give up on our family, even when I told him about Bobby wanting to get married. John said he was going to rely on faith. He didn't get upset or look afraid. He had the same calmness to his eyes that Chaplain Smith had.

I leaned over to the end table next to the bed and slid open the drawer. Inside was a Bible with a red cover and gold lettering. I picked it up and began looking through it.

The words were so small, the pages fragile like onion skin, and the whole thing almost as thick as a phone book. I didn't know where to begin and was totally overwhelmed. I kept expecting the words to draw me in, perform magic on my suffering, and change my life into something I could love again, but instead I was lost. Even disappointed. Wasn't this what John said would heal me and change my life? Then again, he was in prison.

I felt like a foreigner where nothing was comfortable or familiar. Finally, I had to find my own way.

For John's thirty-ninth birthday, we wanted to do something nice, but the guards had already told us no gifts were allowed. The children were disappointed, but I reminded them that our family spending time together was the only gift Daddy wanted. He was very happy with that. But, as we sat through our visit, I could see Vanessa and Mariah whispering back and forth as John and I gave them curious expressions. To make it even more mysterious, Vanessa went up to the front desk and spoke with one of the female guards before returning to her seat all smiles.

"I think it's time for birthday cake," Vanessa beamed. "I'm going to go to the vending machine and see what they have."

Mariah nodded. "It's not a birthday without cake."

They took off with a fistful of change as John broke into a grin. "They look like they're up to something, don't you think?"

It was so good to see him smile. Lines formed at the corners of his eyes as he did so. I had never noticed them before. The years apart suddenly seemed painfully obvious.

"I'm sure they just want to make today special for you. It feels strange not to be able to give you presents or cards. They are probably determined to do something festive."

His gaze melted as he watched them huddling together in front of one of the machines.

"I could have had no better gift than to have you guys here with me today. That's all I want. All that matters."

Whenever he talked like that, I immediately had visions of him with Karen. As eager as I was to hear that he loved me and the children, it also sounded so hollow. If it were true, we would never have ended up here. Tears prickled my eyes as I looked past him to the windows overlooking the prison compound. It was empty. I was empty. Anything I said to him felt empty.

"What are you thinking?" he asked.

It seemed odd he had to hear me say it. I felt as transparent as a glass of water for him and everyone else in the room to see.

"I just wonder how this happened. How we ended up here if you love us so much. Why didn't you ever do something to stop it? You could have prevented all this by cutting it off with her before it got out of control."

He dropped his gaze to the floor. "I wish I had. Believe me, I wish I had."

"How can I ever again believe you love me or our children? It makes no sense, John. People don't selfishly destroy what they hold dear to them."

He looked up at me with a wealth of remorse on his face. "They do, Baby. Unfortunately, they do. Look around this place. It's filled with guys in blue who have done just that. They may be in here for different reasons—burglary, drug possession, forgery, murder—but the outcome is the same. We're all at rock bottom in here and can no longer be with our families. We've all destroyed what we had."

I scanned the other tables where inmates sat with loved ones for the same precious sliver of time that we had. They were all going through the same hell. One day you have your neat little world in the palm of your hand, and the next day it's gone. Something was done that shouldn't have been done. Something that couldn't be taken back and people were hurt. For the first time since the officers came to my home and told me my husband had done the unthinkable, I didn't feel alone. I was surrounded by others who carried the same hurts, and that realization flowed over me like warming sunlight.

The girls returned to the table with a chocolate Hostess cupcake and four forks. The smiles they wore were just as bright as if we were at home, serving John his usual German chocolate birthday cake with candles all lit, waiting for him to make a wish. I watched in wonder as they opened the cupcake and placed it on a napkin. It didn't seem to matter how different the circumstances were. They were happy just to make Daddy's birthday as special as they could.

"This looks great," John said, reaching for a fork.

Mariah tapped his wrist and shook her head. "Wait, Dad. You have to make a wish and blow out your candle."

John and I both looked a little puzzled until the guard from the front desk whom Vanessa had consulted with came over and pulled a book of matches from her back pocket.

"We don't usually do this," she said in a hushed voice. "But your girls are so beautiful and I know you came all the way from Florida just for Daddy's birthday. When they asked for help making it more like a party, I couldn't say no. It may not be a candle, but we can stick a match in the cupcake so you can still make a wish and blow it out. I'm afraid that's the best I can do."

As we sang "Happy Birthday" while the match in the middle of the cupcake flickered and John leaned in to make his wish and blow, it didn't feel as horrible as I expected. I didn't grieve for the big party we used to have or the store-bought cake and presents. Our family was together against the odds. Broken, maimed, bleeding, and fighting for every breath, but we were still sitting here together. On the final day of our visit, my heart felt distinctly changed. I didn't understand it very well and was in complete awe that it was possible, but I sensed our family had bonded again. We had talked, laughed, cried, prayed, and held hands over the last five days, and that process had taken us to a different level. We still had the same obstacles between us with John's prison sentence, the knowledge of the awful things he did, the sting of betrayal and trust in shambles—not to mention Bobby waiting in the wings back home—but something significant had changed. Our family was amazingly still intact somewhere beneath the rubble.

Saying good-bye at three o'clock was the hardest thing to do. The children wept and clung to their father as guards called out for visitors to exit the area. He buried his face in their honey-colored hair, choking with sobs, telling them to be strong and that he loved them with all of his heart. They reluctantly let go so I could also give him a hug. Everything around us disappeared as we simply held each other and cried. I absorbed the warmth of him, the scent of his skin, the way his breath felt fanning against my cheek, not knowing when I'd be able to feel his arms around me again. I didn't know why he had done the things he had or how we ended up in a place like this, but what I did know was that I didn't want to be apart from him. I would have rather joined him in his prison cell for the duration of his sentence than face my freedom without him. I couldn't bear to let him go. I didn't want to turn and walk away. Nothing felt more right than to have all of us together.

"We can do this," he panted in my ear, shaking and swallowing sobs. "I love you and my girls with my life. We're going to make it somehow. Just stay strong and take things one day at a time."

I couldn't speak or think. I could only weep and nod, burrowing my head into his shoulder, showing him I heard what he said. "I love you," was all I could manage to say. "That will never change."

It was then as I went over to the girls and took their hands that I realized all the other visitors had left. The inmates sat alone at their tables, the guards looked sympathetically toward us, and the silence was so thick you could almost touch it. For some blessed reason, we were allowed that extra time without being shooed out like we were supposed to have been. It meant more to me than I could express.

I got our pass at the front desk, and the guard who put the match in John's cupcake gave me a mournful smile. "Have a safe trip home."

Home ... Florida would never be home. "Thank you for everything," I said through my tears. With one last look at John, sitting at his table with his head in his hands, the children and I walked out the exit doors. We held on to each other with every step, crying softly and sharing the same sensation of our hearts breaking in two.

Bobby had missed us. On the day we got back, he was waiting anxiously to welcome us home with gifts for the children and flowers for me. The transition from the dreamlike five days at the prison to the reality of our new life in Florida was like cold water in the face. I couldn't stop remembering. I was dazed on our drive back home. While the kids laughed and played in the backseat, my mind rolled back to every touch, every smile, every tear I shared with John. I kept reliving our last embrace. I didn't understand the things he did to break apart our family, but I felt our love was still true.

Bobby began talking marriage, wanting to become an official part of our family and a stepfather to the girls. When the subject came up, I never felt a burning desire because of a forever kind of love we had for each other. It seemed to be more of a commonsense move to get the children and me off welfare and make our broken family whole again.

After all, Bobby and I were dear friends and lovers. We could make it work. It would be a perfect fit because he was aching inside for children to call his own, and the girls were in need of a father. Together we could give them a better life with two incomes, shared responsibility, and twice the love. It made sense, but I couldn't give him the answer he wanted to hear. It was too much, too soon. As a compromise, we decided he should move in and we could share bills, raise the kids, and give it a trial run. It worked well at first, giving us both what we needed in our hurting hearts. The companionship was nice.

There was laughter in the house again. I had a warm body next to me in bed at night and someone to wake up to. That fourth chair at the dinner table wasn't empty anymore. On many levels, it was wonderful and chased away the past for both of us, but no matter how hard I tried, I couldn't make John's ghost go away. I still felt him with me. Even though I wasn't alone anymore, I'd find myself lying in bed at night, staring into the darkness, feeling lonely and needy. Bobby couldn't fill the places John had always filled. My new life with Bobby was best for the children, but my secret love for John was best for me.

John and I began corresponding regularly. The letters were long, open, and raw, sharing all we felt and thought. He would tell me the things this tragedy had taught him about himself. He didn't pretend to have all the answers yet, but what he had learned from studying the Bible was that he never had a firm foundation to stand on. His newfound faith gave him a rock to lean on now. He'd found the forgiveness and guidance he never had. It took this tragedy and losing it all to find what he needed.

He included Bible verses that had brought him comfort for me to share with the girls, but I knew from trying to connect with the Bible once before that what worked for him didn't do much for me. Again, I felt envious and wanted the peace he'd found. I'd even share that in the letters I wrote to him. I would tell him how torn my heart was, how Bobby was very good to us, and that we were trying to make this living arrangement fit, but that I always felt lonely no matter what he did. That nothing was enough. Nothing filled me. All I wanted was what I used to have with John when I was happy and in love. I didn't see how life could ever be joyous again after all we had lost. I described how Bobby and I drank a lot and that was my only escape. I could try to forget, but in the morning, the hangover and reality would hit me head-on.

My words would grow desperate, begging John to make it right again. I couldn't see a future anymore. All I saw was a miserable existence.

I remember how profound it was when I received a reply to that particular letter. Tears rolled off my face as I read what only a new man, not the husband I thought I knew, would write. It didn't give me the answers I wanted. There was no easy out. Instead, he bowled me over with truth.

> *I can't make it right again. I can't give you what you need. I can love you, I can be your best friend and soul mate again, if you'd let me ... but no person on this earth is ever going to give you what you are looking for. People will always disappoint you. They will let you down. They can't complete that emptiness you're feeling. I know I put it there and caused you and our girls to be in a life you don't want, and for that I will always hate myself. But the healing and peace and joy that you're looking for isn't in human form, Baby. It never will be.*

It's in turning your heart and soul over to Jesus Christ and having his love as a perfect foundation for your life. Only then will you stop looking in the wrong directions for an answer to that empty hole. Your drinking, the relationship with Bobby, your wanting me to make it right—you're trying to fill the hole the same way I did, and it won't work. You can't fill it with temporary things.

God is the only way, and I pray you and the children learn that. I want very much to be a family again and believe that one day we'll be blessed with a miracle if we use this time to work on ourselves and overcome the past. Don't go down the same road I did and self-destruct because of your pain. Let God heal you and lead you to a better place. He'll take you to where you're meant to be.

I must have read that letter ten times before finally tucking it under my shirts in my dresser drawer with the others Bobby had no knowledge of. Ironically, I had my own secret life now. I lived with Bobby day in and day out, playing the role of his future wife and letting him get more attached to the girls, while secretly writing letters to John telling him how wrong it all felt. Telling him my love was still his and his alone.

I realized at that moment that I had become the same lost person John had been all of those years. I reflected on all of those times that I tortured myself wondering how John could have possibly done this. But like light easing into a world that knew nothing but darkness, I no longer questioned him. In fact, I understood him more than I cared to. I had gradually become him.

EIGHT

The Letter

The phone rang one night just before nine o'clock. Bobby had already gone to bed, and the children were watching TV. I answered and heard the recorded message that always precedes John's calls, asking if I want to accept charges from an inmate in a correctional facility. I was stunned and almost forgot to push the "0" button for the call to go through. He never called in the middle of the week or at this time of night. The calls always came on Sundays, when he knew the girls would be home. I immediately thought something was very wrong.

"Are you okay?" I asked him as soon as we were connected.

"Yeah … I just had to call you. I'm sorry it's so late."

I observed the girls looking sleepy in front of the Disney Channel and decided not to let them know it was their daddy on the phone. I had the distinct impression he wasn't calling to hear his daughters' voices. There was something heavy weighing on his mind.

"I didn't know they'd let you use the phone at this time of night," I commented, trying to hide the tension in my voice.

"They don't usually. I had to pull some strings. I just really need to tell you something. I want you to know how much I love you."

At first, I smiled to think he went to all that trouble to tell me he loved me. I knew we had grown close in our letters, but the urgency in his voice sounded strange and desperate. The more I thought about it, the more my joy gave way to uneasiness. This was the kind of thing someone did before disappearing from your life. The kind of *I love you* that meant good-bye.

"John, what's wrong? You're scaring me." I kept my voice low. "Why do you sound so strange?"

He didn't answer. I could hear some voices in the background, sounds echoing from walls too close and suffocating.

"You're going to get a letter," he finally said. "It's going to be hard for you when you read it. I don't know how you're going to react."

"What kind of letter? What are you talking about?"

"I've been working on myself," he answered emotionally. "I never want to be the man I was, and each day I'm getting stronger, but there is still one thing I know I have to do, even if it means risking things I hold dear to my heart. I can't be the man God wants me to be until I confess all of the lies from my past. You deserve the truth, even if it costs me my family and what's left of our love. All I can do is hope that one day you will come to forgive me and see me as a new man and not who I was. I just want you to know I love you and the girls with all of my heart. Just try to remember that once you read that letter, even if you never speak to me again."

My mind reeled. I couldn't imagine anything being as dramatic as he was describing, especially after all we had been through. What could possibly be worse than what I already knew? If I was still willing to have this bond with him after knowing of his affair with Karen, still able to love him even though he killed her, still staying attached to him despite the prison walls between us, what could possibly cause me not to want to speak to him again?

My answer came a few days later when the letter arrived in a large manila envelope.

He didn't even fold it so it would fit in a standard envelope, as if the creases would interrupt the importance of what he had to say. My stomach clenched as I sat at the kitchen table and began to read the first of three pages. What I learned left me so stunned and sickened that I could barely hold myself up.

> *Baby,*
>
> *This letter is the hardest thing I've ever had to write, but I know it has to be done. If I'm going to truly be a new and better man, I have to not only confess my sins to God, but also confess them to you. I can't keep lying to you anymore simply because I'm afraid to hurt you. It's time you knew the man I really was, and I just pray that you'll even want to talk to me after this.*
>
> *You asked during our last visit if Karen was the only one. To be honest, there were many others. For the length of our entire thirteen-year marriage, I have had one-night stands and brief affairs with coworkers and women I met in bars. Anyone who came along just when I needed a sexual fix. I know this will be quite a shock to you since I hid*

it well for all of those years. It was something I wasn't proud of and hated in myself. I loved you and my girls, but something inside of me was so empty and unhappy. Being with other women was a way to escape myself and become someone else. I know it sounds stupid, but that's how it felt. So many nights when you thought I was working late, I was really at a bar picking up one-night stands or spending time with girls I worked with.

We'd have a few drinks, have sex, and then I'd go home. It wasn't what I wanted or needed, but I felt outside of myself. I always told myself that I'd stop. I didn't ever want you to find out or to have us lose our marriage over my secrets. I knew what I had with you was what I always wanted, but I never felt like I deserved it. I always felt like a failure and not good enough, if you can try to understand.

Nothing I can say to you will make up for the wrongs I've done. I know that you will probably hate me now more than ever, and I'll probably lose you and my girls for good. That's been the hardest part about coming clean with all of this. I was just so grateful that you started talking to me again, and then the letters and the visit were a real miracle.

I never expected that much after Karen told you the truth about us. I thought it was over then. But then you started talking to me again, and it seemed like there was still something special between us. I knew I still had truths to share with you, but I never found the right time. I was always afraid of losing you and my girls again. But then I'd read my Bible and get closer to God. His Word tells me that he hates liars and that the truth shall set me free. So I wrote this letter to make myself right in God's eyes.

All I can do is pray that somehow you will come to

forgive me one day. The thought of never talking to you again or seeing you and my girls kills me inside. But I deserve your hatred, Baby. I can only imagine how this is going to hurt you, but I am a new person now. I'm not that sick husband any longer. I love you and my daughters with every breath I have. No matter what happens after you read this letter, that fact will never change.

With forever love,
John

I became aware of Bobby's voice, the smell of hazelnut coffee, his hand smoothing my hair, and the sensation that I was a million miles away. I knew I had to open my eyes, but they felt so heavy. All I wanted was to just be left alone.

"Baby … come on. Wake up. I've made some coffee and toasted some bagels. You really have to eat something."

The television was on in the other room. I could hear Tigger's voice and that springy bouncy sound he makes as he sings about Tiggers being a wonderful thing. It was Mariah's favorite, and she always sang along. I didn't hear her. I wondered where she was. My eyes fluttered and opened. "The girls … where are the girls?"

"They're okay. They're both watching TV. I've been staying home from work to take care of them since you went to sleep. I know they're worried about you, but they are both okay. Your parents have been over, too. They are very concerned."

I went to sit up and became aware of something clutched in my right hand. When I looked, I saw the pages of John's letter. My stomach rolled as I remembered all the filth his words contained. I fell back against my pillows, alarmed at how weak and deathly ill I felt.

"I don't understand," I uttered. "What happened? What's going on?"

His dark eyes glossed over with tears as he cupped my hand. "You've been asleep for the last two days. The only movement you would make is when I tried to get this letter away from you. You held it so tight that I could never free it from your hands, but you still stayed in this sleep. You haven't eaten or had anything to drink. Your mom and dad offered to watch you so I could go to work, but I've been so worried that I couldn't bring myself to leave you. I was about to take you to the hospital today if you didn't snap out of it. Thank God you're okay, Baby. You gave us quite a scare."

Two days? I stared back at him in disbelief, desperately trying to recall the last thing I remembered. The letter came. Three pages. John had always been unfaithful even before the children were born. Our entire marriage was a lie. Karen was far from the only one. *He was getting right with God … getting right with God … God hates liars, and John was finally telling me the truth … he was getting right with God.* My throat ached as I gulped back tears. The pain was like acid in my veins. It was unbearable and made me wish I could find a swift death, but instead Bobby slid the letter from my grasp and helped me to sit up. He kissed my cheek before handing me a cup of coffee.

"It was all a lie," I whispered, barely able to meet his gaze. "The entire marriage was nothing but a lie."

I quietly wept as he read the letter, but it was important he knew the past John was confessing to. It was important for the children to know and my parents to know. My sister and her husband would have to know, too. Everyone needed to see him for what he really was. All of those years we shared as a close-knit family only to find out we never knew the man at all. My soul mate was a virtual stranger. My children's father was a total phony. Over a decade of my life wasn't real after all. How was it possible to fool people so flawlessly and to keep it up for so long? There should have been signs, but instead all I remembered were the most beautiful years of my life.

I contacted my parents, who were very relieved to hear from me. Still, I told them it was urgent that I meet with them. Bobby stayed home with the girls while I went to their house and let them read John's confessional letter for themselves. My mother openly wept as my father clenched his jaw, letting silent tears roll down his face. It had been hard enough on them to accept what had happened in Twinsburg. John was like a son to them, and I knew that their hearts were broken, too. It cut to the core and now to learn there was more—much, much more—it was like the final blow. None of us could comprehend the man John depicted in his letter. "I hate him with all of my soul," I choked to my parents. "I've been so stupid to even speak to him after this thing with Karen. He sat there during our visit in that prison and lied to us even then. He lied straight to my face when I flat out asked him if Karen was the only one. I'll never have anything to do with him ever again. If they gave him the electric chair tomorrow, I'd be more than happy to be the one to throw the switch."

My parents could find no words to say. They opened their comforting arms and held me until I went numb and ran out of tears.

"What will you tell the children?" my father asked. "This is going to be very hard to explain to them."

My heart ached as I remembered how happy they were when we went to visit their father. It felt so good to them to have him back in their lives, even if it meant under the watchful eyes of prison guards. They blossomed as they grew close to him again, sharing hugs, jokes, tears, prayers. Writing long letters when we went back home and waiting by the phone when it was time for him to call. Having that close bond and loving him again had helped a great deal with their heartache. How was I going to tell them their father was gone from their lives? Guilt riddled me, as if I were the bad guy for cutting the ties again, but how could I just let things go on the way they were? John didn't love us. He only knew how to keep hurting us, and I had to cut him loose to protect what was left of our hearts. He was nothing more than a cheat, a murderer, and a pathological liar. My children deserved better, and I was going to make sure that they got it.

I drew a breath and met my father's gaze with a strength that stemmed from my anger. "I have to tell them the truth, Dad. That's all I can do. This family has already had enough lies to last a thousand lifetimes. I'm going to tell them what John wrote in this letter and that this changes things from now on. We won't be having any contact with him. As much as it hurts, it's the only way to heal from the devastation he's caused. I want the girls and me to concentrate on our new life and let go of the past. We'll be all right. We still have each other, and Bobby is now like a part of our family. It's time to close the door on John entirely and focus on a whole new direction."

Back home I found Bobby cuddling with the children on the sofa. The Pooh cartoons were over, and now they were engrossed in a "Brady Bunch" rerun. In my bitter frame of mind, I pictured Mr. Brady smiling like the wholesome family man that he was when all the while he was having an affair with a stripper. If my happy marriage with John was such a sham, it was hard to believe in anyone.

Bobby searched my expression and saw that I needed to get

the children's attention. He squirmed out from the middle of them and walked over to where I was standing, noting my swollen eyes and tear-streaked face. His hand reached out and smoothed my hair as he pinned me with a worried gaze.

"Are you okay?" he asked in a husky whisper.

How in the world could I possibly be okay when the father of my two children and our entire marriage had turned out to be nothing but twisted lies? I wanted to somehow smile reassuringly, just to put his mind at ease. Instead, I kissed him lightly and hoped that was answer enough.

"I'm going to tell the children. They have to know about their father's letter and that I'm cutting him out of our lives."

Bobby looked at them sitting on the couch. He loved them and worried as if they were his own flesh. With a swallow, he nodded and gracefully went into the kitchen to give us some privacy.

Mariah squirmed against the throw pillows and gave a sleepy yawn. "I'm tired, Mom. Maybe I got the same sickness you had that made you sleep for so long."

That must have been what Bobby told them. I hadn't even thought how it must have been for him to be responsible for both of the girls for those two days. They must have been frightened. *Mommy had a sickness. She had to sleep for two days straight. Mommy had her heart smashed into bits by dear old Daddy once again and, very truthfully, didn't want to wake up again at all....*

How I wanted to give in to the bitterness flowing through me, but I had to swallow it down. This was going to be hard enough. I couldn't make it worse by exposing my rage.

"Girls, we need to have a family meeting." I reached for the remote and clicked the television to black. "We need to talk about something very important, and I need you to try to understand."

Vanessa crossed her arms in protective body language. "It's about Daddy, isn't it? Something happened."

Her perceptiveness amazed me, yet showed me how sad the situation really was. Whenever gloom filled the house and our lives turned upside down, her first guess was that her father was behind it. Even though she had gotten close to him again and apparently made amends, a part of her still didn't trust. "Yes. It is about your father. Something very serious has come up, and I need to make you both aware of it." I looked at Mariah, who was so young and impressionable. I had to put it in a way she could understand. "I found out some things from a letter he wrote me. Things that hurt. Things that are hard to get over."

Mariah cocked her head, trying to follow my clumsy explanation. "What things? Is he in trouble? Did he do something wrong in that jail?"

"No, Baby, no. Daddy didn't do anything in jail. He's doing fine, I promise you. I'm talking about things he did before he went to jail. Things that went on when we were a family in Twinsburg."

"What?" Vanessa stiffened as if bracing for a hit. "What did he do? Just tell us. You're starting to scare me."

To my surprise, my throat convulsed with an onset of tears. I didn't think I had any left. John wasn't worth my tears. He wasn't going to hurt me ever again. Abruptly, I mopped the wetness from my face with my sleeve.

"Daddy did a lot of things nobody ever knew about," I explained carefully. "He did things a married man should never do. What I'm trying to say is that your father broke our marriage vows many times while pretending to be true. Now that I've found that out, I feel we can't trust him at all anymore. I know we hoped we could have a friendship with him and continue to write and visit, but things have changed now. I think it's best if we don't do those things anymore. Daddy has a lot of problems, and we're going to get hurt if we continue to hold on to him. It's hard, I know. I'm so sorry for that, but I have to make the decisions for us from now on. We're going to be all right; that I promise you."

There was a brittle silence as my words were digested. Mariah began twirling her hair as she always did when she was thinking, while Vanessa looked more angry than sad.

"I'm going to get rid of his letters," Vanessa said, her voice shaking with anger. "I never want to see them again. All he did was lie to me in every single one of them. How could he have done that? Didn't he love us at all?"

She looked to me for an answer, but I had none to offer. In truth, I had asked myself that same thing a thousand times. I wanted to answer, but all I could do was share what was in my heart.

"I think Daddy had to have been a very troubled person to do the things he did. I don't understand it myself. All I know is that we can't let it ruin us anymore. It's time to move on and concentrate on where our own lives are going. We have to heal and rebuild. I think it's probably a good idea for all of us to dispose of daddy's letters and try to forget all that's happened in the past so we can focus on better things ahead."

Just then Bobby came out of the kitchen, looking at all of us with such sorrow and helplessness. I knew how badly he wanted to help us. He had felt our pain and helped to carry our burdens since the day we first met. It was so typical of him to see how fragile things had gotten and appear just in time to help hold us all together. Mariah wiggled off the couch and went over to put her arms around him. It was as if she felt that if her daddy was disappearing again, she'd just reach out and find another one. Bobby hugged her with all the love in his heart, then looked up at Vanessa and me. No words had to be spoken. It seemed as if we all knew that the four of us would pull together to make a new family. It was time to leave the past behind.

NINE

Another Man's Wife

"It's over."

I needed to say it out loud. I sat on the floor with a mound of John's letters and cards in front of me, knowing this was an important step in truly letting go. Everything related to him had to be thrown out. The letters he wrote from his prison cell, the cards he bought at the commissary, the family photo we had taken in the visitation room. I allowed my gaze to linger on our smiling faces as we huddled together for the camera. *You had it all and didn't even know it, John. What more did you need that led you to betray us so horribly?* I hardened my heart and began to tear the photo into little pieces.

I started on the letters, watching words like "I miss you so much" and "you and the girls were all that ever mattered to me" fall to the floor in shreds. Lies. All lies. Nothing but lies. The more I ripped and tore, the more protected I felt. He wouldn't be able to lie to me again. I wouldn't allow it anymore. A sweet relief filled my heart after I shoved the mess into a trash bag. I was throwing out the hurts. Throwing out the betrayals. Cleaning the junk out of my life.

I went into the girls' room. They were at my parents' house for a visit, but knew what I was doing and had asked if I'd throw out their letters, too. As upset as they were, it was still too difficult a task for them to handle. They both kept shoeboxes with their dad's letters and cards inside. They had to go just as mine did. I didn't want his lies tainting my family's clean slate anymore. First, Mariah's: "Daddy loves you and misses you … I can't wait to hold you again … I'm so sorry for hurting you and Vanessa and Mommy … one day I'll come home and make everything okay.…" His words made me gag. I ripped the letters and cards with an anger that felt wonderfully refreshing. I wasn't fragile anymore.

I felt empowered by my hatred and knew I was done cowering in a corner because of him. I was going to build a new life even bigger and better than before. Then he'd see that we didn't need him. We'd be the ones with a happy home and a family that loved one another, and he'd have absolutely nothing. It satisfied me to picture him suffering and alone. His hurting was almost humorous … *I bet you're not feeling like such a sex stud anymore, are you, John? Where did all your bed buddies get you?*

Next was Vanessa's collection, which was held together by a large rubber band. She had more letters than any of us. I let them fall into a pile on the middle of her bed, sickened by the sight of his handwriting and knowing how he manipulated her heart. He knew how she was suffering. He knew he had hurt her so badly that she wasn't even able to go to school. He kept on writing that he loved her and never meant to hurt her. That he would never do it again if she only gave him a chance.

My heart ached as I tore up the letters, remembering how much they had helped her. She clung to them like a saving hand when getting buried in depression, her father's reassuring words of love and remorse a salve to her wounds. Why did I ever allow the two of them to communicate after all John had done? I may not have known at the time about the rest of his affairs, but he had one with Karen and murdered the girl, leaving us shattered and struggling to survive. How did I ever soften after that and let him back into our hearts? I hated myself for not being stronger. I cursed as I dumped all the torn letters into a trash bag. "You'll never manipulate us with your lies again. I hope you burn in hell."

That day was a turning point for all of us. Psychologically, ridding the house of traces of John helped the children and me to find the strength to move on. It cut the cord that kept us connected to him so we could learn to function without him. It was hard at first. Vanessa had more frequent sessions with Peggy, and Mariah developed sleep problems. I burned with anger nearly every moment of every day, but gradually we began to feel lighter and stronger. The excruciating pain lapsed into a dull ache. As hard as it was to completely let go, I could see it was doing some good. The children were adjusting to Bobby being the father figure in their lives now. There was laughter again.

Mariah showed interest in becoming playmates with a little boy across the street instead of fearing to leave my side. Vanessa was open to the idea of returning to school if her counselor thought she was ready. Even I was doing better and felt more productive, which resulted in more writing assignments. Without John weighing me down, I actually allowed myself to get closer to

Bobby, too. He wasn't the kind of man who set my heart on fire or made me feel like a lovesick schoolgirl, but our relationship was wonderfully comfortable. His love was safe and stable. I knew we could depend on him.

After all John had put us through, a man like Bobby looked pretty good to me. He certainly wasn't perfect. He drank a bit too much. He was simple and didn't make a whole lot of money, but he was the rock we needed. He was the one who loved us when everything else fell apart. I considered myself blessed to have him in my life and was determined to dedicate myself to making him happy from then on.

"I've got an idea," he said one night as we did dinner dishes. "How would you like for me to whisk you away for a weekend at the beach? We could make it just the two of us, or we could bring the girls. What would you say to that?"

A smile slid on my face. Bobby wasn't one to do more than go to work six days a week and enjoy his time off being at home, but he was happy. Having things going so well with me and the children made him want to break away and do something special. A little swimming, tanning, and scouting for shells seemed like just the perfect treat.

"Don't you have to work Saturday?" I asked.

"I'm taking the day off. I've already told my boss. It's time to romance my beautiful lady by the seashore for a couple of days and have a little fun."

My parents happily agreed to take the children for the weekend so Bobby and I could have some time alone. I could tell by my father's enthusiasm every time he was around Bobby that he was elated I had a reliable man in my life. He'd pat him on the back, offer him a cold beer, and wear a smile whenever he saw how nicely Bobby filled the gap in our family. "Be good, okay?" I hugged Mariah close before Bobby and I started for the coast.

She acted a little nervous, but when her grandpa had promised to show her how to fish in the canal, she got all excited. Besides, Grandma made the absolute best waffles. I was very proud of my little girl. It wasn't so long ago that I could barely go into another room without her by my side. My heart swelled to see the progress she was making.

"And you be good, too. I'll miss you." Vanessa felt stiff in my arms as I hugged her.

Knowing Bobby and I were going to be at the beach for the entire weekend alone without her and her sister cast a whole new light on things. At least around the house, Bobby was more the friend and the handyman, the comforter and the rock. It felt harmless and even helped us all heal. But the vision of him taking her mother to a romantic place so that he could have her alone meant that he would be doing things with her that Vanessa didn't want to think about. It brought back all of the hostility she first felt when she saw me kissing Bobby that night. It wasn't supposed to be him in her mother's arms. No one should be there except for her daddy.

Bobby noted Vanessa's discomfort and gave her a hug. "Don't worry. We'll even bring back some surprises for you and Mariah from the gift shops. Maybe next time we can all go, and you can do a little shopping for yourself."

She smiled nicely enough, but I knew my daughter. Inside, she was angry. I felt a tug of guilt as Bobby and I said our goodbyes to my mom and dad, then got into the car.

"It'll take time," Bobby assured me as he drove. "There's still a lot of healing to do. We'll get there. It's going to be just fine."

I snuggled up against him, leaned my head on his shoulder, and watched the scenery pass by. Something dark nagged me even though I was excited to be on our way. I wasn't even sure what it was. I felt dirty for some reason, as if I were betraying someone. Thoughts of John played in my head. I started to think about our family trips to the beach and how special those memories were. We had only Vanessa then, but the three of us would hunt for shells; make sandcastles; and go swimming in the cold, foamy waves, laughing when one knocked Vanessa over, even though the shock of it made her cry. John would hike her up on his broad shoulders and turn those tears into giggles. *Touch the sky, Spunky … reach right up there and grab hold of a big fluffy cloud … don't be afraid … Daddy's got you … Daddy won't ever let go.*

"Look what I brought," Bobby said, interrupting my memories. He reached under his seat and retrieved a bottle of champagne. "The cups are in the glove compartment. I thought we'd get this trip started off right. Let's make a toast to our first weekend alone."

He popped the cork while keeping the steering wheel under control with his knees. With a smile, he filled my Styrofoam cup and then did the same with his.

"To us," he said, touching my cup with his and lovingly glancing into my eyes.

"To us," I repeated, rushing to take my first two sips. It would numb me. It would relax me. It would chase away those irritating thoughts of John, which weren't supposed to be there. My next few sips were more like gulps, and pretty soon I got a lovely warm feeling all over. *I'm not going to let you ruin anything more for me…. I refuse to let you win.* I downed the rest of my first one and poured myself another. This was my first weekend alone with the new man in my life, and I was going to enjoy it.

We checked into a lovely hotel on Clearwater Beach. I immediately opened the sliding glass doors to the terrace as we unpacked, letting in the sound of the gulls and the salty sea air.

After the three cups of champagne, my spirits were high. Happily, I wrapped my arms around Bobby and gave him a passionate kiss.

"Wow," he uttered, tracing my cheek with his finger. "Is that a preview of what I have to look forward to this weekend?"

"Oh, that's nothing. What I have in mind for you is a whole lot better than that."

"Really? And how long do I have to wait?"

I giggled. "Maybe at least until after dinner and a long sunset stroll on the beach. I'll save my plans for you until later tonight just to keep you in suspense."

He groaned as if being tortured, but let his mouth hold a grin. "I'm looking forward to it, lady. And you'd better look out. You just might get a few surprises of your own."

It felt wonderful to be alone. There was no clock to watch. No sneaking in steamy kisses when the children weren't looking. No dishes to wash or boring domestic chores to worry about. Just time for us to have fun and get closer.

We started off with a wonderful dinner at a Chinese restaurant on the strip and then browsed a few gift shops on our walk back to the hotel. We also stopped into a convenience store and bought a six-pack of beer to take it on our walk along the beach. I hadn't felt so free in a very long time. Even Bobby was extra adventurous.

"Let's go skinny-dipping," he suggested as we walked along the shore. "It's dark. There's no one out here except the fiddler crabs and us. There's no way we'll get busted."

I laughed as the wind whipped my hair behind my shoulders. "You're crazy. We can't do that. Sometimes people walk the beach at night. We saw a few up by the hotel."

He looked back where we just came from. "They're gone. It's

just you and me. Or do you need another beer to get you in the mood?" Without waiting for my answer, he opened another bottle. "One more and you'll be ready. I dare you to catch up."

On a wild impulse, he sprinted for the crashing waves. It was a side of Bobby I'd never seen before. He didn't usually do the unexpected. I chugged my beer, let out a few giggles, then took a few more swallows. The wind felt good on my face as I gazed up at the stars. They were as brilliant as diamonds sparkling against the blackness. Countless and endless as far as the eye could see.

My love for you is endless, Mrs. Nichols ... just like those stars overhead with no beginning and no end ... that's how I'm going to love you from this day forward ... just like the sky and the stars ... forever and ever and ever. I saw John's face clearly in my mind and heard the very words he said to me on our wedding night. I had believed him. I shook my head as if that would scatter my train of thought and then gulped what was left in my bottle. It didn't matter how or why anymore, and I had to stop those inner voices from asking. My marriage was over and behind me. I was with a new man now. A man who didn't lie to me and would never cheat. A man who appreciated a family. I had the real thing this time and was going to be very happy.

"It's cold out here," Bobby yelled, waving his arms from the surf. "I think I need someone to jump in and keep me warm!"

Without hesitation, I ran out to join him. It was our time. Not time to let thoughts of the past drag me down. Squealing as the icy rush of the waves engulfed me, knocking me off my feet, I swam blindly until Bobby appeared out of nowhere and pulled me into his arms. It was as if we were the only two people on earth.

The sensation of being out in the ocean under a breathtaking star-filled sky was like a fantasy. All that existed was the ocean, the stars, and us. All that mattered was the man in my arms.

We spent the next day lazily tanning on the beach and then had a casual dinner at an Italian place across the street. By nightfall, we were in the mood for some music and found a nightclub with a live band. Suntanned and happy, we cuddled together in a booth. Bobby made fun of the people on the dance floor and got me laughing so hard that my stomach hurt. It was the greatest time we'd ever had together. In fact, the weekend had been so heavenly that I hated to go back home the next day. As much as I missed the girls and knew we had to get back to reality, a part of me longed to stay. This was as close to happy as I had been in a long time, and I was afraid to let it go.

In the morning, we packed up our things before taking a last walk along the beach. We wanted to get back to Auburndale fairly early to have time to spend with the children and to give them the T-shirts we had bought. Holding hands, we strolled along the shore, knowing this would be the last time. It made us both more quiet than usual. It was hard to make the transition from a carefree, awesome weekend to going back to responsibilities. I thought going home was causing Bobby to be so serious. I was wrong.

"I have something to talk to you about and I hope it's the right time." The wind played in his silver hair as he turned to look at me. "Before we go back, I want to see what you think of this. I want us to get married. It would be better for the children, and we can knuckle down and start saving for their future. Besides that, if you become my wife, I can add you and the girls to my health insurance. You won't need the Medicaid benefits anymore. Our two incomes will be enough to live comfortably and even save a little. The girls are growing quickly, and it won't be long before they'll be looking at colleges. I want to be a part of that and help to plan for their future. We can't do these things by playing house like we've been doing. I want to make it legal."

My breath caught as my steps came to a halt, both feet sinking into the sun-warmed sand. Looking into his eyes, I could see he was dead serious. Why did it feel more like a business merger than a marriage proposal?

"Bobby ... I don't know what to say. How do we know it's the right time?"

"Because the girls need a dad and you need a husband. I want to help. I want the children to have a better life than your being on government assistance and always just scraping by. You can write, and I can go for that promotion at the steel plant. Together we can give them more than you struggling by yourself. It's a logical step, Baby. It's a good solution to a lot of problems. Will you marry me?"

Something stabbed me when he called our marriage a "good solution to a lot of problems." He didn't say I was the love of his life and he wanted to marry me because he couldn't live without me. In fact, the word *love* was never mentioned. I knew that we didn't have a sizzling-hot love affair and that it was something nicely comfortable, but the way he proposed was like a bath with tepid water. It saddened me, somehow. Yet, what he said made perfect sense. What could I offer the girls on my own? My writing brought in a meager income, and I had no insurance for protection. I had hoped one day to break into writing novels where my income would be far better and we could finally become secure, but no telling when that would happen or if it would happen at all. Perhaps Bobby was right in his thinking.

"Yes," I answered, squinting in the sun as I looked up at him. "I will marry you. Thank you for asking."

He swept me into his arms and spun me around, making people passing us on the beach pause and stare. "We'll be happy," he whispered against my ear as he held me close. "You, me, and the children, we'll be a real family now. Things will be a lot better from now on, you'll see."

Our families took the news of our engagement very positively. My parents, although concerned that it might be a bit too soon, gave their blessings and welcomed Bobby into the fold. Bobby's mother and stepfather were absolutely thrilled, knowing how happy it would make Bobby to be a father to my two girls after losing Mandy from his life. Even the girls were accepting, especially Mariah, who'd never been to a wedding before and was excited to be a flower girl. It was Vanessa who simmered and stewed. She understood why this change was going to make our lives better, and in a way, she was happy that I'd have someone by my side. But she never smiled about it or even spoke about it as openly as her sister did. Instead, she kept her thoughts to herself. We went ahead and planned a small ceremony to take place in a neighborhood church. Bobby knew the pastor and he had offered to marry us. By January, we would officially be husband and wife.

On our tight budget, Bobby could afford only a small, modest diamond, which he proudly put on my hand. It made our plans real and cemented our commitment. The ring felt strange on my finger after wearing nothing for so long. At least, that was what I told myself.

As plans for our wedding progressed, I began to suffer from bad dreams. They were always of John cheating on me and coldly laughing over my pain. Sometimes, after I had one, I'd walk around the house just to shake free of it. Other times, they would come in continuous strings until the morning light broke the cycle. How real they were. I could actually feel the sickening blow of his betrayal as if it just happened at that very instant. I'd wake up perspiring and hurting inside and often spend the rest of the day shaken. I couldn't understand why I'd be plagued with nightmares like that when my life was going so well. Sometimes I wondered if John would ever be out of my system completely.

"You look tired," Bobby commented, seeing the shadows under my eyes. "Are you getting enough sleep?"

I tried to brush it off. "I'm fine. I just have all the wedding plans on my mind and can't turn my thoughts off at night. As soon as we're married and everything gets settled, I'm sure I'll be sleeping much better."

Dreams weren't the only things tying my thoughts to John. It seemed that everywhere I went, my senses were assaulted by memories of him. I'd go to the gas station, and the car at the next pump would be identical to the one John used to drive. I'd be in a restaurant, and a man would walk by wearing the cologne John used to wear. There'd be someone who looked like him in a crowd. His favorite, dutch apple pie, would be on sale at the bakery. Some of our favorite songs would magically play in the mall or on my car radio. I felt as if his shadow was tacked to my heels, constantly following me.

At that point I decided to get some counseling. I wanted to figure out why I still couldn't shake John from my life. Having your ex-husband in your dreams and constantly on your mind is no way to start a marriage. I contacted the mental health clinic Vanessa went to and made an appointment.

"You still have unresolved issues," Sharon, my counselor, said after listening to my story. "These dreams and the reminders that haunt you every day stem from questions you still have from the past."

"Yes, I have questions." I folded my hands in my lap to keep them from fidgeting. "I have enough questions to last a lifetime."

"Like?"

I drew a breath and felt an ache rise in my throat. *Damn you, John … how many more times am I going to cry over you?* "Like why. I want to know why. Why did he do all of this when we were so happy?"

"You may never get your answers," Sharon replied. "I think what we need to work on is how to get you to a healthy place without them."

I expected more from a woman with a psychology degree displayed on her wall. She couldn't explain John's behavior? She had studied people like him. His warped actions should have a name. How could she charge me thirty-five dollars for a half hour of her expertise and simply tell me there may not be any answers?

"How can I ever let go of the past if I can't understand what happened? I had thirteen wonderful years with a man who fathered my children and was my best friend and soul mate. Then, he turns into this monster that I can't even fathom. I find out I spent all of those years with him thinking we were as close as two people can be, and it turns out I didn't know him at all. How am I supposed to just shrug it off and walk away? Do I simply start over from scratch and forget my tough luck?"

The sound of Sharon's pencil tapping on her steno pad filled an awkward pause. "What are your other choices? I suppose you could hang on to the questions you have and let them drive you into a depression. You can make the choice to stay stuck in the past instead of moving ahead to a new future. I know it's not easy.

I'm not saying it is. What happened to you and your children is very traumatic. But you're a young woman. You have a lot of life left to live. Instead of asking yourself why John did what he did and never finding an answer, start asking yourself what you want to do with this new beginning. You're about to get married and start over with a nice man who wants to be a father to your children. I'd say that's a good place to begin. You deserve happiness, but only you can make that happen. It's a choice. That's all it is. A choice to be a survivor or a victim of someone else's actions."

I left, processing all she had said. Maybe she was right. There never would be an answer to why John destroyed the life we had. I had to make the choice to let it go and find happiness again. With my new marriage on the horizon, I had the opportunity to do that. I had to stop messing things up by clinging to the past. It was time to focus on the hope of the future. I sighed and felt better, sliding my key into the ignition. But as soon as I turned on the radio, my positive thinking took a drastic dive. Blaring from the speakers was a song by Foreigner that John always used to sing to me. A sudden shiver feathered over my skin.

It was crazy, but I felt him as if he were seated right beside me, singing those words from his heart. His presence wasn't something conjured up in my mind to keep from moving on. I was willing. I was determined. I had a diamond ring on my finger that proved I wanted to escape. I had been telling myself to stop holding on to the past. A professional therapist had just told me to stop holding on to the past, but it actually felt more like the past was holding on to me. It would see me breaking free and going my own way and then reach out and grab me in its clutches with a song, a dream, or a memory. Tears burned my eyes as I snapped off the radio. Whatever this curse was that kept following me and throwing thoughts of John in my face, I'd outrun it.

I'd outsmart it. I'd totally ignore it. Before turning down our street, I stopped at the corner store and bought a bottle of wine. If I couldn't drown out the past by my own doing, then I'd get a little help.

I may have still been struggling with hidden emotions, but the girls showed great improvement. Mariah was far more relaxed and hardly felt the need to cling to me any longer. Seeing things stable in our lives and having Bobby around helped her to let go of the fear that she'd lose more people she loved. She made friends in the neighborhood and even started kindergarten in September without any trace of separation anxiety.

Vanessa, who had also shown a world of recovery, went back to school. Although she still missed her father and had issues of anger from all that had happened, she was able to handle things far better than before. She started making friends in her new class, got fairly good grades, and was in positive spirits most of the time. The only thing that tended to bring her down was the thought of having to be a bridesmaid in my wedding. As much as she cared for Bobby and loved him in a way, a part of her felt loyal to her dad.

"I feel like a princess!" Mariah exclaimed just before the wedding ceremony. She twirled before the dressing-room mirror, admiring herself in a flowing pastel pink dress with her blonde hair done up in curls.

I fumbled with my bouquet, eyeing my own reflection, and tried to feel like an excited bride. Even though I looked the part with my beaded white gown and two-tier veil trimmed in satin flowers, I didn't feel anything like I wanted to feel. I was just going through the motions. I glanced over at Vanessa, who was as stern as a soldier in her long pink dress.

She was approaching this wedding with dread that harbored in her heart. Honestly, so was I. Instead of joy and excitement, I felt a cold and empty void inside. I think we both wished this were some kind of dream and her daddy would magically appear. "Are you okay?" I straightened one of the flowers in Vanessa's hair. She looked so grown up even though she was only thirteen. It wouldn't be long before she would be a bride at her own wedding.

A weary sadness clouded her face. "I'm not into this wedding, Mom. I can't help it. I'm sorry if that hurts you, but it doesn't feel right, and I hate having to be here."

"I know you're not happy about this, Baby. This was never how it was meant to be, but I know this is the best move for us now. Bobby loves us and wants to help to make a better future for you girls. He's not your father. He doesn't intend to try to take his place, but he wants to be your friend. That's okay, isn't it?"

Mariah grinned, exposing a missing front tooth. "I'm glad. I'm getting a new daddy."

"Well, he'll never be a dad to me," Vanessa scowled. "You can marry him, and he can be your husband, but I'll never ever let him be my dad."

I hugged her and left the last word at that. Deep in my heart, I'd never consider Bobby to be my true husband. I was marrying my friend. He was only taking these vows today to afford a better life for my children. Today was about survival and making it the best way I knew how. But the only husband my heart would recognize was the man sitting in a prison cell serving fifteen years to life for murder. The ceremony was brief, with only our family and some of Bobby's coworkers in attendance. Everyone seemed genuinely happy for us and showered us with well wishes in the church hall at our reception. We danced to music on a portable CD player, ate wedding cake, and sipped champagne. Even Vanessa managed a smile or two until it was time for Bobby and me to leave for our honeymoon. We reserved that same hotel on Clearwater Beach for an entire week this time.

"We'll call you," I said to the kids as I hugged them good-bye. "Be good for Grandma and Grandpa, okay? I love you. I'll miss you so much."

Mariah hugged Bobby tight as he hiked her in his arms. Then she planted a kiss on his cheek. "Will you bring me back another surprise?"

"You bet," he promised, grinning ear to ear. "Something extra special because you were the world's most beautiful flower girl today."

I waited for Vanessa to soften, but she kept herself guarded and her posture rigid. If our last weekend away ticked her off, the thought of a honeymoon for an entire week was making her boil. "It'll be okay," I said, touching the arm she kept tightly by her side. "You'll see. Once we get back, things will be better than you think."

Bobby beamed at her proudly. "You did beautifully today. Your mom and I will be sure to pick out a very special present on our trip for you, too."

"Great," she uttered. As bitter as she was, it would sure take a lot more than a T-shirt or a beach towel to make her happy.

As usual, Bobby had a stash of champagne hidden under his seat to make the one-hour ride to Clearwater Beach more festive. At times, it bothered me how he involved alcohol in most of our activities, but at that moment, as we left my children at my parents' house, I was happy to see the green bottle with the white label. I even offered to pop the cork.

All the way to the beach, I tried to comprehend what had happened that day. It was my wedding day. I was now married. I had a gold band to go with my little diamond.

Bobby and I were no longer roommates who spent every evening together. We were now husband and wife in the eyes of the law. I belonged to him from this day on.

"What are you thinking, Mrs. Beauregard?" He smiled over at me as he kept command of the steering wheel.

Mrs. Beauregard? Diane Beauregard? The sound of it didn't fit, like wearing shoes on the wrong feet. I grinned back, then took two large gulps of the wonderful, bubbly concoction in my cup.

"I'm thinking that it feels good to be out of that wedding dress and back in my jeans and on the way to a whole week at the beach. I never like to deal with all the formal stuff. The honeymoon is more my idea of fun."

"Did you bring something special to wear on our wedding night? That's tradition, you know. At least, that's what I've seen in the movies. I can't help but picture you in something naughty and lacy."

I guess I should have. It was, after all, my honeymoon, but it never occurred to me to buy something sexy to heat up our first night as husband and wife. Not like when John and I got married. I actually ordered something in sheer black lace with garters and fishnets out of a lingerie catalog. *You're beautiful, Mrs. Nichols ... the most beautiful bride in the world ... seeing you dressed like that and knowing you're mine forever is like a fantasy come true.* Three more gulps. Another. Then another. Just what I was afraid of. John's ghost was still here and all geared up to be a part of my honeymoon.

By the time we checked into the hotel, I was buzzed. I drank my share of the champagne faster than usual, and it went straight to my head, which suited me fine. It was my head that was driving me crazy. As soon as we unpacked, I asked Bobby if we could get more champagne. He was more than happy to fulfill my wish.

"I'll be right back, Mrs. Beauregard," he said, kissing my lips before setting out for the market across the street. "Feel free to wait for me under the covers if you'd like. I intend to start our wedding night festivities a little early."

The door closed behind him, and tears instantly blinded my eyes. It was as if they had been contained all day and finally felt safe to surface. I didn't expect the idea of being officially married to Bobby to hit me so hard, but every time I looked at the set of golden rings on my finger or whenever he proudly called me Mrs. Beauregard, I died a little inside. I mourned for what could have been if John had only loved me like he pretended. I loved him like no one else before him and was so happy in the life we created. To be married to another man was like facing the truth of what happened head-on. There was no hope this was all a mistake. John wasn't coming back. Our life was over. It was legal and official now. I was now another man's wife, and that man wasn't the one who owned my heart.

Hot tears ran down my cheeks as I closed my eyes and gave in to them. I missed the anger that had allowed me to function before. It had helped me to be strong and capable of making it through each day. But now I was back to where I started. Confused and aching for something I had lost.

"I wish you could tell me why," I whispered, needing a world of things I couldn't have. "Why did you need love from other women when I loved you more than life itself?"

Bobby got his wish when he returned with more champagne. After drinking two more glasses, I was numb enough to play the role of his brand-new bride. We made love until we lay in each other's arms, bathed in a film of perspiration. Bobby sighed with contentment, but something made me crumble.

"Baby, what's wrong?" He propped himself on one elbow and stared helplessly as I cried. They weren't silent tears. It was more like removing a finger from the dike and letting the flood begin. I felt totally out of control and couldn't help but share my pain with him, even if it was our wedding night.

"It hurts," I sobbed, still reeling from the champagne. "I don't know how John could have done the things he did. How could he have sex with those girls and then come home smiling to me and the kids? Didn't he love us at all? I can't understand it."

Bobby hesitated. "I—I don't know. I wish I could help you make sense of it, but I can't."

"It felt so real." I began shaking and rolled on my back to stare at the ceiling. My tears flowed backward, soaking into my hair. "We had something special. How could I be so wrong about something like that? Am I that stupid that I can't tell when a man is lying to me about these things? Shouldn't I have felt it in his touch? Or sensed something missing in his kiss? How could there have been nothing at all?"

Another man might have gotten angry, but Bobby gently took me into his arms and rocked me to calm me down. I was drunk, and I tasted the champagne as I breathed. Why wasn't it killing the pain?

"I don't know," Bobby whispered. "All I know is that he was a fool. And that he'll never know how badly he hurt you."

I must have fallen asleep in his arms. The next thing I was aware of was fighting to open my eyes as my tongue stuck to the roof of my mouth. Hung over and confused, I searched the room for Bobby and found it totally empty. The TV was on, but he wasn't anywhere in sight. I swung my legs over the side of the bed, then stood and wrapped the sheet around me. It smelled of Bobby's cologne and stale champagne.

"Bobby?" I took slow steps as my head swam in circles. If only I had stopped drinking after the first bottle. "Bobby … are you here?"

Something drew me to the sliding glass doors that overlooked the ocean. The moon was full and cast a glow on the beach like a spotlight of luminous silver. In the distance, I could see him sitting alone in the sand, just staring at the raging surf. His dark silhouette showed a man defeated. I knew I had hurt him with tears over John that poured out in my drunken stupor. I wanted to go to him and apologize, but the words would sound so lame. The worst of it was, I couldn't promise that it wouldn't happen again. I couldn't promise that John would leave my heart. In fact, I was so messed up that I had no business promising Bobby anything. But it was too little too late, seeing that only hours ago I had promised the man my life.

TEN

Cries and Whispers

I stood by the stove, smiling as I stirred a pot of spaghetti sauce. Bobby and the children played a tickle game in the living room, laughing hysterically. In moments like these I had real hope. Maybe things would finally fit together and we wouldn't have so many rough spots. We could feel like a normal family without the darkness of the past pulling us back down again. After my doing so much drinking and crying about John on our honeymoon, things were a bit fragile between Bobby and me. We did have some good times as we sunned ourselves on the beach and swam in the ocean. There were romantic evenings with candlelight dinners and dancing until dawn at the nightclub. We browsed the gift shops and enjoyed picking out special things for the girls. We made passionate love like typical newlyweds, but never without the aid of a bottle of champagne and a six-pack of beer. It was getting so that we always had to have a drunken high just to feel free and relaxed with each other.

Although Bobby was understanding and comforting with my crying jags, I knew I had wounded him deeply. We thought getting married would be a good way to take better care of the children, but we had even higher expectations. We also hoped it would help to leave old memories far behind. We'd make new ones, better ones, which would leave no room for the past to interfere in our relationship. We could finally be a real husband and wife with a family to take care of. But after the honeymoon and seeing how I only seemed to be hurting more, we both had newborn fears that we were aiming too high. We didn't talk about it much. I knew better than to try to make Bobby put into words what my emotional roller coaster must be doing to him. In fact, we didn't talk about anything to do with John or even Mandy anymore. It was a fresh start for both of us, and we didn't want to soil it with past hurts. What we did instead was drown our struggles in alcohol.

"Do you want dessert?" Bobby looked at me from across the table in a Chinese restaurant. We had left the children at my parents' for the evening so we could catch dinner and a movie, but there was something strained about our mood. He had been quiet all night, while I felt strangely restless.

I shook my head and played with my fork. "I'm full."

He continued watching me intently. I wanted to crawl under the table, knowing what he saw was probably what he was hoping would be gone by now. We had been married three months and felt more like roommates sharing bills than husband and wife. Although we made love, it was usually after an evening of drinking. "Maybe we should talk about it." His jaw muscles jumped with tension. "I can feel it all the way over here."

"Feel what?"

"Him."

"Who?"

"You know who I mean."

My heart skipped in my chest as if I would die on the spot. I kept my gaze on my silverware. I couldn't bear to see the hurt in his eyes that I knew I was responsible for.

"Why are you starting this?" I asked, desperate for any other topic of conversation.

We could talk about Mariah and her kindergarten drawings. How nice it was that they always depicted our happy family, complete with her new daddy with the silver hair. Or how wonderful it was to see Vanessa doing so well in school and volunteering at the Humane Society on weekends. She was such a huge part of their team that she was even named Volunteer of the Year. Those were wonderful things to talk about. Safe things to discuss. Why would he want to strike a match and hold it so close to a mountain of dynamite?

He leaned forward to pin my gaze. "It kills me to see you hurting, Baby. I was hoping the counseling would help you sort through the things that still trouble you. Does Sharon have any idea what can be done to rid you of the past once and for all?"

I shrugged. "We don't really pay a lot of attention to the past anymore. We talk a lot about the future and how good it's going to get. She's so glad to see that I've remarried and moved on. She says that's a positive sign."

"Sometimes I wonder," he remarked sadly. "I love you and the girls to death, but I think I pushed you too fast. You didn't have time to heal all the way before I asked you to marry me.

Even your parents warned me, but I didn't listen. I thought if we had a piece of paper saying we belonged to each other, that we truly would. But … I think you still belong to … him."

"What did my parents tell you? I wasn't aware you talked to them about this."

"It was when I was thinking of proposing," he answered. "I went to their house and asked their permission. I felt that after all your family has been through, I shouldn't just spring my intentions on them. They said that they thought I was a good man for you, but that you hadn't had time enough to heal. They told me you still loved John. That you probably always will, and they asked me if I could be happy in a marriage like that."

I was stunned. My parents had seen how enraged I was after getting John's letter of confession. How could they tell Bobby something so ridiculously off target? It wasn't love I felt for John. It was an all-consuming hatred that was making me die a little each day no matter what I did to try to save myself.

"I'm sorry they told you that. They were wrong. I don't love him anymore. How could I after all he's done?"

"Because he's the father of your children." His answer was quick and ready. "That is a difficult bond to break no matter what the circumstances."

"Does that mean you're still in love with Denise? After all, she's the mother of your daughter."

Just the mere mention of Mandy made me shrivel at his expression. He looked instantly wounded. "No. That's not the same thing. You and John truly loved each other for all of the years you were together. I told you that I was never in love with Denise. The only bond I have is between me and my little girl. Even though I'm not allowed to be a part of her life, she's in my heart and always will be."

A ponderous silence fell between us as the waiter came with the check. "But, it wasn't that way with me and John," I said, hating to even say the name. "You said we truly loved each other all of the years we were together, but now I know that wasn't so. It was just a lie. He cheated on me the entire time. He couldn't have loved me and done that, could he?" I wanted to take back the question as soon as it hung in the air. Bobby reached across the table and took my hand. "I'm sorry, Baby. I just don't have the answer to that question."

It was going to drive me mad. My counselor claimed no answers. Bobby didn't have them. Even the alcohol I had come to depend on never brought one to light. If I didn't make some kind of sense of it all, I feared it would kill me.

Life rolled on with a steady rhythm. Bobby got up early and worked at his welding job all day. I took Mariah to kindergarten and then Vanessa to her school before settling down in front of my computer to write magazine articles.

I'd quit by midafternoon to pick up the children and then run some errands. By five o'clock I had dinner on the table and a welcome-home kiss for my husband. When nothing tender was brought to the surface, our routine would flow just fine. It was only when reminders of the man I was trying so hard to forget came up that it knocked me back down again.

"Hello, I'm Mr. Hatcher," the man on the phone line said. "Is this Mrs. Nichols?" I hadn't legally switched my name to Beauregard yet. Hearing him address me as Mrs. Nichols reminded me to do that.

"Yes. This is she."

"I spoke to you two days ago about your life insurance policy.

I needed information on the children and you supplied that to me?"

"Yes ... of course ... I remember. Is there a problem, Mr. Hatcher?"

He paused as if looking at papers in front of him. "Well, I may have made a mistake in the last names of your children. The computer isn't accepting them as Vanessa and Mariah Beauregard. I distinctly asked if they had the same last name as your husband, and you told me they did, but I'm still showing them as Nichols."

My memory whirled back to the conversation he was referring to. I had been updating my life insurance policy since I was now newly married, and he had asked about the children's last names. Of course he would need to know if the beneficiaries were still Nichols or Beauregards, but when he asked if the children had my husband's last name, I thought of John instead of Bobby.

It came so easily and naturally, as if my marriage to John was still intact and he was the man I was bound to for life. Not once did I catch myself and realize that Mr. Hatcher was asking if the children took Bobby's last name since my new marriage. I was stunned to see how my heart didn't even recognize him. How the word *husband* still meant no one but John. By the time I apologized for my mistake and explained that the children were keeping their names and not changing them, my guilt was hitting full force. After all that Bobby had done for the girls and me, he deserved more than the kind of love I was giving him. To wear his wedding band, sleep in his bed, share every aspect of his life, and still not consider him my husband was absolutely horrible. I hated myself almost as much as I hated John. I hated the lie I was living.

I began drinking my beer a little earlier than usual that afternoon. I wanted to get calmed down enough so that Bobby wouldn't be able to detect anything was wrong. I picked up the girls from school, masking my pain with a smile, but as soon as they were at home and busy in their rooms, I cracked open my first beer and chased it with my second as I set the table and prepared dinner. With each swallow, I waited for that wonderful calm feeling. It was the only thing that ever took the edge off and made things better. And today it would help me to face the good man I had disrespected by forgetting that he was my husband.

As it turned out, I needn't have worried so much about covering up what happened. Bobby came home glassy eyed and half drunk himself, with a six-pack under his arm. He had stayed after work and downed a few beers with a coworker, which he was doing more and more of lately. Before, he couldn't wait to get home to the kids and me at the end of his day, but now he delayed it by drinking with a friend. He had his own hurts to camouflage.

That night ended as many did before. I went to bed alone and slightly hung over, leaving Bobby on the couch to sleep it off. I was glad to have the bed completely to myself. I needed room to breathe. As I lay in the peace of darkness, staring at the red glow of the digital clock on our dresser, I felt lonely. Hopelessly lonely, even though I was now married and had a partner. But it wasn't a partnership built on real love. It was more of a mutual arrangement for the children's benefit. Yet, I wondered if what Bobby and I were doing was hurting them more than helping them. The girls were seeing a lot of drinking going on between their mother and new stepfather. They could feel the strain. It wasn't something we hid well. The children didn't ever bring it up or show signs that anything was wrong, and that worried me more than anything. When did they stop talking to me about things that hurt them or things that worried them? Our new lives with Bobby changed everything between us to where Bobby and I numbed our pain with our beer, but the girls numbed their own with pretending.

I looked over at the empty pillow next to me, remembering another lifetime when the husband I loved slept by my side. I didn't have to pretend or drink to dull the pain. The love was real and wonderful. Life was so happy and only got better with every passing year. While I knew it had been a lie, I missed that blissful contentment. I would never know that kind of love again. It wasn't just because I married a man who was a family friend more than a husband, but because something vital had died inside after all that went on in Ohio.

I touched the vacant pillow where I ached for John to be, hot tears slipping down my cheeks. It didn't have to be this way. There was one solution. It would stop my constant hurting and free my children to be raised in a better place. If I were to die, my sister and her husband would take them to live in their home. Maybe the kindest thing for both the children and me was if I committed suicide. It would end this suffering. Hadn't I struggled like hell for over three years now, trying to make this whole mess work out? I had tried everything I could possibly imagine to do, yet the misery and the pain were still very much a part of our lives. There would be no end to it.

Bobby shuffled into the bedroom, still groggy with booze, and crawled into the bed with a weary groan. I could smell the stale beer on the air he exhaled, and I winced at the sound of his throaty snore. Curling into a fetal position on the edge of my side of the mattress, I closed my eyes and tolerated it. I knew I wouldn't have to live this way much longer. I had a new plan. A better plan. I finally had some hope. This whole unbearable nightmare was about to vanish.

Maybe I should have felt anxious over what I was about to do, but oddly, I didn't. That next day as I sent my children off to school, worked on my articles and finished the laundry, I thought about how I would carry through with it. I decided the best way was to combine my prescription sleeping pills with alcohol. It seemed peaceful and painless, which suited me just fine. I was ready for a rush of complete nothingness.

Tonight would be my last night. I would do it tomorrow after Bobby went to work and the children went to spend the day with their grandparents. I would write letters first. Long letters to everyone explaining how I truly wanted it this way and not to grieve because I was finally free from suffering. I would tell them how very much I loved them and tell my daughters how I will always watch over them. To know that they were the light of my life. I just wasn't strong enough to go on anymore. I'd tell them that they will be better off with their Aunt Dee and Uncle Tom.

There'd be a letter to Bobby apologizing for ending a life we had only just begun. But he had to know it wasn't right. He was feeling it, too. I would tell him I did love him for being such a friend, but sometimes friends just aren't enough to make the pain go away. I'd wish him well and hope that one day he will see Mandy again. I know his heart won't mend until his little girl is back in his life.

I'd write my parents and beg for their forgiveness. After all they had done to help us survive this nightmare, I felt guilty that I was letting them down. I'd tell them how much I loved them and that I was so very sorry. I wish I could have made them proud.

Last, I really didn't know if I should send a letter to John. I hadn't contacted him since reading his shocking letter. He at least had the sense not to write or call anymore. He knew that what he told me had cut the last thread we were hanging from. I'd have nothing to say, really. Nothing civil. What do you say to the man who pushed you to suicide?

"Bed, kids," I called out that night. "Turn off the TV and go brush your teeth."

Vanessa rolled her eyes from the floor to the ceiling and then widened them on me. "Why can't we stay up, Mom? Tomorrow's Saturday. There's no school. I want to see this emergency vet show."

Bobby stretched from the corner of the couch where he was dozing. "You lucky kids got off tomorrow, but welders have to get up early. I guess I'll say my goodnights."

I watched as he bent over and kissed Mariah and then Vanessa, both girls never letting their gaze stray from the television screen. He then walked over to me and planted a soft kiss on my forehead. *It's our last night, Bobby. Tomorrow at this time, I won't be on this stinking earth any longer. Can't you at least give me a better good-bye kiss than that?* I snagged his sleeve as he turned to walk away and ignored his puzzled expression. All I wanted was one more for the road. I kissed him long and hard.

"Whoa! Now I really wish I had tomorrow off so I could make it a late night." He winked at me, and his face melted into a smile.

"I love you," I told him, an ache blossoming in my throat. "I just want you to know that. You're a wonderful man."

His face clouded with uneasiness. "You're wonderful, too. I love you, too."

I know he was about to ask if something was wrong. No matter how strained our marriage was and despite the many beers he downed that night, he still had the ability to read me like words on a page. God knows, this was one time I didn't want him to.

"Off to bed with you," I playfully scolded. "I don't want you to sleep through your alarm in the morning."

He hesitated before he turned and went off down the hall. It was to be the last thing I ever said to him. The last time we looked into each other's eyes. I didn't want it to crumble me or make me second-guess my plan. I had postponed it too many times before.

My gaze settled on the girls, sitting casually in their pajamas in front of the emergency vet show. Vanessa was watching in fascination as a pregnant bassett hound endured a lifesaving C-section, while Mariah scrunched her face up and hid behind the throw pillow in her hands. Her muffled voice could be heard saying, "That's yucky" and "How gross."

I love you girls so much … you don't know what's about to happen, but I can only hope one day you'll understand.

"Mom?" Vanessa was suddenly staring at me with inquisitive eyes. "You okay? You look a little funny."

Unwelcome tears surfaced, and I brushed them away. I couldn't possibly explain. I knew what I was about to do would be better for them in the long run, but it hurt to know I wouldn't be with them anymore. This was our last bedtime together. *Don't do this. Don't wimp out. You know there's no other way to end this. They'll be fine … just give it a chance. They'll be a whole lot better off.*

"I'm tired," I said, hoping she believed me. "I guess I'm anxious to go to bed."

She sighed and grabbed the remote, clicking the TV off. Both girls went to the bathroom and took turns brushing their teeth, and then I walked them, single file, to the bedroom they shared.

"We go to Grandma and Grandpa's house tomorrow, right?" Mariah climbed into bed, gathered her blankets around her and then blinked up at me from her pillow. It was astounding how much she looked like her sister.

"Yes. I think they mentioned something about taking you to the park. It's supposed to be a nice day. It'll be great for you to get out and enjoy it."

Vanessa got under her covers and then clicked the switch on her lava lamp that sat on the night table. She loved to sleep by its gentle light as the purple globs slowly floated up and down. "Why don't you come with us? You should take a day off from writing and have a little fun yourself, Mom."

I swallowed something acid and avoided her eyes. "I can't, Baby. I've got too much to do. Maybe another time." *There'd be no more time … time is running out … the clock is ticking … ticking … ticking … the final minutes are almost here.*

"I hope I get an ice cream," Mariah said, smiling at the thought of it. "Last time they took us to the park, I got that pretty blue cotton candy ice cream that had pink swirls all in it. It made a mess on my shirt, but it was soooo good!"

I remembered. I scolded her for not using a napkin and staining a perfectly good shirt. Now I wish I would have held her instead.

I smoothed her covers and then sat on the edge of her bed. "I'm sure Grandma and Grandpa will spoil you both with ice cream and everything else. But if you don't quiet down and get some sleep, you'll be too tired to enjoy any of it."

She smiled and closed her eyes. "I'm sleeping now. Good night, Mommy."

I rigidly held my tears in check as I traced a silky lock of her hair. "You deserve to be spoiled. You deserve to be happy. Always be happy … okay, little angel? Just promise Mommy that you'll always be happy."

Her eyes still closed and already near slumber, she only gave a sleepy nod. With an aching heart, I leaned forward and kissed her lips, so soft and deliciously sweet with traces of peppermint toothpaste.

Vanessa watched me as I approached her. I felt rather transparent and tried to cover it with a smile, but she saw the glimmer of tears behind it. "I'm sorry you're having a hard time, Mom. I hate to see you sad. Is it anything you and I can talk about?"

I sank down to the edge of her bed and admired how mature she had become. "No, sweetie. I'm really okay. I don't want you to worry."

"I worry because I love you. That's what you say to us all the time."

"I love you, too," I whispered, anguish almost overcoming my control. "And I'm so proud of you and the young lady you're becoming. You're only thirteen, but yet you seem so much more mature than that to me. I know you're going to do great things with your life."

"I hope I can get into vet school," she said, uncertainty clouding her expression. "What if my grades aren't good enough or I faint when I see a real operation like the one on TV?"

"You won't. It's what you were meant to be. You've loved animals ever since you were a baby. It will come naturally, you wait and see."

She grinned. "Thanks, Mom. I guess I'm worrying too much, huh?"

"I think so," I replied, patting her leg bundled under her comforter.

"I think that's what you're doing, too. You're worrying too

much, and it's making you unhappy all the time. Both you and Bobby."

She was so perceptive. We hadn't been fooling her with our charade. I drew a deep breath and found a clever way to speak the truth. "I'm not going to worry anymore. Things aren't going to go on this way. So just get some sleep, and don't think about anything but how much fun you're going to have at the park tomorrow."

I leaned over to kiss her cheek, so velvety warm to the touch. She reached up and hugged me for a moment. "Mom … just don't let Daddy do this anymore. Don't let him bring you down. Be happy, okay?"

It had been forever since she had mentioned her father. I envied her ability to block him out of her mind and concentrate on the here and now. If I had been able to do that, my marriage to Bobby might have stood a chance. Vanessa didn't have to worry about my letting her daddy bring me down. She didn't have to worry about it at all.

"I won't, Baby," I assured her, meaning it more than she realized. "I won't let him hurt me another day longer."

My side of the bed felt chilled as I slid in under the blankets. Bobby was lying on his back, snoring. I couldn't help but lie there in the gray shadows of the room, hating myself for the suffering I was going to inflict on my loved ones tomorrow. I thought of my parents, who had been so strong for us, always there to help in whatever way they could. This would destroy them. I knew it would break their hearts. The children would be worst of all. First, Daddy went away, and now Mommy disappeared, too. Mariah would be clingy again. This would bring back her old fear that people do vanish in the blink of an eye. She may even blame herself for letting go of me. I remembered how sweet her lips tasted as I kissed her. Would she ever forgive me for betraying her so?

And Vanessa—already a teenager and able to comprehend so much. She'd reel our last conversation around in her head, blaming herself for my taking my life. Maybe she'd replay how she told me not to let Daddy bring me down any longer and feel like she was the one who gave me the idea. What would that do to her, just when she was finally getting stronger? It would be a setback she'd never recover from. Tears streamed from my eyes and soaked into my pillowcase. I stared at Bobby's silhouette in the darkness, remembering how warm and safe his arms once felt. *Hold me again like you used to do, Baby … please … make me feel something … just hold me and don't let me go …* but his snoring continued, and I realized how foolish this was. He couldn't make this better. No one could make it better. I was asking the impossible.

Then I remembered what John told me on our visit with him in prison. That God hears prayer. He is the comforter and the healer and the miracle worker in all things. I saw such a difference in John once he had that belief. It seemed foreign to me. How do you believe in something you can't see or touch? There couldn't really be anybody up there listening. Despite my doubts, the guilt I was feeling over my suicide plans was tearing my soul apart. I had to talk with someone. Anyone. Even if that person was faceless and unfamiliar. I brought my hands together and folded them tightly.

Dear God … please help my family forgive me for what I'm about to do. I can't go on hurting anymore. It's more than I can bear. I can't go on living like this. Taking my life is the only way to find the peace I long for. Just not to feel anymore. Not to think. Not to struggle. I need to disappear. I'm sure of what I want, yet I worry so much about my children. Please, help them to understand somehow. Help them to be okay and to forgive me. Help my parents, too. And Bobby. It's going to be very hard on all of them. I feel selfish by shattering their hearts like this, but I just can't go on hurting anymore. I'm so tired, and there's nothing that will ever free me from this pain. I want to die. Forgive me. Help everyone to understand. Amen.

Amazingly, the next thing I remember is waking to my bedroom bathed in sunshine. I had somehow managed to sleep soundly despite all that weighed on my mind. In fact, I didn't even dream. It was the most restful sleep I could remember experiencing for a very, very long time. Outside my window, birds chirped and squirrels chattered from high in the treetops. A dog barked somewhere down the road. I heard the whisper of a breeze. All I could think of was how clear everything sounded, as if I hadn't noticed how alive the morning hours were until right at that very moment. And the rays of the sun pouring through the sheer curtains at my windows were absolutely beautiful. So radiant, bright, and lemon yellow, spreading a lovely warmth. I felt joyous inside to be experiencing it all. Every part of my body tingled and pulsated; I felt the invigorating rush of blood pumping through me and the awesome drumming of my heart. It felt so wonderful to be alive. Not just alive, but alive and happy. My spirit was light instead of burdened, and it soared as if it had wings.

I sat up, puzzled as to what was causing such a lovely reprieve from all of the anguish I felt. Then, I heard it. The voice. The words. It was as bold and crystal clear as if someone were in the room with me. *Suicide isn't the way to free yourself from your pain … forgive John and you will find your peace … forgive him … trust in me … I will show you how.*

It startled me. I wasn't sure what I had just heard or where it came from, but I knew it was the absolute truth. This wonderful lightness in my heart, the joyous feeling in my soul was what I would be able to hang on to if I forgave John for all he had done. It was never an option before. In our divorce group I remembered a part of the course dealt with that very topic, and I was one of the first ones to speak out with my bold opinion. To forgive meant doing the person who hurt you a giant favor. It meant letting him off the hook, and I would never do that in a million years. I wanted John to pay for all he'd done. Yet, now, in the brilliant light of my room as I felt a blissful smile on my face, I realized I was sampling how it would be if I did forgive and let it all go. By some miracle, I was being shown a preview. And I liked it. I loved it. I felt reborn. Charged with excitement, I kicked my covers off and dashed from my bed to the children's room. I didn't want to examine it or question what had just happened. All I knew was that I was happy and this wasn't my dying day.

"Girls," I called, first shaking Mariah and then rushing over to jostle Vanessa. "Wake up. It's a beautiful day and we have something special to do."

Mariah rubbed her eyes and grumbled something under her breath. She was never a cheery morning person. It used to be a chore to get her out of bed, but I found myself laughing and loving her all the more for it. She looked at me as if I had lost my mind.

"What's gotten into you?" Vanessa asked, kicking back her blankets and dragging herself into a sitting position. Her hair was wonderfully disheveled. She looked an absolute mess. I stared at her with my heart overflowing, wanting to climb up on our rooftop so I could shout to everyone that I had the most beautiful daughters in the whole world.

"We've got a mission to complete today," I happily told them. "Instead of the two of you spending the day with your grandparents, you're going to spend every minute with me.

We're going to the store to pick out a very special card for Daddy. Inside the card, we're going to write that we forgive him. That's the only way for us to be able to heal from the past and learn to be happy again. Then we're going to go out and celebrate by having lunch at Dairy Queen. I think we deserve the biggest hot fudge sundaes they have."

"With a cherry?" Mariah chimed, suddenly bouncing up from bed.

"Two," I answered. It was a day to live it up. I laughed and enjoyed the feeling of it.

Vanessa let a grin play on her lips. "Mom … I don't get it. What brought all of this on? I thought you were really mad at Daddy."

"I am mad. He hurt us very deeply, but something's changed. It's … wonderful."

She hesitated, blinking in bewilderment. "What? What's wonderful?"

That I'm not going to die today. God gave me the hope I was looking for. I swallowed tears of joy and answered as best as I could. "It's wonderful that now I know the way to true healing. Forgiving. Letting it all go. We're finally going to be okay."

After a breakfast of waffles, we all got dressed and went to the store to choose just the right card to send to their dad. I knew Hallmark didn't have a card for forgiving someone who destroyed your life, but we did find one that said what we felt. There was a photo of a wrinkled bulldog puppy looking worried and forlorn. The inside verse read, "Nothing is right without you."

"How do we sign it?" Vanessa asked once we got back to the car. "I don't know what we should say."

We thought silently for a moment, but then I scrambled in my purse for a pen. Vanessa read my words out loud as I wrote them inside the card.

"What you did really hurt us, but it hurts worse to hate you for it. We want to forgive you. Can we write to each other again?"

I gazed at the girls. "So what do you think? That says it all, right?"

Mariah nodded. "Good job, Mom. Can I write my name and draw a smiley face?"

By the time our card was signed, sealed, and stamped, I felt a great rush of enthusiasm. I wondered how John would react once he got it. It had been nearly a year since the devastation of his last letter. So much had happened. There was so much to say. I was excited and couldn't wait to hear back from him. I drove to the post office and dropped it in the box. There was no turning back now. Our mission was completed. The card was on its way to Mansfield, to a gray dismal prison cell where a wrinkly bulldog puppy and our words of forgiveness were going to let the light shine in.

ELEVEN

A Private Truth

"I can't believe the change in you," Bobby commented, chewing his broiled chicken thoughtfully. I had made a special dinner complete with fresh flowers on the table. It felt good to primp and fuss.

Vanessa smiled. "Yeah, Mom. You haven't cooked a real dinner in a long time!"

I had to laugh. Living with a writer meant lots of frozen pizzas and microwave meals, but now that I was feeling so much lighter in my spirit, it felt good to do things for the people I loved. I even baked a batch of double-fudge brownies for a surprise dessert.

Mariah poked at her chicken and looked rather unenthused. "I don't like it. I'd rather have hot dogs."

"That's what we'll have tomorrow night, then." I made a mental note to get the works with baked beans and brown bread. "If you'd rather, you can make a peanut butter and jelly sandwich."

"Really?" She broke into a relieved grin. "Can I eat it in front of the TV?"

I was trying to get us to eat dinner together as a family but decided it would be okay this one time. I gave her a thumbs-up, which made Vanessa want to watch some TV, too.

Bobby and I sat alone at the table, holding hands and smiling at each other. It was so good to feel this close and happy. When I looked into the depths of his dark brown eyes, I saw a calm that hadn't been there in too long a time. We were finally enjoying the comfort of our relationship without anything else in the way.

"You're like a whole new person," he said, gazing at me lovingly. "Since forgiving John, I can see such a difference. The children, too. They seem far happier, and I'm sure they're relieved to see their mother finally doing so much better."

"I feel … I guess … unburdened," I tried to explain. "I never thought I could feel this way or come to a place of forgiving, but it's what I needed to do. I was literally dying inside. I can't get over how that voice came to me that morning and told me that forgiving was the way to heal. It was so clear, Bobby. So real. You must think I'm pretty crazy."

"Oh, I think you're pretty, all right," he answered lightly. "But I don't think you're crazy. I think this voice you described was merely your subconscious telling you what you were needing to do all along. It didn't feel good to hate someone you were once so close to. I think it broke your heart to be enemies with John."

"I don't think that's it. It felt more miraculous than that. More like it came from a place far bigger than me and was showing me the way out of my pain."

"Like heaven?" His chuckle made me feel a bit foolish. "God spoke to you?"

"I don't know," I answered. "Maybe. I don't know how else I could have made this change."

He settled back against his chair. "I think God is something people hold on to when they've lost all faith in themselves. Is he there? I don't know. With all the bad things that happen to good people and the tragedies going on all around the world, I can't see how any God could just sit by and let them happen. I really don't think there is a higher power. If there was, we'd see proof of it. I think God would make sure we knew he was there. What happened with you was that you were so hurt and emotionally battered that you lost all faith in your own abilities to survive this. But underneath it all you had a fighting spirit. Your subconscious kicked in and told you what to do. That voice was nothing but your own survival instinct."

It made sense, but something wouldn't let me buy into it. What I experienced that morning was far more powerful than just my subconscious speaking. I know it didn't come from me. Something else was at work in my soul, responding to my prayer. Not only did I hear the words spoken to me that morning, but I also felt a presence, a distinct comfort, as if someone were right there with me. Whoever was speaking, whatever this was, I knew without a doubt that it was telling me the absolute truth.

In the past, I had set opinions about people who would forgive those who did awful things to them: they were weak, foolish, and gullible, and by forgiving, they were saying that the wrong done to them was okay. I never wanted to be that way, especially not where John was concerned.

But then this voice spoke to me like a teacher correcting a student, saying *I* was wrong. It told me that holding on to hatred and anger trapped me in a prison of my own. Instead of feeling weak or foolish, I felt empowered by my ability to let it all go. I felt like a drowning victim breaking loose from a cinder block, swimming to the surface, and gulping fresh breaths of air. I had another chance. Life was pumping through my veins.

My discussion with Bobby made it painfully clear that I was alone with my newfound beliefs. His views of God were scientific and calculated, while I was becoming more and more hungry for the true meaning of what had happened to me.

On Sunday morning, I left the children with Bobby so they could plant a vegetable garden. I left the house and drove several blocks to a beautiful church I had passed many times. With its stained-glass windows and modern architectural design, it commanded a person's attention. A sign out front posted the message: *The family that prays together stays together.* Several cars filled the parking lot, and people entered the building in a steady stream. My stomach grew fluttery as I parked. If I was going to find out about the power of God, and if it was truly real, this was the place to do it.

I was immediately greeted by a woman handing out bulletins, and then I continued into the massive sanctuary. Never before had I seen anything so beautiful. The carpeting was a plush lavender, the pews polished oak, and the ceiling frosted glass with a giant dove in the center. The altar was decorated with an assortment of potted ferns and lilies with the focal point being the podium from which the pastor would speak. Behind that, choir members dressed in deep purple robes filled the risers. I slid into the back pew, not wanting to be noticed.

A band off to the left of the altar joined with the choir in music that took my breath away. Then Pastor Edwards took over the podium and began his message of God's faithfulness. He read from the Bible and then explained the meaning in more modern terms. I was riveted to my seat, absorbing every detail like rain to parched soil. I felt thirsty for something I couldn't even identify. I knew the reason I came that morning was for some clues as to what God was about. If anything, I expected to find out how to tell if he was for real. What I didn't expect was for the words of the sermon to switch paths so that it seemed God was speaking solely to me.

"I had a lot more to the message today that I was going to deliver," Pastor Edwards said. "But God is impressing me to take a different direction. There's someone here who has been in a world of pain. Something has happened in your life to make you want to give up. You've been in the grip of depression and have even planned your own suicide. God is reaching out to you now. He wants you to step forward. Please come to the altar so my wife and I can pray with you."

I couldn't believe it. Like a wind at my back pushing me up from my seat, I stood and walked down the aisle. No one else moved. The entire church was totally silent, but I wasn't embarrassed or nervous by having all eyes on me. All I was focused on was Pastor Edwards and his open arms.

"Bless you," he whispered, as I sobbed up against him. "God wants to heal your hurts. He wants to give you hope."

Mary, Pastor Edwards' wife, also came to the altar, and I told them about John's being in prison. I told them that I had planned to commit suicide, but that a voice in my soul stopped me. I didn't know what it really was. As soon as I said that, they both smiled. I could see they had the answer.

"In our darkest moments, God works his best miracles." Mary offered me a tissue. "He knows our trials and he watches our suffering, but he allows it so we can turn to him and develop a love relationship. That voice you experienced was exactly how God speaks to us. It will come to us like a whisper in our soul, guiding us and offering us his hand. You were saved from suicide because you heard God's voice and responded. What you heard was his message directly to you to show you a way out of your pain."

"I felt so light as if my troubles were immediately lifted," I choked. "I felt free."

The warmth of Pastor Edwards' smile echoed in his voice. "Only God can take our burdens and free us from all the pain. Rejoice in the wonder of his love."

My heart soared. This was real. I felt it so very strongly. Then I became aware of so many others from the congregation coming up front to pray in a circle around me. People wept and laid hands on me, praising God for bringing me forward. They prayed for the children. They prayed for John. They warmly embraced me and offered me hope. One woman told me that she gave her heart to God after her daughter was killed by a drunk driver. God's comfort was the only thing that helped her to live again. Another man told me he was once a drug addict who lived on the streets and stole to support his habit, but Jesus changed him. Now he was married and a deacon at the church. Another woman once had cancer and was told she wasn't expected to live, but God cured her. An elderly man shared with me how his own son was in prison and that because of it, his son was now saved. He assured me that God has John in a place where he needs him to be right now. With a sparkle in his small gray eyes, he told me that God is working miracles. To have faith in his plan no matter how dismal it feels at times.

Those words replayed in my mind as I drove home elated. I could have stayed there for hours more, absorbing the joy and the hope in that place. I had heard stories of suffering, yet it wasn't pain and anger that prevailed. The joy and comfort all of these people had found weren't only the result of antidepressants or counseling. They came from God, and they were as real as the sun. I finally saw what John had tried so hard to tell me. I couldn't wait to start writing to him and sharing the wondrous things that had been happening.

I arrived home to find a modest little vegetable garden on the side of the house and the man I married sound asleep on the couch with the remote control still clutched in his hand. The children were in their bedroom, playing a board game and listening to music. No one knew anything more than I was back from the store. I wanted to share it with them. I wanted to shout and sing and dance with the joy I felt firing up my spirit, but Bobby wouldn't understand, and the kids would just think I was nuts. Only one other person could relate to the newfound strength I felt inside, and I couldn't wait to share it with him. I didn't even bother to think how ironic it was: he was the very person who had destroyed me in the first place.

When I got my first letter from John in response to the card we sent, I was so excited to read it that I tore it open right next to the mailbox. It made me smile as he told me how he whooped and hollered the day the card came. He said the entire cell block heard him weeping and thanking God. He told me how the guys in his Bible group knew about the last letter he wrote and urged him not to lose hope. John admitted he didn't have much faith that such a miracle would ever happen.

I knew what I told you in that letter was going to hurt you and ruin what was left of our relationship. You don't know how I wept the day I mailed it off, knowing that while I was being faithful to God in confessing my sins and cleansing the lies, I was revealing to you a part of myself that I am so very ashamed of. I felt dirty as I wrote it. I don't like to remember the person I was. That man was dark and troubled, tempted by evil and too weak to turn away from it no matter what the cost. I'm no longer that man, Baby. I've been redeemed and reborn. I wish you could learn what I'm learning in here. To let go and let God. To lay it all at his feet and find peace in the love he so unconditionally gives to us. This Bible group I'm in has been so very powerful in teaching me how to be the man God wants me to be. The kind of man I wish I could have been the day I met you, so I could have been the husband you deserved. You don't know how it tears me apart to know how badly I've let you down. I didn't deserve to ever hear from you or our girls again. Then this card comes out of nowhere like an answer to my deepest prayer, telling me you want to forgive me and we can start writing to each other again—how incredible is that? How can I ever thank you, Baby? All I can do is to tell you that you won't regret this decision. I respect that you have a new life now, and I won't intrude on anything you're trying to do. As much as I would love to have a new start with you as your husband, I know I have no right to that. I'm very happy to just be your friend. Believe me, that's more than I thought I'd ever have the privilege of being. So, write back to me and let me know how you feel about all that I've said. I can't wait to hear from you next, just to convince me this card isn't some kind of a dream. I love you, Baby. Right or wrong, I love you with all of my heart. You and the girls are my life no matter what happens....

Getting John's letter made me all the more eager to correspond with him. I had so much to tell him. So many things to catch him up on, including my marriage to Bobby. I didn't expect that news would come as a big shock. As much as he didn't like the thought of another man being my husband, he understood it.

I also wanted to let him know about the children and that they were doing so much better. To send him Vanessa's report card and a photo of Mariah painting at an art easel in her kindergarten class. I had a world of news to put in my next letter, but I knew I had to talk with Bobby first. He was my husband now. We were trying to make this work, and I didn't want to do anything that would hurt or disrespect him.

"I don't see anything wrong with it," Bobby responded after I explained things to him. "In fact, I think it would be very positive if you and the children could have contact with John again. Forgiving him has made such a drastic change for the better. I have to believe being friends with him would be a positive move, too. There's no reason to cut him out of your lives. I never wanted that to happen. He's Vanessa's and Mariah's father. I know more than anyone how it hurts to have that bond broken, and I never wanted the girls to have to grow up without him in their lives. As long as it doesn't hurt you, I'm all for it. It's actually what I was hoping would happen."

"You were?" I blinked in disbelief. I doubted I could be as understanding if it were Denise coming back into the picture.

"I think if you can find a comfortable friendship with John where you can tell him what's going on in the children's lives and let them communicate with him again, it will be healing. Healing for all of us, actually. We'll finally be in balance, so there won't be any more rough spots to knock us off course."

When he smiled at me, I took a long look into his eyes. They were gentle and kind, never accusing or jealous whenever John popped back up between us. It was a delicate situation and I expected more discussion, but Bobby had made it easy. Even though our new marriage got off to a rocky start, he still believed that John would find his rightful place in the picture. Being a friend to me and still being a dad to the girls was a place we all could live with.

"Thank you," I whispered, adoring him with my gaze. "You're a special man who has a very understanding heart. Sometimes I wonder how you handle it all. I don't think I could if I were in your place. I know all this has been very hard on you."

"Loving someone means going through the storms. I never expected our life together to be only good times. I'm here for you and for the girls. We're a family now, and I just want all of us to be happy."

That word would have seemed out of reach before, but finally I began to believe in it. I had learned to forgive John through God's grace, which freed me to move on with my life. That life was going to be spent with a man who had a heart of gold and never wavered in his love or commitment to us. Bobby was my future; John was my past. Now it all finally jelled.

The children and I enjoyed our letter writing. Anytime we got mail from their daddy, it made the day special and put smiles on our faces. He'd send Mariah cartoon pictures to color and letters saying how much he missed her. She loved it when he talked about how big she must be getting since she was in such an awful hurry to grow up. He wrote letters to Vanessa filled with praise over her grades and warned her to stay focused and not get distracted by the boys. She'd roll her eyes and break into a grin, enjoying the sweet annoyance of having a dad who nagged at her. My lengthier letters dealt with more complicated issues. He explained how my marriage to Bobby only emphasized all he'd lost, but that he brought it on himself. We also shared a great deal about what we both were learning about God. His Bible study had helped him to grow as a Christian, and he encouraged my own faith journey. He shared Scripture and inspirational verses he thought would strengthen my soul, while I sent him clippings and quotes of a spiritual nature to help hold him up.

He was happy that I was going to start taking the girls to church, but disappointed we couldn't talk Bobby into it. He told me to be patient. Some people need more time to open their hearts to all God has to offer. He also went to chapel on Sundays, and he said it made him feel closer to me to know I was in God's house, too. I also had to promise that I'd get the children into the youth programs so they could learn about Jesus, too. He wanted them to learn now while they were young, not later on as we were doing. "If our family had a firm foundation in Christ," he wrote, "evil never would have won out. I'd be holding you now and watching my daughters grow. I just want them to know the love of God while they're young, before they go down the wrong path. If they can learn from my mistakes, it will help with my own struggle to forgive myself. At least, some good came of all this."

The coming months went smoothly. John faithfully sent us letters and began calling the children again, which added to their improved spirits. He and I grew more comfortable, talking on the phone and sharing more and more of our feelings in letters. It felt good to be in a positive place with him again after all that had happened. Not only could I tell him the good things going on in our lives, but I could also express myself when I wasn't having such a great day and was sliding back on my forgiving feelings. It tended to be a constant exercise instead of a onetime deal. I'd have to forgive over and over, having occasional bad dreams or facing reminders of the past. I'd have to tell myself that those things were of another time and place. We were all different people. John had been saved and had given himself to Jesus, and the children and I were beginning that journey, too. Yet the past was still knocking on my door. Forgiving wasn't as simple as I expected.

After that morning when God showed me what forgiveness could do, I thought I was cured of my misery. But in reality, it was much more complicated than that. Every day was a test. I'd hear the name "Karen" at a school function and feel my insides churn. I'd see a movie where someone was shot. On TV I'd see talk shows featuring men who were unfaithful to their wives. Dreams of John's secrets still haunted me from time to time. With each test, my strength would be shaken as if I could so easily slip back into a tunnel of despair. I constantly found myself repeating my vow to forgive over and over as a way to fend off the negative. I came to see what forgiving really consisted of: daily choices, daily successes, one baby step at a time.

When school let out for the summer, the children began asking to make the trip to Ohio for another visit with their dad. Bobby was working long hours and we couldn't plan a family vacation, so I thought perhaps another visit up north would be a good idea. With things going so well with the letters and phone calls, it seemed like a logical next step. I ran it by Bobby, and he agreed. It was time for the girls to see their father again.

We were less anxious on this trip than we were on the first one we made. We knew more about what to expect. And best of all, we'd have five wonderful days to share with their daddy. No blessing was more cherished than that.

"I can't believe you guys are really here." John hugged me tightly. He then blinked back tears and turned to his daughters, drawing them into his arms. I wanted to freeze that picture in my mind.

The children looked just like him with their amazing pale blue eyes, Vanessa especially. She even had his long straight nose. My heart melted to watch them all embrace together.

We sat at that same little table in the back, holding hands and talking about everything under the sun. Although it felt strange to wear Bobby's wedding rings in front of John, it wasn't a factor. I didn't notice that John even looked at them. He was too busy soaking up the sight of us with an eager gaze. It wasn't a photograph to make do with. It wasn't a letter or a long-distance call. We were here and together, able to touch and to be close. Mariah sat on his lap, and while he held Vanessa's hand on one side he held my hand on the other, not wanting to break the connection in any way. Even when Mariah wanted to buy him a candy bar.

"I want to get you a Snickers, Daddy." She dove into the plastic bag of change we were allowed to bring in and fished around for a few quarters. "I know it's your favorite. I want to go get you one. Vanessa, come with me and help me."

Her older sister rolled her eyes in frustration. "Why can't you do anything by yourself? You're not a baby anymore. Man … why do you have to be such a pain?"

They went off together as John chuckled and watched them. He was fascinated by their every move. He returned his focus to me and leaned closer to my chair, his hand still holding mine. He squeezed it tightly and smiled, reminding me how petite I was next to him. I stared down at his fingers laced with mine and remembered a marriage that once felt so right.

"You look wonderful," he said, interrupting my thoughts. "I can't thank you enough for doing this. I miss you guys so much every day. Being able to see you again means the world to me. I'm thankful, also, that Bobby is okay with all of this. I kind of wouldn't blame him if he wanted to keep you all to himself."

It was strange to hear John comment on my marriage and Bobby. Although my relationship with Bobby was definitely much better, I still struggled to accept him as my true husband. I knew in my deepest heart of hearts that I wasn't in love with the man. I wanted to be. "Is this bothering you?" John referred to our hands still holding tightly to each other.

I should have pulled away and said it wasn't appropriate, but the words just wouldn't come. "No," I answered, smiling. "It feels nice." Mariah was the first to come back with not only a Snickers bar, but a packaged wedge of apple pie. "Here, Daddy. Vanessa told me you love apple pie, too. I don't remember. Do you really?"

"You bet I do," he answered, delighted when she crawled back up on his lap. It wouldn't be much longer before she'd be too big for such things. "Thank you, sweetie. I'll save it for when we all have lunch together. Then we can share it. How would that be?"

She nodded and laid her head on his shoulder. "I love you, Daddy. When are you coming back home?"

His expression softened as if she spoke to a dream he held in his heart. His eyes searched mine, asking for help, but all I could manage was to swallow back tears. Seeing how hard it was for her father to answer the question, Vanessa reached out and held his hand. Wordlessly, we sat together with emotions we didn't know how to handle. "I don't know, pumpkin," he finally said. His voice was hoarse with emotion. "But I want you to know that I'm always with you inside your heart. Every moment of every day, I'm there."

"But I don't want to go home and leave you here," she argued. "Can't you come home with us? Can't the jail people forgive you, too?"

My heart plunged to the floor. If only it were as simple as her childlike world. How lovely it would be if horrible things could disappear in a puff of smoke, clearing the way for what we wish for. Things wouldn't be so tragic or complicated. People wouldn't have to hurt anymore. Children wouldn't have to grow up with a substitute daddy because their real daddy was locked up in a prison.

"Bobby does fall asleep a lot." Vanessa sat back and crossed her arms. "And he drinks too much. I don't like it—it makes me mad. I wish he could go for just one day without having to drink so many beers. That's why he's always tired."

"He's tired because he works long hours," I said, jumping to his defense. "And he has cut back on the beer since we've been doing better at home. A lot of that was all the hard times we've gone through."

She acted as if she had more to say but decided against it. John stared at her and then looked over at me as Mariah blinked sleepily in his arms.

"Is this true?"

I shrugged. "He does have a few drinks every day. It's something all of our rocky times haven't helped, but it isn't anything that harms the children. He mostly just sleeps it off."

"That's not right," John countered, frustration growing in his tone. "He's head of a household and responsible for our children, and he drinks every day? How do I know that he's not driving with our girls in his car when he's had a few too many? How do you allow him to—"

"Cut it out, John," I interjected. "Don't start pointing fingers when we're doing the best we can. It's you who put us in this situation. It's you who blew our lives completely apart. Bobby is there for us and takes good care of us. If he drinks a bit too much, then that's just part of the package. I know how it feels to be hurting so much inside that a few beers is your only escape. I was there, too. I drank a lot every day just to kill the agony you were putting us through. At least Bobby is helping to raise your children because you disappeared from their lives. At least he's there to hold us and protect us and take care of us. Where are you? How can you afford to judge anyone?"

I was breathless. Where did all of that come from? I thought I had made more progress than that, but that sudden burst of rage made me feel like I slid all the way back to the starting point again. *I have forgiven … we are new creatures … I have forgiven just as God forgives me … honestly, I have … I forgive … I do forgive …*

My strength, my courage, my ability to sit calmly in a prison visitation room were all being worn a little bit thin. Just being near John again brought up such want. I wanted to erase all of this. I wanted to hold him. Make love to him again. I wanted no spaces left between us. Just a wonderful life where everyone was happy. What made him destroy something that felt so perfect? *I'm asking questions again, Lord … I thought I had forgiven and washed the slate clean. Why am I back to needing answers I know don't exist? Where is the strength you blessed me with? I can't fall apart now that he's sitting in front of me.*

He checked to make sure Mariah was almost asleep, then looked to Vanessa, who was now old enough to comprehend. He wondered if she had such anger, too. He seemed to almost welcome it.

"It's okay to let it out," he assured us. "I know the hurt I've inflicted on you guys isn't going to just go away because you've chosen to forgive me. Especially when we get to see each other face-to-face like this so rarely. It's easier to write letters and talk on the phone. We make small talk and don't have to deal with more important issues. But now that we're sitting in a circle like this, hard emotions are bound to break free. I'd rather we talk about them than try to ignore them."

It struck me how incredibly calm he was. I noted his obvious pain and guilt, but nothing like a hardened edge or sign that he needed to retaliate or defend himself with sharp words. I expected an argument, but all I saw was a quiet acceptance and that same glow of peace in his eyes. Just like the people in church who prayed for our family. I wanted that same sense of faith that would keep me on even ground.

Vanessa squirmed uncomfortably against her chair. "I don't know if I'm still mad. I guess deep inside I am, but as long as Mom does okay and doesn't look like she's falling apart, I do okay."

"And I am okay," I insisted. *At least, I thought I was until today.* "I don't know where any of this came from. I thought I had gotten over … I guess I'm worn out from the trip."

John shook his head and reached out for my hand. Mariah cuddled closer against his shoulder. "I hope you're not disappointed in yourself because all of a sudden you feel like tearing my head off. This is going to be a process, Baby. A long, hard process where we all have to work through what this nightmare has done to us. Forgiving isn't a onetime thing. I've found that out in trying to forgive myself. It takes doing it over and over again, especially when the anger resurfaces. We have to forgive and keep forgiving as many times as it takes and realize that it's natural to struggle with it. I'm so proud of you and the girls for how strong you've been, and you should be, too. This isn't a setback. It's only a part of the forgiving process that we're all going to have to go through."

Forgiving is a constant, ongoing process, John said. There will be times when you question yourself. The key was in holding strong to your commitment to let go of the past and forgive as often as it takes.

With a smile, I examined his face. It was like seeing a whole new man. "You're so different now. You have that same peaceful-ness about you that I saw in those people at church. So many of them had problems far worse than mine, yet they were steadfast in their faith and glowed with joy."

"It's there for you. It's there for the girls. All you have to do is reach out for it."

"How?" I asked. I prayed daily. I went to church. Still, I was riddled with self-doubt and fear.

He turned to Vanessa and then pointed toward the front desk where the guards were. "Spunky … do me a favor and go get a Bible. They're in the bookcase over there."

When she brought it back, John carefully adjusted Mariah on his lap. He then opened the Bible on the table between us, point-ing out several Scriptures that had helped him through the most difficult times. Vanessa and I listened intently as he read them aloud. As I listened, I felt the familiar comfort that God's mes-sages bring. Like a baby just starting to take those first steps, I wanted John to show me and lead me. With John so on fire for what his newfound faith had done for him and his eagerness to pass it on to us, I was charged up inside. It felt great to have some-one to believe with. He could tell me how to understand it all. We connected and had this hunger in common. Believing gave us both what we needed to survive.

By the time our visit was over that day, we had grown closer as a family. I was glad that we actually experienced a little turmoil because it brought us to where we needed to be. We had started to understand what forgiveness really is. I couldn't wait to go back and see him again tomorrow. We shared a world of pain, but things still felt so close between us.

We spent a glorious week together, laughing, talking, joking, praying, and simply soaking in the joy of being together. John introduced us to a few of his friends in the visitation room with their families. It didn't even bother me that John always introduced me as his wife. Nothing else would have sounded right. I was actually glad that he still saw me that way. The longer I spent with him, the more I felt the same about him. My husband. The love of my life. The man who blessed me with two beautiful children. The good things started to come to the surface again, pushing the hurtful things aside. We started touching more and holding hands longer. His hugs got closer, and his good-bye kisses tasted sweet. He kept them short so as not to give the impression that it was meant to be anything but a caring gesture, but I knew. I felt it. Nothing was taken for granted anymore, especially every minute of our final visit that Saturday.

"I don't understand this," I admitted, gripping his hand as the children cuddled close on either side of him. "How could we still feel so right as a family? It's as if this bond between us never breaks."

"I'm so thankful," John answered. "I can only give God the glory. I believe he's got a plan for us that we can't even comprehend, but I've got a feeling it has to do with granting us a miracle. If we stay faithful and continue what we're doing, I believe we're going to be together again."

I almost wished he hadn't said that in front of the girls. It was impossible to dream such things, let alone give them hope that would only let them down. There was no way we could end up together. The obstacles were too great. The best we could hope for was what we had right now: a loving friendship with periodic visits.

My hand went to let go of his, but he held on tighter and wouldn't let it slip away. "John, it's impossible. How could that work? You're here, and I'm married to Bobby."

"I just believe," he said with conviction. "I think somewhere inside that you believe, too. This love between us isn't a mistake or something that's going to go away. We've been through the worst that life has to offer, yet look at us. I love you and the girls more than ever before. And whether you say it to me or not, I know that you love me, too. I was sick before, Baby. I did things that shattered our entire world. Evil knew my weakness and used it to destroy us. But evil isn't winning. We're finding our way back to being a family. I don't know how. I don't know when. I know how impossible it looks right now, but I have to believe that God has preserved our bond for a reason. He intends to reunite this family."

"You mean you want to marry Mommy?" Mariah broke into a toothy grin.

John glanced at her and then settled his gaze on me. "I'd marry Mommy in a heartbeat, but I know I have to be patient. Just make it our secret, okay? Don't talk about it to anybody."

"Like Bobby," Vanessa warned, knowing her little sister had a very big mouth. "I don't want to hurt his feelings."

I grew uncomfortable. This wasn't right. We couldn't talk like this, no matter how wonderful it was. Bobby deserved better, and I already worried about how I'd face him when we got home.

"Your father and I are not going to get remarried," I insisted. "It's not good to start fantasizing like that. But I am very happy that we have gotten this close again. We have something special that no one can take away."

The girls went on to other subjects, but John's attention kept drifting back to me. The pull of his gaze made me feel wonderfully vulnerable. How I ached to have his arms around me and to bury my face in his shirt, inhaling his scent, absorbing his warmth, hearing his heartbeat, and never having to leave him again. But the clock didn't cooperate. When the guards called that all visitors had to leave, we knew this was it for a while. He'd go back to his life behind bars, and we'd go back to our home life with Bobby. Back to lives that didn't fit, no matter how hard we tried to accept them.

Mariah shed tears as she hugged her daddy as tightly as she could. He wept, rocking her back and forth, telling her to be good and to say her prayers. That he was always there in her heart. He then embraced Vanessa, who cried openly against his shirt, leaving wet spots where her tears soaked in.

"I love you, Spunky. Be good for Mom and help look after your little sister. I'm so proud of you for all you've been through and still being so very strong. Go to church, okay? Start learning about the power of the Lord. With his help, we're going to make it through this."

Once they broke apart, John turned toward me. The pain of saying good-bye was as acute in his eyes as it was in mine. "I love you, Baby. You're my soul mate and my wife. I'll never give up hope that we'll end up together."

In a blur, he kissed me. This time it wasn't short and polite, but long, deep, and heated. Everything around us seemed to disappear. We didn't curb our emotions to decipher right from wrong. All we knew was that something beautiful was happening and we never wanted it to end. Nothing else mattered for that one wonderful moment.

"Nichols!" The guard shouted from her perch at the desk. "Time."

I pulled back, but John still held me close. "Forgive me. I know you're married, but it still feels so very right."

Tears flooded my face. "I know. That's what scares me."

"Don't be scared. Just keep praying. God is leading us somewhere special."

With one last embrace, I took the children's hands and walked out of the visitation room. We wept as we walked, each step taking us farther away from a man who was still a part of us. As we checked out at the main gate and heard the steel door slam behind us, locking us out of John's world once again, I wondered how I'd ever be able to go back home and face Bobby. Our life together was more of a lie now than ever. These last five days proved that my heart was anchored right here in this prison and would never belong anywhere else.

TWELVE

Exploring the Darkness

Bobby was happy when we returned, genuinely glad that we had such a positive, close visit with John. The children told him all about the places we saw on our three-day drive home and how cool it was to sleep in hotels. They talked about their daddy and how good it was to see him. Nothing was said about anything else. Even the children were now playing a role around Bobby so as not to hurt him with the truth. They knew, as well as I did, that my relationship with their dad had changed.

"Why do we have to go to church?" Mariah whined as I fixed her hair one Sunday morning. I straightened the pink ribbon on her ponytail. "Because I want us to go as a family."

She scowled. "Why?"

"Because what God has to offer us is very, very special. I want you girls to join me in learning more about it."

"Why won't Bobby go?" Vanessa asked. I could tell by the way she kept tugging at the hemline of her dress that she missed her faded baggy Levis.

I sighed, finally letting Mariah run off to find her best shoes. "I don't know, really. I've talked to him about it several times, but he doesn't believe there is a God. I wish I could get him to at least have an open mind, but he seems against ever setting foot inside a sanctuary. We'd best leave it alone and just go on by ourselves. Maybe one day, he'll change his mind."

I didn't believe it, even as I said it. The drinking helped to chase away Bobby's pain and was, in a sense, his religion. Now that I had pulled away from that, our relationship was even emptier. We didn't have anything in common besides our dedication to the welfare of the girls.

I wanted faith in something bigger than myself. I believed that what saved me from suicide that day was the voice of God. It strengthened me in ways nothing else had, and I wanted more of it. I wanted it for my children. I felt on fire for that wonderful sense of peace that was so obvious within John and the other believers I had met. Nothing could keep me from gathering my girls and going to that awesome house of worship to learn more about the miracle of God. We needed to be inspired. To sing. To pray. I wanted Vanessa and Mariah to experience the same kind of blessing I found when I sat in that place. It was the most important thing I could expose them to if they were to have the promise of a bright future.

Mariah was welcomed into a Sunday school class with other children her age, and Vanessa and I went to the main sanctuary. After several songs by the choir and a brief prayer, Pastor Edwards introduced the guest speaker for that day, a man who had been consumed by a life of sin but was saved by turning his life over to Jesus. He seemed just like one of us. He spoke of his years gripped by alcohol and drugs and how he eventually became involved with the Mafia. After over five years of self-destruction in a lifestyle of senseless killings, he was finally caught and sentenced to twenty-five years in prison. It was there, in that claustrophobic cell, that he first learned about another inmate who had spent most of his adult life incarcerated. He was trapped by the same bars and was surrounded by the same concrete walls, yet his spirit was joyful and thankful. It was then that this man's life changed as a result of the hope he found in Christ. He now dedicated himself to traveling around the country and sharing his testimony. I glanced over at Vanessa, who dabbed at tears trickling down her face, and my heart rejoiced. This was what she needed to hear. This story was similar to her daddy's, yet just another confirmation that people can change. The man's story gave such hope and comfort to everyone sitting around us that several people wept, raising their hands in praise.

After the speaker concluded, Pastor Edwards invited anyone else who had a testimony to come forward and share it. A woman told of her drug addiction and that she lost custody of her child because of it.

"But then God took a hold of me and showed me a better way," she beamed. "I'm clean now, going on twelve years. I've got a great job in management at a hotel and married a man I met in my Bible study. My daughter has just started college and is going to be a doctor. There was a time I never would have believed it, but my life has been restored to something more than I ever dreamed. I'll never be the person I used to be ever again. I've kicked my habit, and my past is gone for good!"

Vanessa perked up when a teenage boy stepped forward. He was shy at first, but eventually grew more comfortable making eye contact with those filling the pews. More than once, his gaze settled on my daughter as if he somehow knew her pain.

"My dad ruined our family when I was really young," he explained, nervously holding the microphone. "He wasn't ever home for us. He ran around with lots of women and really shamed my mom. She cried all the time. I don't remember a lot because I was only like six or seven, but she was always tired and depressed, sometimes sleeping most of the day. I took care of myself and my baby brother. She ended up having a really bad breakdown and was admitted into a mental hospital. I vowed to myself on that day that I would hate my dad for the rest of my life for what he did. He moved, and we kids went into foster care until my mom was able to come back home. It was hard. Real hard. I wasn't sure that we'd ever be okay again, but then my dad came back last summer and wanted to talk to us. I didn't want to, but it turned out to be a cool thing because my dad was really different. He had found out how sick he'd been for so many years with a sexual addiction. He got treatment and then found a really good church that helped him to get stronger inside and make changes. Now, we live together as a family again. We've all gotten saved and owe a lot to God. That's it, I guess ..." He shrugged shyly and handed the microphone back to Pastor Edwards.

Vanessa and I held on to each other's hands. I was trembling so badly over this young boy's story that I thought I'd fall out of my seat. There was something very powerful at work in that room. It was no coincidence that we felt the impact of these stories. God knew what we needed. The messages were the lifeline we needed to hold on to. We had made great strides in getting closer to her father, but the wounds were always there. I knew this young man's testimony was God's gift to us. It hit so close to home that it got me to thinking about John's dark side and how he described it as an empty hole he could never fill. I began to wonder what a sexual addiction was and if John possibly suffered from such an illness. Maybe it actually had a name.

The library was filled with the hushed whispers of students studying for tests, friends chatting at square tables, and children asking their mothers for just the right picture book. My shoes echoed on the tile floor as I made my way to a computer station. I was thankful that no one seemed to notice. My mission felt dirty and frightening, but I knew I couldn't go on wondering. I had to know about sexual addictions. If there was an illness that made people give up everything for sex, then there may be reasons for the nightmare that happened to us. I carefully typed *Sexual Addictions* into the search window. My stomach clenched as I waited several moments for possible book titles to appear on the screen. After what seemed like forever, a string of titles appeared. I quickly jotted each title and its catalog number down on an index card and then deleted the request. My knees felt rubbery as I walked over to the nonfiction section, scouting the vast array of self-help books. I found the titles I wanted—four books written on sexual addiction. And one was meant for the wives of addicted men. I found a secluded table in the back corner of the library and immediately sat down to scan the pages. I wasn't even sure if this pertained to John. The thought of his unfaithfulness being anything more than a selfishness that got out of control was a stretch. After all, a cheater was a cheater, right? The words unfolding before me rocked my foundation. One author was a recovered sexual addict and plunged the reader into an in-depth exploration of this compulsive disorder. He compared this illness to alcoholism or drug abuse. Certain personality types were extremely prone to sexual addiction, and factors from one's childhood also played a role. The type of person who usually became addicted to sex was a person who never found reward in anything. No job was enough. No amount of money could satisfy them. Even the best of marriages and the closest of families couldn't fill the addict's heart. No matter the cost, no matter how they hated themselves for taking risks with their careers and home life, they had to have that "fix."

"This is it," I uttered, staring down at the pages now dotted with my tears. "It's him. It's John. This is why he did the things he did."

After so many years of searching for an answer everyone told me didn't exist, I now held it in my hands. I was ecstatic and desperate to read each book from cover to cover. In a rush, I went to the checkout desk and fumbled through my purse for my library card. I couldn't wait until I got back home. I had to find out what this addiction was all about. I had so many questions tangled in my mind, but I also felt such hope because all of these books offered real solutions for survival.

The authors spoke of addicts recovering and broken families being restored. One book mentioned a twelve-step program similar to Alcoholics Anonymous. To my pleasant surprise, the program involved having a faith in God. It was the faith foundation needed to reconstruct a more positive life, which John had already begun in his transformation. There were reasons why this happened to people, and more important, there was a definite cure. Families did survive. Marriages were mended. Once the addiction was recognized and the work had been done to reverse it, people did actually put back the pieces of their broken lives. I wanted hope like that for my family, even though I felt as if I were betraying Bobby with these heartfelt desires. But if the people in this book could climb out of their illness and reconstruct their world despite all the pain and demolition, then perhaps we could clear the way to becoming a happy family again. I was married to a man I wasn't in love with, and John was incarcerated possibly for life in a maximum security prison, but something told me not to rely on my own understanding. I was to simply trust. By now, I knew exactly where that voice was coming from. There was a master plan, and all I had to do was follow.

I finished one of the books within three hours of getting home. What John tried to describe as his dark side was a sinfulness related to sexual addiction that many people suffer from. While this addiction has various degrees, the condition often stems from early childhood wounds that never heal. The real-life examples in the book portrayed several men who had loving marriages and stable, successful careers. The need for sexual relations outside of marriage was so strong that the addict knowingly risked it all. The author described the illness in such vivid form that I could look back and see John in this pattern.

Tears streamed down my face as I closed the book and set it on the table by my bed. I got up to check on the children when Bobby unexpectedly stepped into the doorway. I hadn't heard him come home from work.

"What's wrong?" He sat down beside me. His gaze then drifted to the books on the table, examining their titles in confusion.

I dabbed my eyes. "I didn't know it was this late. I'll go make dinner."

He shook his head and picked up a book. Slowly, he flipped through the beginning pages. "It looks like whatever you were reading really upset you. What's this about?"

I swallowed a pocket of air and realized there was nowhere

else to go but straight forward. He could read for himself what the book was about. We had more than enough untruths between us, and it was getting harder and harder to manage.

"I went to the library today after hearing a young boy talk about his father's sexual addiction during Sunday's sermon. One book is written by a man who suffered such an affliction and ruined his life and the lives of his family because of it. It helped me to understand what made John do the things he did. Another book I found was written to the spouse of an addict, showing that the affairs and sexual behavior have nothing to do with the marriage. It's a sickness. Just like alcoholism or drug addiction. It also responds to treatment and has a cure."

He wasn't prepared for so much information. "So why do you need to know all of this? I understand that you've always wanted answers, but it sounds like you're almost wishing you could change things. We're married now. There's no fixing anything that went wrong with you and John. We've moved on, remember? The past is in the past, and now we're supposed to be concentrating on our life together."

"We are," I answered defensively. "I just needed to know what made John do the things he did. Is that so wrong?"

The lines of his face softened as he slowly shook his head. "No. It's not wrong. Just hard for me to deal with."

"I'm sorry. I don't mean to hurt you with this."

"And I don't mean to make you feel guilty. I know you're always going to hurt and wonder why John did those things, but just once I'd like to see that our marriage is taking the place of all that. Just when I think we're getting somewhere and we're actually happy together, John pops up again."

I hated what I was doing to him. He deserved much better. I took him in my arms and held him close. "I'm sorry, Bobby.

Honestly, I am. I just don't know if I can ever be what you want. Maybe I just can't let it all go. It's inside me like a constant ache. I know it's hard on you when I'm supposed to be your wife and dedicated to you, but I feel like I'm still searching for answers. I'm still hoping for some peace. These books helped me get closer to that goal."

Drawing back, he stared into my eyes. "And I want you to find that peace. Believe me, I do. I just don't want to lose you in the process."

I should have assured him that he wasn't going to lose me. That this new life we built with the children was as solid as Gibraltar, but I couldn't. The words wouldn't come. Not after feeling such fire from John's good-bye kiss the last time he held me in his arms in the prison visitation room.

"Things will work out," I managed to answer. It seemed generic enough. But as he got up and walked away, I knew it wasn't the answer his heart needed, and I knew I wasn't being completely honest.

In the next letter I received from John, he shared with me the work he was doing with Chaplain Smith in private sessions. He opened up to me about how long he had carried feelings of resentment toward his mother. He was faced with finding a way to forgive her. Since John had been in prison, the two of them had written letters, and she expressed great remorse for her behavior. She felt partially at fault for John's situation and was riddled with a nagging guilt. Seeing her own up to part of the problem helped him to want to move forward and work on a new relationship with her. It would take time, but he joked that he had plenty of that. He also wrote about how good it felt to be a changed man and to understand what led up to the murder. It was a tragedy that Karen lost her life and so many people he loved were destroyed in the process, but he firmly believed that, had he not lost everything, these changes would never have taken place. I responded to his letter immediately with the same honesty.

I hate lying to Bobby, I wrote in closing. *I'm feeling more and more guilty about my growing feelings for you while having to go through the motions of my marriage to him. He knows something isn't right. I think he senses that my heart hasn't gotten over you, and I don't know how to handle this. He's been so good to us and such a friend. I just wish I were free to explore these feelings that still exist between you and me. I have no idea where in reality they could lead considering our current situation, but they are so strong. The bond our family has is still there. When we were all together again during our last visit with you, it felt as if my heart was finally home. I didn't have to pretend something I didn't feel. I was sitting with my children's father and the man I love with all my life. Bobby is a good man and genuinely cares about the girls and their welfare. As much as we feel bonded with you, you're still not here with us. You can't help me to raise the children or pay the bills or save up for a more stable future. If there was an emergency, you couldn't be here. What sense would it make to let go of the marriage I have and put my heart in your hands again? But, at the same time, I'm not happy. I've tried so hard to fall in love with him and make this relationship work, but you're there. I can't let you go, and I'm hurting him because of it. I feel confused and torn. My head tells me to make this work with Bobby, but my heart tells me that there's something unfinished between us. I don't know how much longer I can go on balancing this kind of a lie. To be one man's wife and still be so tied to another is going to drive me crazy. How do I do this? What do we do with what's happening*

*between us? Do you have any answers? All I know is that it
feels good to be close to you again. I'll love you always.*

His answer came in a letter the following week. His advice:
Whenever you can't find solutions and things don't make sense,
lean heavily on God for direction. What we don't understand, he
sees very clearly. It is his plan and his timing. He is at work at the
potter's wheel, molding and shaping us into the people he wants us
to be and choreographing our lives according to his purpose. John
told me he had been praying heavily on it, too. He admitted that
the message he kept getting was to regain his family and things will
fall into place. I wondered if that would be God's answer for me,
too. If ever I needed to hear his voice loud and clear, it was certainly
now. *What do I do, Lord? Which way do I go? Why do I love John so much
when having any kind of a future with him is impossible?*

Mariah squirmed in her dress sitting in the pew alongside me
before that Sunday's sermon. Vanessa looked more comfortable in
a pair of black slacks and an ivory silk blouse with a lace collar.

"When is Sunday school?" Mariah scratched her nose and
stared at a little girl her size in the third row. "Why do we have to
sit in the big church today? It's boring in here. I think it's just for
grown-ups."

I patted her knee. "I'm not sure. The Sunday school room was
locked. The teacher may be running late this morning."

Just then the choir members rose to their feet, and the sanctuary filled with song. Listening to the rich harmony and comforting
lyrics soothed away the stress that had been churning inside me.
The doubts, the questions, the need to know which way to go all
dwindled to a wonderful calm.

Once the musical portion was finished and Pastor Edwards took the podium, he burst into an ear-to-ear smile. He said something special had happened concerning the children's Sunday school, and Mrs. Meredith and her husband would share it with everyone.

"Hey," Mariah whispered, pointing with her small finger. "That's my Sunday school teacher!"

The petite blonde woman positioned herself behind the microphone, carefully making room for her husband to stand alongside her. They both appeared very happy and anxious to speak.

"Good morning," she began. "I have a very joyous announcement to make that will call praise to our Lord and Father. A very special prayer has been answered for Don and me. We've just learned that we're expecting our first child. For those of you who may not know us or understand the history behind this blessed announcement, you may be wondering why the big fuss. Don will tell you a bit about the road it took to get here and what we've overcome."

Her husband had the glow of an expectant father. The sanctuary was silent as everyone waited with anticipation. Even Mariah sat still and listened instead of wriggling like a worm.

"There was a day I thought my wife and I would never share such a miracle." His piercing green eyes grazed faces in the congregation. "In fact, I didn't even think I'd have a wife to share with at all. Two years ago our marriage was extremely rocky. I had brought a lot into our life together by having a problem with alcohol. I wanted to kick the need to have a drink, but the craving was overwhelming. It pushed my relationship with Amy as far as it could go, and we eventually got a legal separation. That was when God got a hold of me. I prayed endlessly for God to help me to stop my drinking. It wasn't until I was alone in a depressing little hotel room with nothing but a whiskey bottle staring me in the face that I found the courage to change my life forever and break my losing cycle." He paused to blink away tears of emotion. His wife lovingly took his hand for added support. "From that day forward I've been a changed man. I have never taken a drop of the evil that nearly stole my wife from me. I turned away from the addiction and never looked back.

"Now we just found out that we are going to have the baby we always dreamed of. We wanted to share this with all of you for one reason today. To tell you that no matter how broken your marriage may seem or what problems are holding you apart from the one you love, God will work to restore the relationship if you let him. He will make troubled marriages new again and hold families together against all odds if you hold strong to your faith and don't let go."

Applause rang out as Pastor Edwards hugged them both. He shook his head with delight and scanned his church.

"Is God good or what?" he asked, drawing cheers from those around us. "I think this testimony is touching a lot of lives today. If you have a marriage that has been falling apart and it seems the problems are too heavy to bear, just trust in God to restore what you've lost and make it better than ever. I don't care what your circumstances are or how hopeless it may seem, if you trust in God and his power to hold families together, you'll see miracles coming your way. Let's bow our heads today and say a special prayer for Amy, Don, and their unborn child. Let's give God all of our praise in this miracle."

I bowed my head and wept. Vanessa was so worried about my emotional reaction that she slid closer and put her arm around me. What I just heard was an answer to the prayer I had been lifting toward heaven. Now I could see which way to go. No matter how impossible it seemed or how many obstacles stood in our way, our family could still stay together. Divorcing John and marrying Bobby were the results of my trying to control the situation, not what God ever wanted to have happen. I was unhappy. Bobby was unhappy and drinking more because of it. And the children could see how it wasn't working, no matter how accepting they acted. It was time to stop lying to myself and everyone around me and trust in the direction I felt pulled in. John was still where my heart felt at home. Our family was still bonded and unbreakable even with prison walls between us. We survived such tragedy because what we had was real and worth saving. Our family was to stay together even if I couldn't see a way. I knew in my heart that this love wasn't supposed to die and that our story would serve a purpose one day.

"Are you okay, Mom?" Vanessa squinted at me with worry. "Is something upsetting you? Do you want to leave?"

I gathered myself and controlled my stifled sobs while taking both of my daughters' hands. "We're not going anywhere, girls. This is exactly where we need to be. Right here where there are stories of hope and proof that miracles do happen."

THIRTEEN

An Imperfect Circle

The joyous message from church that day was mixed with a heavy dread. It was time to make some major decisions that would hurt Bobby. I prayed for guidance in how to face him with everything I had on my mind. As it turned out, I wasn't alone in wanting our relationship to end.

He came home from work Monday afternoon, obviously agitated over something. Instead of greeting the children with his usual hugs, he wordlessly passed by them and went straight to the closet in our bedroom. I wondered if he had lost his job or something, but by the time I caught up to him, he had most of his clothes off the hangers and was piling them on the bed.

"What are you doing?" I kept a safe distance, not daring to get too close.

He glared at me with burning, reproachful eyes. I had never

seen Bobby so enraged. "What I should have done a long time ago."

"What are you talking about?"

"Getting out of here. This game we've got going won't work."

I wanted to talk with him about that very same issue, but certainly not like this. I had no idea what was causing his huff, just that it seemed serious. Something must have gone very wrong to make this man with a gentle heart act as if he had no heart at all.

"I don't understand," I said, braving it and taking two steps closer. "If something's happened, why can't you talk to me about it?"

He swung around from the pile of work shirts he was stuffing into a duffel bag. "You want me to talk about it? Well now, maybe I should. After all, I guess you sure weren't going to do it."

Totally bewildered, I could only wait and watch as he stalked across the room and yanked open the drawer to my nightstand. Pushing aside my Bible, some note cards, and a pen, he brought out the manila envelope that held all of John's letters. I hugged my arms around my waist as he opened it and dumped a mound of letters on the bed. Letters that were never meant for anyone but me to see. Words of undying love from a man behind bars.

"How long were you going to lie to me?" he shouted. "You said you were only going to have a friendship with John. I believed it was a good thing for you to see him and write to him again, but you played me for a fool. You're still in love with each other. What am I here for?"

I stood there blank, amazed, and completely shaken. It wasn't supposed to happen this way. I wanted to tell him in my own way so that he would understand. In my own time when things were calm and the children weren't within earshot. Not like this. Not with him shouting and throwing all of my secrets in my face, leaving me with nothing to say.

"I'm sorry." It sounded so lame. It was all I could think of to say. I owed him so much more than just two empty words.

"I'm sure you are. I'll bet you're sorry that I'm here instead of John. If he walked up to our front door and rang the bell today, you'd be back with him in a heartbeat. All we have would just be thrown aside. I'm nothing but a replacement until he gets out."

I desperately shook my head. "No ... that's not what it was at all. I never meant for things to turn out like this with us."

"Really? That's funny when you're writing love letters to John behind my back. How else did you expect it to turn out?"

"I didn't expect to fall in love with him again," I blurted, my heart racked with guilt. "I thought everything between John and me was finished, but ... things have changed. I wanted to talk with you about it. I was going to tell you, but not like this."

"How then? When? What on earth were you waiting for?"

"To be sure," I answered, gaining strength and holding his gaze. "I needed to be absolutely certain that what I was feeling in my heart was real. I've been so confused for so long that I wanted to be sure before I spoke to you about it. But now I know that John and I still have a strong bond between us. Our family needs to stay together no matter how many obstacles we face. Trying to build a new life with someone else so soon was a mistake. You have been my dear friend and a wonderful father figure for the girls, but I was scared. Now I know that trying to take control and going against what feels right only makes things worse in the end."

Bobby blinked through his tears and let his rigid shoulders relax, a sense of relief taking over his anger. He raked a hand through his thick silver hair and drew a weary sigh. "We were both at fault. It wasn't just you. Your parents even tried to warn me, but I was like a bulldozer trying to make things work when I knew we both had serious issues from our past that hadn't been resolved. I couldn't fill John's shoes any more than Vanessa and Mariah could fill Mandy's. We married for reasons that guaranteed disaster. I guess we just had to get to this point to see that."

I stood back as he gathered his things and walked out of the room. It was hard not to call out to him, telling him to wait and that there was so much more to say to one another before our relationship came to an end. As strange as it seemed, I wanted to thank him for all he had done. I wanted him to know that we did love him, that we would never forget him. I wanted to tell him so many things, but before I could, he was gone.

"Where'd Bobby go?" Vanessa sat on the couch, baffled after seeing him leave with all of his belongings. She grew even more concerned once she saw my tears.

I glanced at Mariah, who wanted an answer, too. I sat between them and grappled for an answer. "Bobby went back to live with his brother down the street. It's just going to be the three of us from now on."

"Why?" Mariah's eyes were as wide as two vivid blue Frisbees.

"Because of a lot of things, really." I paused and gently swept her hair behind her slender shoulder. "Things that might be hard for children to understand. It's just that things between your father and me have changed since our last visit with him, and that makes my marriage to Bobby unfair. My heart isn't where it should be to have Bobby as my husband. Both he and I wanted this to work, but it just can't. We got married for the wrong reasons and have decided to end it here. Don't worry. I think the three of us are going to be just fine. We'll be a good team and, I hope, be able to remain friends with Bobby once things smooth out a little."

Tears fell from Vanessa's lashes as she swiftly brushed them away. "I loved him and everything. He was really good to us, but he never felt like my dad. It was just weird having him instead of Daddy here."

Mariah nodded. "I miss Daddy, too. I thought having Bobby would make that go away, but it doesn't. I still want my daddy home."

Both of my girls had said exactly what my heart had been feeling. As much as we loved Bobby, trying to fit together as a family was more like fitting a square peg in a round hole. It never worked no matter how hard we tried. John was the only one who belonged.

"I'm just so sorry," I said, choking back my emotions. "I didn't want to have you both go through more losses, but this was bound to happen sooner or later. This isn't the union God wants for us."

Vanessa pulled back from my embrace and dabbed at one of my tears. "Is that why you were crying so hard in church last Sunday when that man was talking about God saving families? Did that make you think about Daddy and us? I was thinking about it a lot."

"Yes. I believe that testimony was meant especially for us to hear. Maybe this is a good time to talk about it. I need to know how you guys feel about something."

Mariah shifted against the couch cushions to sit up as straight and tall as she possibly could. She liked it when we had these special discussions.

"Is it about Daddy?" She twirled the end of her shoulder-length hair, waiting for my answer.

"Yes," I answered. "It's about all of us, really. Some amazing things have been happening, and I want you to know about them. I've found out why Daddy did the things that made our family fall apart. He had a sickness. It's an addiction that many people have. It makes them do bad things that hurt the people they love. The good news is that Daddy and I are learning all that we can about it, and that there is treatment so bad things like that will never happen to us again."

"Does he need a doctor?" Mariah asked.

I smiled. "Well, actually I think he's found something better than that. I think God has been the answer to curing Daddy's addiction. Daddy is better now, and he no longer hurts inside like he used to. What I want to ask you girls is how you would feel if we tried being a family again, even though Daddy has to stay in prison. We've worked through a lot, and it feels good to love each other and still be together in spirit. Forgiving Daddy has actually made us a stronger family. I think that being so close now means we were meant to survive this and not let the pain of the past win. I don't know what the future holds. I don't know how long Daddy will be gone, but I do know that we all still love each other very much. I guess I need a vote on what you guys think."

A big grin crossed Mariah's face. "Do you mean you and Daddy would be getting back together?"

"In spirit, yes." I returned her smile. "We'll still live apart because he's in prison and we have our lives down here, but we can be together in our hearts and our souls. In a way, I feel closer to him than ever before because we're surviving the unthinkable together. With God on our side, I really believe we can do this."

"My vote is yes," Vanessa offered, giving a thumbs-up.

Mariah copied her sister. "Make that two!"

I took them in my arms and savored the joy of the moment. As hard as it was to have Bobby walk out of our lives, it felt wonderful to be open and honest again. I didn't have to feel guilty for talking about John with the children. There was no need to keep our love for him inside like a dirty secret. Now we could be honest with our hearts and get in perfect line with what the future had in store.

"What's your vote, Mom?" Mariah squirmed inside my arms.

Vanessa made a clucking sound with her tongue as if her little sister were getting on her last nerve. With seven years' difference in their ages, she tended to do that quite a bit. "Duh, blockhead, what do you think it is?"

"It's not fair until we all vote." Mariah tipped her chin back with defiance and then looked at me. "So what's your vote, Mommy? Yes to being a family with Daddy, or no."

I reflected on the last time we all sat together in the visitation room of Mansfield prison. How close it felt despite the walls that had separated us for so long. How perfectly miraculous it was to sit in a circle as a loving family. It still worked, and I had a feeling the best was yet to be.

I gave a thumbs-up and burst into laughter. Suddenly, my spirit felt as light as air. "My vote is yes. A definite yes. I know we can make this work. Nothing will ever break our family apart again."

It was freeing to be alone to raise my children. I hadn't been solely responsible in a very long while with all the help I had gotten from Bobby, but having to handle my writing, the household chores, the shopping, the cooking, picking children up from school, and helping with homework was good for me. The more I saw I could actually do on my own, the better I felt about myself.

The fear that I couldn't be a good mother on my own was now replaced by a sense of pride. I enjoyed the challenge this time, instead of cracking under the weight of it. I had more faith in myself as a person and all I could do.

While working in my office one morning, I began to think about the story we had to tell. I had written other people's stories for years in various magazines to inspire readers with hope, but the more I thought about it, the more I felt the need to share all our family had been through. I wasn't sure how my editor would take it. She had no idea about the trauma in my personal life, nor did I know if others would accept it even if it did get to be published. Perhaps the fact that John had killed someone would make it impossible for them to understand how a family could still stand beside him. The topic of sexual addiction, along with a true account of how it destroyed a marriage, could just be too heavy. As uncertain as I was about how people would react, I still felt our testimony had to be shared. If it could open one person's eyes to the healing power of forgiving the unforgivable, then I knew it would all be worth it.

To my amazement, every magazine I submitted our story to accepted it for publication. Titles like *God Sent My Husband to Prison so He Could Be Set Free* and *His Sexual Addiction Destroyed Our Lives* and *I Forgave My Dad For Murder* all appeared on various covers on newsstands all over the country. The shameful secret we once guarded so closely was now hung out in the open for all to see. Photos of our family were included with each article. *Guideposts for Teens* even put Vanessa on its cover. Our story was now public knowledge, and as much as I wanted it to touch people's lives, I was scared to death that it might come back to hurt us. I began to question what I had done, even though it felt so right. Our story could serve a purpose. It could change hurting lives. The healing that took place after we forgave John was miraculous, and it could happen for other people, too.

My doubts began to ease when the magazines forwarded mail from readers. Instead of criticism or hateful judgments, we received letter after letter of thanks and praise from many others who were facing issues of forgiveness. Vanessa got letters from teenagers telling her that her forgiving her dad changed their lives. I received letters from couples with broken marriages who found hope in reconciling. We even got letters from other families that also had a loved one in prison.

One letter was from a young man incarcerated in Texas, saying that he realized for the first time by reading our story the hell he had put his family through with his actions. He now understood how his being in prison was hurting his wife and children and made a promise to himself to change. That he'd straighten his life out so he could come home to them. In all the outpouring of mail we received, not one letter was critical or cruel. I was overwhelmed by the response and more convinced than ever that the message of forgiving and healing broken relationships was something people were in need of. I wasn't sure how, but I decided I wanted to take it to a whole new level.

"How would you girls feel about going on a TV show to talk about what we've been through with Daddy?"

"What show? Would we have to talk or just you?" Vanessa was the first to offer questions. She wasn't one to jump into something she wasn't informed about.

"Actually, it's a show for people who are facing problems in their lives. It's called the 'Dr. Joy Browne Show.' I've contacted their producer, who invited us to fly to New York City to appear on a show that deals with families broken apart by sexual addiction.

They want us to speak about how Daddy's actions shattered our lives, but that forgiving brought on healing. The producer said they even want to try to get permission from the prison to have Daddy on the show by speakerphone."

"What's a speakerphone?" Mariah asked.

"It's so your daddy can be heard on TV even though he can't be there," I explained. "It would mean our whole family could talk to millions of people about the miracles God has done in our situation and tell them that forgiving is the key to healing."

"I'd be scared," Vanessa admitted. "It's one thing to have our story in magazines where people just read it, but now we have to be up in front of everyone talking about everything. What if I say something wrong? I make mistakes when I'm nervous. What if I cry when I hear Daddy's voice? I don't know if I could really do it."

I took her hand and held it for a moment. It didn't feel childlike in mine anymore. She was blossoming into a beautiful young lady with thoughts and fears of her own.

"There is no way I'd force this on either of you," I explained. "If you don't feel right about it or good about it, we won't do it. It is pretty scary, and I understand your reluctance, but at the same time, this is an amazing opportunity to reach a lot of people with our story. You saw the impact the magazines had on everybody. It's like turning our nightmare inside out and making something good come out of it. If you decide that you think you'd like to do this show, I can only imagine how many more people will find hope because of our story. God wants us to use our trials so we can better the world. This is our chance to do that."

"Do we get to stay in a hotel?" Mariah asked.

I broke into a grin. "Yes. We even get to ride in a limo."

Her eyes flew open and she bounced up and down. "Let's do it! I want to go! Say yes, Nessa!"

Her big sister edged into a smile. "Okay. It sounds cool. Let's take our story to New York."

I made an emergency call to the prison to have John phone us at home. Once I told him about the show and that they were going to have him be a part of our interview by speakerphone, he was pretty excited about touching millions of people with his heartfelt message of facing your wrongs and making a change before it's too late. Maybe someone else with an addiction or a sinful lifestyle would find hope in what he had to say. The thought that he could actually make a difference from the gray surroundings in which he was trapped made him feel as if he could give back something to the outside world. New York City was spectacular even though we didn't have much time to enjoy it. We were picked up at the airport by a white stretch limousine and whisked to the heart of the city to check in to our hotel. Taping would be that next morning, so we barely had time to grab dinner, see a few sights, and then get to bed early. Upon arrival at the studio, we were briefed on where in the show we would appear and that John would be on the speakerphone. They also decided at the last minute that Mariah was a bit too young to put in front of the cameras.

Vanessa sat in the front row of the audience where Dr. Joy would ask her some questions, but I was seated in the center of the stage to tell our story in front of the cameras. I wasn't prepared for how hard that would be or how frustrated I would feel.

"How did you find out he was having an affair?… What was that phone call like?… What did you do once you learned John had shot her?… How did you tell the children?"

My hands clasped tightly in my lap as I answered each of her questions with tears stinging my eyes. The cameras zoomed in for the emotion. The audience whispered. I kept praying that she'd move on and get to the main message of our story, but once she finished hearing about that horrible day from me, she moved on to get John's version.

"Where did you get the gun?… What made you pull the trigger?… Didn't you know when you had the affair with her that something terrible would most likely happen?… Did you fear losing your family?… Why didn't you tell Diane the truth?…"

My heart broke as I listened to John answer each question. His voice boomed into the room, making me long to reach out and hold him. A photo of him grinning ear to ear was splashed on a nearby monitor. I instantly regretted getting our family into this whole thing and hoped that Vanessa was holding up okay.

Dr. Joy went over to my daughter and made her stand up. "What do you have to say? How does what your dad did make you feel?"

I cringed as the camera closed in on all the suffering on her face. "P——d off," was all she said. Two words made up her television debut.

Dr. Joy put a sympathetic arm around her shoulders and offered a bit of psychiatric advice. "Just don't let what he did poison the rest of your life. You need to be okay, and so does Mom. Would you like some counseling once you get back home? I'll pay for it if you go."

Not knowing what else to do, Vanessa silently nodded. That was Dr. Joy's cue to cut to a commercial now that she supposedly found a cure for us. My stomach hit the floor as I was ushered to sit near Vanessa in the front row of the audience. My portion of the show was finished, and all I had to do now was blend in with the crowd. Not one word was spoken on what God had done for us or how far we had come because of that awesome morning when a heavenly voice told me to forgive. Not one point was made about how even the deepest hurts can be healed by forgiving and letting go. All we ended up doing was making John look like a monster.

"I thought you were amazing." A young girl seated next to me broke the train of my thoughts. She offered a gentle smile. Her large brown eyes reflected something that was hard to identify. It was as if she were smiling through her sorrow. "I listened to you up there and thought how strong you've been. To keep going after all that happened and to take care of your children by yourself had to have been hard. You've helped me a lot. I've been hurting over something lately and thought I really wouldn't make it, but after seeing how you survived everything … well, it's made me believe I can make it, too." She reached over and hugged me. "Thank you."

In that moment, I felt so grateful. Now I knew our mission wasn't a waste. What we said was enough to make one young girl want to hang tough and survive her own issues. Her thanks was the gift I had prayed for.

Coming forward with our story only added to our healing. Each one of us seemed to be stronger because of it. We thrived as a family, but as happy as we were to have our bond restored, it was all the harder not to be together. We missed John so. The miles between Florida and that little visitation table in Mansfield made our hearts feel like they were breaking in two. It was especially hard when Christmas rolled around. I began to wonder if even Santa's wonderful gifts could put a smile on my daughters' faces.

"I wish Daddy were here." Mariah hung an ornament on the tree with her lips drooping into a frown. "It's not right without him. I wish Santa would bring him home."

Vanessa straightened the angel on the top and then stood back to admire it. "He always got so silly when he put up our tree. I remember how he'd sing along to the Christmas songs in this really goofy voice and make us laugh so hard."

"He wouldn't want us to be sad," I said. "We have to just hold him in our hearts and try to have the best holiday we can. One day he'll be home to decorate the tree again. One day things will be like they should be."

Even as I said it, I wasn't sure I believed it. With a fifteen-years-to-life sentence, there was a very real probability that John would never walk free again. I prayed every night for a miracle that would somehow open those prison gates and let my husband come home, but I still wondered if that day would ever come. My fears and worries began to smother my faith.

I got the mail one day and noticed an interesting envelope from Prison Fellowship. I had received mailings from them before, since I subscribed to one of their magazines, but this one was different. It had a photo of a little boy clutching a Christmas package on the outside. The caption that went with it read, "Be an angel to a prisoner's child!" I tore it open and read about a wonderful program called Angel Tree, a worldwide outreach to deliver Christmas presents to children of prison inmates on behalf of their incarcerated parents. The people who volunteered to deliver the gifts would also leave coloring books and brochures about the love of Jesus so the broken family could find hope in his love. Between preserving the parental bond with gifts and spreading the Word of God to needy prison families, I knew I wanted to be involved. Perhaps getting involved in this program would help us get through our own Christmas.

"I can't thank you enough for volunteering to be an Angel Tree angel this year, Mrs. Nichols." The Prison Fellowship coordinator who phoned me sounded as energetic as a child herself.

"You just can't imagine the need we have for people like you. So many of these children go without simply because we don't have enough volunteers."

"That's awful," I said, amazed at her statement. "I hope the kids I'm sponsoring covers the Auburndale area at least. I actually wondered if you'd have even that many."

"The truth is, I could have given you hundreds of names in your area. There are prison families in virtually every neighborhood. So many of them fall between the cracks. All I can say is God bless you for helping. Thanks to you, these fifty children will have a very special Christmas this year."

I had no idea that the neighborhoods all around us housed others just like us. Behind the locked doors and closed curtains were more single-parent and grandparent households raising brokenhearted children who also wished that Santa would bring their mommy or daddy home for Christmas.

Thanks to the incredible help from our church, all fifty of our Angel Tree children had presents wrapped and ready for us to deliver. After we put up a little artificial tree in the church's lobby and hung the paper angels on the boughs, people could choose which child to buy for by reading their names, ages, and clothing sizes on the paper angels. The children ranged in age from newborn up to teen, but the warm and caring people of our congregation made sure no one was left out. It was heartwarming to load the mountain of brightly wrapped packages into the back of my car, knowing that each one would put a smile on the face of a prisoner's child.

It took two days to deliver to all the families, but it was an experience we would never forget. Vanessa and Mariah wore their bright red Santa hats and thoroughly enjoyed the happy squeals of each child as we distributed the packages one by one. Some lived in comfortable homes, while others were barely getting by. One grandmother was raising her daughter's four children in her one-bedroom apartment in a very bad section of town. It was obvious they had very little. There wasn't even a Christmas tree, but all four of her grandchildren wore the biggest smiles once we told them we had brought presents from their mom. They each took the package that had their name on it and hugged it to their chests as the grandmother blinked tearfully with silent thanks. It was all they would get this Christmas.

"My husband is in prison, and I'm raising our two girls alone," I told her, wanting her to know that we understood her pain. "It's very hard, especially on the children. I just hope you know that God will see all of you through."

Her small brown eyes lit up as soon as I said those words. She was obviously a firm believer. "We're blessed," she said, her face nearly glowing. "I make it a point not to lose sight of that. We're healthy, and we have each other. I know God will bring their momma back when he feels she's ready. It's drugs. She's hooked. She just can't get off them and stay off long enough to come clean. This is her second time getting locked up."

"Just don't give up," I said to her. "She can beat her problem. My husband also had an addiction that was hard for him to break free of, but he did it because God worked so powerfully in him as he sat in a prison cell. I think as sad as it is to have so many people behind bars, it can also be a place where all is stripped away and real work can be done to finally make a change."

A tear dribbled down her wrinkled face as she reached out to give me a hug. We stood for several seconds, drawing strength from one another. "Thank you," she whispered against my ear. "I had no way to afford presents this year."

"You gave me and my children a wonderful gift, too," I

answered. "Now we know we're not alone."

After that busy weekend of nonstop deliveries, we relaxed by our tree with our arms around each other. We felt such a major change. Each and every family we met, spoke to, and prayed with made an incredible impact on us. It made our own hurts far easier and put the spirit of Christmas back in our hearts instead of feeling empty without John. We especially learned how very much we have to be thankful for.

"I used to hate this cheap little artificial tree." Vanessa gazed at the twinkling lights while propping her feet on the coffee table. "I thought it was small and ugly. It made me mad that we didn't have a huge real one like Daddy used to get us. But after seeing those kids who barely had anything, I feel pretty lucky. We have a whole lot. I guess you don't know how good you have it until you see somebody worse off than you."

Mariah cuddled sleepily into the crook of my arm. "Can we do it again next year, Mommy? I liked feeling like Santa Claus. This is the best Christmas ever."

"I think we will." I nodded, my heart welling with joy. "And I agree this has been a pretty wonderful Christmas."

At the beginning of the new year, I knew I needed to take care of something. It had been five months since Bobby moved out, and it was time to officially file for divorce. Since he left, we had not communicated. I'd see his truck drive by periodically, but he kept his eyes straight on the road ahead. I had hoped we could be friends once the dust settled, but I realized that it probably would hurt too much. It was best to leave things as they were and get going on the process of legally dissolving our marriage. In my heart it had been over for a long time.

"It's official," I said to John one Sunday when he made his weekly call home. "I got the final divorce papers in the mail today. I'm now legally a free woman."

"Legally," John repeated, stressing the term. "But I hope you don't feel like a free woman in your heart."

I smiled into the receiver, wishing I could crawl straight through and feel the warmth of his arms around me. "In my heart I'm with you. Don't you ever question that. I just thought you'd be happy to hear the news."

"I am. You'll see."

I paused with confusion. "What do you mean?"

He chuckled and repeated himself. "Just that. You'll see."

Two weeks later, a package arrived. The girls excitedly helped me open it. We dug through a sea of foam packing chips and found a long, narrow white box buried underneath. It looked like the kind of box you'd get from a florist. My heart skidded to a stop as I lifted the lid.

"What is it, Mommy?" Mariah looked on with interest.

Vanessa stepped closer to steal a peek. "Who's it from? Is there a card?"

Laying against dark green tissue paper was a beautiful bouquet of red silk roses surrounded by sprays of baby's breath. A small card rested between the stems. I anxiously opened it and read the question that John had first asked me more than a decade ago: *Will you marry me?*

"That's so beautiful," Vanessa exclaimed, bursting into tears of her own. "I can't believe he did this."

"What?" Mariah asked, standing on tiptoe to see the card she wasn't old enough yet to read. "What's going on? Who is it from?"

I cradled my roses and wore a wide smile. "It's from your daddy ... the man I'm going to marry."

FOURTEEN

Just Like Cinderella

As if John's surprise proposal wasn't enough excitement, I got an unexpected phone call one morning from a producer of the "Montel Williams Show." She saw our story in a magazine and wanted to know if we'd be interested in being guests on the show. The topic would deal with family secrets that resulted in shattered lives. Two other families that were dealing with issues of a father's betrayal would be featured. We would be an example of how broken families can overcome the damage and end up stronger because of it.

"I'm not sure," I answered truthfully. "The last time we did a talk show it was very disappointing. I don't want to put my children through anything like that again. I only want to share our story with the media if it's going to be told in the way we want it."

"I understand," Kristin told me. "Montel isn't anything like that. He cares about his guests and really believes in helping people solve their problems. The last thing he would want to do is to make anything harder on you. I can promise you that this interview wouldn't be anything like your last. Montel truly wants to show how far you all have come and talk about what you see in your future."

I softened somewhat. "Actually I see a wedding in our future. John has proposed to me, and we're getting remarried in the prison in June."

"That's wonderful!" she shrieked. "How amazing! You've got to share that with our audience. What a touching piece to add to your interview. I think you could make an incredible impression on our millions of viewers by showing that happy endings are still possible after horrendous suffering. The other families on the panel will certainly benefit, too. Of course, we would want you to explain what happened to you back in Ohio, but I assure you that this show is to focus on the healing process. With so many divorces and families falling apart in today's society, your story will be such an inspiration. Can we include you and your children on the taping next Tuesday? I can promise you that it will be a good experience."

At first my impulse was to gracefully say no, but then I began to think about the impact such a story could have.

The "Montel Williams Show" had a large following. We could reach millions more people with what we had to say. If this show was dedicated to giving hope to broken families that had been torn apart by a loved one's hurtful betrayal, then our message would be needed. We could give hope to so many by telling them that no matter what they are going through or how deeply they have been hurt, healing and happiness can be found in the act of simply forgiving. Would God lay this opportunity in the palm of my hand if he didn't want us to go back out and tell our story?

"What do you think?" Kristin asked. "Will you let us fly you to New York for the taping next week?"

I smiled. "Tell Montel that we'll want an autograph."

"Done!" she exclaimed. "We'll even throw in a mono-grammed baseball cap. I'll call you tomorrow with your flight arrangements."

Our experience with the "Montel Williams Show" was like a refreshing breath of spring air. Not only did he spend very little time discussing the crime itself, but he gave Vanessa and me a chance to talk about our healing process. We didn't have to relive all the dark places we left behind. He allowed us to focus on the good things that had come out of our nightmare. His style was gentle and compassionate, allowing us to show that even though John did the unthinkable, it didn't have to mean the end. That a family can still hold together after the worst of wounds have been inflicted. That it's never too late to rebuild a relationship as long as you have faith and a forgiving heart.

The camera followed Montel as he walked over to where I was sitting. He wanted to be closer to me as we got to the happy ending. "And you've not only forgiven John for all he's done, but you're planning on getting married to him again … am I right?"

I smiled and held my head high. "Yes. We're exchanging our vows this coming June. It's going to be the most beautiful day of my life."

"And what was the turning point here?"

Tears welled in my eyes. "When God spoke to me and told me not to commit suicide. That forgiving was the way to be free."

He then turned to the panel members who'd already had their interviews. Families torn apart by hurtful secrets. Children angry with their father for his betrayals. Hearts that were yet to be healed and were still bound in anger and hurt.

"Then, that's the thought," he said, meeting their gazes. He paused a moment before repeating the message that literally saved my life. "To be free of the pain, you forgive."

"Maybe you can learn something from Diane's and John's story," he said, scanning all their faces. "Forgiving could be the answer to the pain all of you are struggling with. Give it a try. You just might end up celebrating some miracles of your own." The audience applauded warmly even after the cameras were off. It was a very powerful show and delivered just the message I was hoping for. I wanted to have a chance to thank Montel for being so compassionate and focusing on the positive things in our story, but another show was about to be taped and we were quickly ushered out of the studio. Before I knew it, we had souvenir bags and were escorted to the limo that would take us to the airport.

I began to have dreams shortly after returning home from New York. They interrupted my sleep almost every night the closer we got to the wedding. They were joyous dreams in which I was walking into the prison in the most beautiful wedding gown I'd ever seen with my long veil flying in the wind behind me. I walked proudly and felt peace in my heart. I looked as elegant as a princess marrying her prince. I woke each time with a feeling of pure elation.

We set the date for June 24, when the children would be out of school for the summer. It seemed like plenty of time to prepare, but once I started making all the arrangements, I was pressed to get everything done on time. The most complicated part of planning a prison wedding is the process of getting the marriage license. Since the groom is incarcerated and can't appear at the courthouse in person to sign the legal documents, the bride has to hire an attorney to take the papers to him. I wasn't prepared to have to pay such a large fee just so we could get the license, but I had little choice. Then there were wedding bands to buy, dresses for the girls, and a wedding gown for me. The expenses for our special day mounted fast. I knew I couldn't afford anything fancy, but I still wanted something special. After all, this was our miracle. Our family was going to be united again after nearly losing each other forever. I wanted a dress that would take John's breath away. A dress just like the one I had seen in my dreams.

"This one is four hundred-twenty-five dollars." The woman at the bridal consignment shop read the price tag from the sleeve of a white satin gown. It was full and lovely with some beading on the sleeves and pearl trim around the neckline. Unfortunately, it was completely out of my price range. I had less than half that to spend.

"You might try Goodwill," she called out over her shoulder as she hung the gowns back on the rack. "They sometimes have wedding gowns donated that are in pretty fair condition."

I went into the thrift store trying to convince myself that it really didn't matter where I found the dress. All I needed was something simple. It was the joy of the day that was going to make it beautiful. It wouldn't matter if I didn't wear a real wedding gown. I may have looked like a princess dressed for the ball in my dreams, but in reality I was a single mother who was broke and had to make do with whatever she could get.

It wasn't a wedding gown. It wasn't even close, but the dress I finally decided on was the same shade of ivory as the girls' dresses. With its simple style and chiffon sleeves, it would be lovely coupled with flowers in my hair. The tag said thirty dollars, which was a far cry from the gown back at the upscale consignment store. I tried it on and stood in front of the mirror, waiting to feel enthused. I didn't look like a bride. I looked more like I was going to a cocktail party, but I kept trying to imagine how it would look if I spruced it up. Maybe with a pearl necklace and a matching veil it would be more suitable.

Before I made it to the cash register to write out a check, a voice sounded in my ears. It was the same dynamic voice that spoke to me so clearly on the morning of my planned suicide. *Put the dress back!* It was so loud and commanding that I looked around the store, expecting the other shoppers to be just as startled as I was. My pulse began to race as I turned back toward the rack. I didn't understand what was happening, but I knew better than to argue. Swiftly, I hung the dress on the closest rack and sprinted out of the store.

My heart rate was up and I felt a little dizzy. It was nearly lunchtime, and all I wanted was to go home. I began driving in that direction when I suddenly had an overwhelming urge to make a U-turn. I barely looked for cars first and didn't bother to use my turn signal. Now things were really getting crazy. Perhaps I was cracking under the pressure of all the wedding arrangements. I kept going for several miles, scanning storefronts, gas stations, and fast-food restaurants and wondering what it was I was actually looking for. As strange as it sounds, it didn't even feel as if I was the one in control of the car. I expected it to come to a sudden halt all on its own whenever I arrived at the final destination. A thrilling sensation surged through me, as if I were on the brink of something wonderful. All I could do was go along for the ride and hope I hadn't totally lost my mind.

Twenty minutes later, in an unfamiliar section of downtown, I saw a huge two-story bridal boutique on my left. It was very ritzy, with double doors, smoked-glass windows, and a large neon sign welcoming brides inside to see the designer gowns. It was the kind of place where rich girls get their wedding dresses.

"You must be kidding," I uttered to myself as I pulled into the parking lot. I felt a bit dazed and didn't really want to go into the store. I'd have to make it a point to slow down and get more rest … right after I went inside.

"Welcome. My name is Lisa. Can I help you find anything today?" A lovely blonde girl greeted me after I climbed the spiral staircase.

I was in awe of the size of this place. With the lower level for grooms in need of tuxedos and formal wear, the second level was dedicated to the bride and also had formal gowns for pageants and proms. There were mirrors everywhere and a giant carpeted pedestal in the center of the room where the bride could admire herself in her expensive wedding gown. I'd never seen so much white lace in my life as I gazed at the miles of racks surrounding me.

I cleared my throat and apprehensively met her gaze. "I'm getting married and need a wedding gown."

"Wonderful. Do you know what style you're interested in?"

"No," I answered, tempted to turn around and go back down the stairs. I had no business taking up this nice girl's time.

"How about price range? What are you looking to spend?"

That was the million-dollar question. I felt like a fool. I shifted my stance and shoved my perspiring hands into the front pockets of my jeans as a rush of heat traveled up my cheeks. I wanted to leave. This was a mistake, but my sneakers felt tacked to the floor.

"I don't have much. Actually, all I have to spend is two hundred dollars."

Her expression sagged slightly, but then she headed to a sale rack. Only one gown was in my size. It was plain and stiff with a large bow at the waist. I would have been better off with my Goodwill cocktail dress.

"I'm afraid this is all we have in that price range. I'm sorry. I wish I had more to show you."

It was ridiculous. I didn't know what possessed me to come into this fancy showroom in the first place, thinking I could find a dress in my price range. Out of fatigue and embarrassment, my eyes welled with tears. For some reason, I decided to dump on her.

"I don't know what brought me here," I told her. She looked rather startled by my sudden breakdown. "I knew I couldn't afford anything in a place like this. It's just that this wedding is going to be the most miraculous day of my life. I'm marrying my children's father again after six years of devastation. He's serving time in a prison in Ohio, and this nightmare has torn our family apart. But we've forgiven him for the past, and now we're stronger because of it and are going to get married again. I guess I wanted some fantasy dress like Cinderella would wear to the ball, but I don't think that's possible." I paused for a moment, rather embarrassed. I couldn't imagine what possessed me to tell her all of that. "I'm really sorry for wasting your time. Thank you for trying to help me."

I started to leave, but the girl caught hold of my shoulder. "Wait. Can you just wait here a minute while I go get Michelle? She's the owner, and I think she'd like to meet you."

"Sure." I stood awkwardly while the girl hurried off to a back room. I couldn't figure out why the owner would want to meet me, except maybe to enjoy a good laugh. I walked over to a mannequin on display in the far corner, smiling in her designer gown of white satin and french lace. The rhinestone tiara on her head sparkled like a regal crown. I turned over the price tag dangling from her sleeve and let out a muffled groan.

"Pretty, isn't it?" A woman stood behind me with a warm, welcoming expression. She wore a burgundy floral pantsuit with a matching scarf draped over one shoulder. Her ears sparkled with wine-colored jewels, and her fingernails were manicured and polished. A french twist showed off her platinum blonde hair. Just the kind of woman who would own a stylish boutique.

I stepped away from the mannequin and her obscenely expensive gown. "Yes, it is. It's very beautiful."

"I'm Michelle," she said, extending a hand. "Lisa told me all about you. I hear you have a pretty important day coming up."

My smile felt stiff. "In two weeks actually. My daughters are also going to be allowed to be a part of it, so they're pretty excited."

"That's unusual for prison weddings, isn't it?" she asked, cocking her head in question. "The ones I've heard about didn't allow children. Only the inmate and the bride, along with one other adult witness, are allowed."

"Yes." I wondered if she also had a loved one behind bars. "I had to write a letter to the warden asking for special permission. She wrote back that she would grant permission for them to be there. We feel very blessed because she usually doesn't bend the rules."

Her perfectly penciled brows shot up in amazement. "No. Usually wardens aren't known for their soft hearts. You must have a pretty remarkable story."

Why was I so emotional? I didn't want to cry, but tears spilled freely before I could respond. Perhaps it was her caring gaze that made me feel I could open up to her. Something told me she genuinely wanted to know.

"John was arrested six years ago, and it tore our family apart. I ended up raising our children alone and surviving on food stamps. I divorced him and vowed to hate him for the rest of my life, but the anger and bitterness only destroyed me. It took a while, but I learned that the only way to be free of my pain was to forgive him. It's unbelievable, but now we're closer than ever. This marriage is a gift I never expected."

Michelle didn't bother to brush away the tears streaming down her face. She looked at me for several moments and then called out for Lisa. Immediately, the girl appeared like a faithful servant. Michelle whispered something in her ear, and then Lisa smiled and walked over to one of the racks. I stared in confusion as she selected an exquisite ivory gown that sparkled with sequins and pearls. It was the most incredible wedding gown I had ever seen. It made the mannequin in the corner look like a bag lady.

Michelle winked at me. "Just for fun, why don't you try this one on?"

I sucked in a breath, not knowing what to say. It certainly couldn't hurt anything. Why not put it on just to dream for a little while? It might be fun to see how the other half lives. The gown was so full and had so much beading that it weighed a ton in my arms as Lisa escorted me to the dressing room. My stomach fluttered with excitement once I got behind the closed the curtain. I felt like a little kid playing dress up with two girlfriends.

Nothing prepared me for the sight of my own reflection as I stood on the pedestal. I looked like royalty in a fabulous ball gown of luxurious ivory silk, the bodice twinkling under the lights with gorgeous ivory and silver sequins. A six-foot train spread out behind me cascading to the floor. It was nearly identical to the gown I had seen in my dreams. If anything, it was even more spectacular.

"It's so beautiful," I gasped. "It's exactly the kind of gown I had fantasized about. I feel like Cinderella ready to marry her prince!"

Michelle smiled. "It's funny you should say that because that gown is actually called the Cinderella gown. It's one of my favorites."

Lisa came forward and straightened my train, making sure it was evenly spread out behind me.

"It's perfect on you," she said, looking to Michelle to second the motion.

Michelle responded with a smile. "Yes, it is. It's perfect."

Never had I worn anything so extravagant, and I hated to take it off. I knew I had to. Our little game of pretending had to come to an end. We all knew the dress cost much more than I had in my wallet. Still, I loved them for letting me fulfill a part of my fantasy just to see what I would have looked like if I could have married John in the gown of my dreams.

"Well, this was special," I said, taking a last look in the mirror. "Thank you both. It was fun to pretend for a while."

I went to step down from the pedestal and change back into my clothes, but Michelle motioned for me to stay. She walked over and straightened the flow of my train, then stepped in front of me and met my curious gaze.

"How much did you say you have to spend?"

I felt foolish to repeat it. "All I have is two hundred dollars. I think that would probably buy the right sleeve of a dress like this. I'll find something, though."

"Lisa," she said, placing her hands on her generous hips, "write up this sale for two hundred dollars. This Cinderella is going into that prison to marry her prince in this gown."

"You can't mean it," I choked, growing weak in the knees. "This dress has to cost a fortune!"

It was then that Michelle joined me on the pedestal. She took both of my hands in hers. "Let me do this for you and John. It would mean so much to me. You see, my husband and I used to live in Ohio and did prison ministry in all of the area prisons. I'm sure we've prayed with inmates in the very same prison your husband is doing time in. That was years ago, but we still remember their faces. I can only imagine what this wedding means to your family after all you've endured. It is a miracle. It's a fantasy. God has blessed you with your own happy ending, just like Cinderella, and Cinderella needs a fairy-tale gown to marry her beloved prince in."

Never in my wildest dreams did I expect such an extraordinary gift or think that I'd end up meeting such a special woman. A woman with a heart of gold for prisoners and the pain their families endure. I didn't understand what led me to this place, but now I knew why I was meant to be here. God wouldn't allow me to buy that thrift store dress and to compromise on what I had dreamed about for so long. I was pulled here to find this spectacular gown that was a replica of the one I saw in my dreams.

I carefully loaded the beautiful gown into my car, still amazed at all that had happened. I was ecstatic, and I couldn't wait to get home and show my dress to my parents and the girls. This wedding was going to be the event of a lifetime. Like Michelle said, it was truly a fairy tale. And now I could marry the man I love while wearing a gown as miraculous as our wedding day.

After starting the engine and pulling out of the parking lot, I glanced skyward with tears of joy streaming down my face. "Thank you, Lord," I whispered, overwhelmed by the miracles he kept showing me. His presence flowed through me and brought complete peace to my soul. I was ready to marry the man he had led me back to. Ready to trust and follow his plan.

FIFTEEN

Forever This Time

OHIO WELCOMES YOU! The girls and I cheered as we read the big green sign. It had been a long three-day trip with our car packed high with luggage, blankets, pillows, floral bouquets, beautiful dresses, and my three-tier veil. My gown alone took up the entire passenger side of the car. I kept looking at it as I drove, touching it to make sure it was real. It was finally happening. In only two more days John and I would exchange vows, promising forever.

The wedding ceremony was scheduled for nine the following morning, and the hours oozed by like molasses. Since it was such a perfect day and we were feeling pretty energetic, I suggested a trip to Malabar Farm. I loved the wholesome charm of the place and thought it would be a great treat on the day before our wedding.

I had forgotten how beautiful Ohio is in the heart of summer. Only a few clouds feathered the brilliant blue sky, and the songs of robins and cardinals filled the air. Just walking outdoors rejuvenated my soul. Malabar Farm was a breathtaking 914 acres of lush green land and rolling hills. The sweet smell of hay wafted through the air as visitors toured the working farm and visited the shops. The girls didn't spend much time reading the display signs of how the farm works or gazing at the display of antique farm equipment. They had a favorite place where you could sink your fingers into the wool of a baby lamb or get kissed by a brown-eyed cow. The petting barn was always the highlight of our tour through this wonderful farm.

"Look, Mom!" Mariah ran over to a pair of huge hogs chewing grain. "They make grunting noises when they eat. Come here and touch one! They feel all prickly."

I broke into a laugh as I petted one, causing the other to nudge him over jealously.

"Check out this turkey!" Vanessa leaned over the railing of a pen where a majestic white turkey proudly strutted.

As I watched the girls, all I could think about was how much John would have enjoyed this day. It had been six years since he was put behind bars. Six long years since he could feel the grass under his feet or look up and count the stars at night. It never got any easier for me to comprehend. I couldn't imagine an existence in prison. It was like dying, but still breathing and functioning. All the things that are nourishing to one's soul have been taken away—love, laughter, family, friends. All that's left is a barren cell and a stretch of time that offers nothing but years of seclusion. Yet, he had God—the one thing the inmates could keep. Maybe

God was his blue sky and fresh air. Judging from the sparkle in his eye and the peace in his heart, his faith was what kept him alive in that place.

We had never explored the Malabar Farm Victorian farmhouse, and I thought it might be interesting for the children to see. We waited with a small group on the sprawling front porch before being led inside. Mariah hung on to my hand as we climbed the wooden steps holding on to a creaky banister that wobbled.

The rooms were magnificent with the four-poster beds, colorful hand-sewn quilts, and sitting tables with etched mirrors, where we imagined a young girl once brushed her long hair before blowing the lantern out at night. We viewed the sewing room, where an ancient Singer machine was displayed complete with antique dresses that women wore in that time period. Vanessa took a close look at the lace-up corset and gave thanks that we females no longer have to cinch ourselves like that.

"Once we get downstairs," our guide said, "you will see the sitting parlor and the kitchen. There is also a rather large library. After that, we'll have refreshments on the front porch."

As soon as we all filed into the sitting parlor to admire the magnificent furniture, the old player piano in the corner jumped into song. The "Wedding March" blared loudly, making everyone gasp in surprise and cover their ears. The tour guide rushed over to try to stop it.

After fumbling for several moments while the piano played on, she turned to us and seemed a bit flustered. "I apologize," she shouted. "This has never happened before. I don't know what's making it play, and I can't seem to turn it off. Just follow me, and we'll go into the kitchen where it won't seem so loud."

The group hurried away, but my girls and I stayed behind. We stood there and listened, laughing through our tears. This was no coincidence or freak glitch inside the old piano. Like the tour guide said, it had never happened before. But we knew it was happening now because a miracle would take place tomorrow. The "Wedding March" was coming from the heavens straight to our ears. The girls and I joined hands and danced in a circle as the notes continued to sound loudly through the air.

"It's spooky," Mariah called out. "It's like a miracle just for us!"

Vanessa laughed. "Maybe we should leave and see if the music finally stops. I think it's going to drive everyone crazy!"

Breathless from dancing, we headed out the door, and as soon as we did, the old piano fell silent. I looked to the sky, feeling God's presence so near.

"Thank you," I whispered in heartfelt prayer. "That was the most beautiful wedding gift in the world."

The morning of June 24 dawned as perfect as they come. The sun was glorious and streamed through the hotel curtains as I prepared to put on my gown. John and I learned the hard way what it truly means to commit to each other through sickness and health, for better or worse, for richer or poorer without quitting. Surviving the past meant that there was nothing to fear in our future. This time we were going to go the distance.

Once I was dressed and nearly ready, thoughts of Karen Romano began to cloud my head. I usually didn't allow myself to think of her and would immediately push images of her away, but not this morning. It seemed oddly appropriate for her to intrude on my wedding day. She lost her life while trying her best to ruin the love John and I had.

Until now, I had crammed unresolved feelings about her into a deep, dark hiding place. I didn't want to imagine who she was or what she looked like. My anger. My hatred. I couldn't deal with the awesome power of these emotions, so I chose to simply ignore them. But today, I felt as if she were standing next me, close enough to adjust my train and fluff my veil. For once, I didn't feel hateful, as I always had before. I could think of her and not push her away. It was then that it occurred to me that even though I had forgiven John, I had never forgiven Karen. Now was the time to face her straight on and do the same thing for her that I had for my husband—forgive the unforgivable. I closed my eyes and whispered words that were long overdue.

It's not easy to tell you what I know I need to say. So much hurt and devastation have occurred. I never knew you. I will never know what made you want to hurt us so deeply, but I can only imagine that you were a very troubled young woman. Something made you need love so badly that you would stop at nothing to steal someone else's.

I can't go on hating you for all you've done. I've learned a lot through this and have come to realize that people don't do such hurtful things for no reason. It comes from somewhere. I have no idea what your life was like. I remember your father at the trial weeping over your death. Your uncle stayed by his side, reeling with grief. There were others there on your behalf that I didn't know. Friends of yours from college came to testify. I know you had people who cared about you in your life, but I can't help feeling that it wasn't enough. You needed more, but you looked in all the wrong places. A married man with two children. We became your target, and it changed all of us forever, but I don't believe anything you did was from a healthy mind.

I'm sorry for your problems and all that they cost you. You didn't deserve to die. You deserved a second chance to find happiness and inner peace just as John has done. I've forgiven him for the past just as I know I have to forgive you. I'll always have a darkness in my soul if I don't. So I choose this day to do that because it is a day of new beginnings. It's a time to let go of the past and focus on the future. I will be marrying John this morning with our two daughters beside us to reunite what was never meant to be broken. We'll officially be a family again. Nothing you did accomplished what you had hoped. It hurt us. It shattered our lives. It changed us in ways we'll never forget, but today we come full circle and take vows as husband and wife.

Still, as joyous as this celebration is to us, I do feel a private sorrow. You weren't successful in your attempt to destroy all we had. If anything, the love we share is now deeper than ever before. It was all so senseless, and I grieve for your family. I can only hope that somehow you've found peace wherever you are and that before your final breath, you had a chance to ask God for forgiveness. It's taken a lot for me to get to this point, but today I can offer you mine. I forgive you, and now I can let you go.

Walking toward the prison in my fairy-tale gown was like reenacting my dream. The girls followed behind to carry my train, looking like angels in their ivory chiffon dresses with halos of silk flowers in their golden hair. I savored every step as I lived out the fantasy that had been in my heart for so long. With pride, I lifted my chin and smiled as the wind caught my veil. My prince waited on the other side of the wall.

All eyes were on us once we entered the security area. It wasn't every day that the prison guards saw a bride and her two bridesmaids going through the metal detector. We got smiles and thumbs-up. A few of the guards knew us from previous visits and wished our family well. Once we cleared security, we met up with Mayor Reid, the mayor of Mansfield, who waited for us by the door. She looked lovely in a pastel pink suit and wore a genuine smile. I liked her the moment I met her.

"What lovely daughters you have," she said while we waited for the steel door leading to the outside courtyard to be buzzed open. "I'll bet this is quite an exciting day for all of you."

"It is," I answered, dizzy with happiness. "There was a time when we never thought this would happen."

"There's not much to celebrate in here." Her ice blue eyes looked over my shoulder to the window behind us. Row upon row of cellblocks could be seen from where we stood. "I used to do a lot of work with prisoners and their families and traveled to many of the institutions throughout central Ohio. Now I just do weddings, which is very rewarding for me. It's always wonderful to see love strong enough to survive something like this. I admire people like you and am always happy to be able to be a part of the ceremony."

The door buzzed, and she pulled it open, holding it for us as we paraded through. In just a few minutes I would stand beside my groom and also meet Rick, John's cell mate, who was going to be our witness. In the years they had shared that tiny cell, they had become brothers in Christ and cultivated a close friendship. Rick's family didn't choose to stand by him when he began his sentence more than ten years ago, so he often wondered how his daughter looked. It had been a long time since he last saw her. She'd be about Vanessa's age. He kept the only photo he had of her on the wall next to where he slept, creased and worn with many years of admiration. John told us in one of his letters that being a part of our wedding meant the world to Rick because at least he could meet me and the girls. He was happy that John had not lost his family. It gave him hope that one day he'd get his own back.

The first thing I saw when I entered the visitation room was John with a delirious smile. He watched us as we crossed the courtyard before we entered the visitor building and drank in the sight of his girls in their beautiful dresses.

The children rushed over to him to get their long-awaited hug. I blinked back tears of joy as I waited for my turn.

He gathered them into his arms, careful not to crush their bouquets. "You look so pretty. You're both so grown up. I've missed you so very much."

"Today's the day!" Mariah cried out. "Doesn't Mom look just like Cinderella?"

The blue of his gaze melted into mine, holding a world of joy and love. "Yes … she's beautiful. I think I'm going to have to pinch myself to see if this is a dream."

"It's no dream," Vanessa joked, trying to break up the emotion. "I'm a wreck after riding three days in the car with this brat."

"You're the brat," Mariah tossed back. "She hogged the whole backseat!"

John gave our girls a playful scowl, then drew a breath and walked toward me. He seemed almost afraid to touch, taking only my hand at first, but then drew me into the warmth of his arms where we molded perfectly together.

"It's really happening, isn't it?" I whispered against his ear.

"Yes. We are blessed."

"It's for real this time. Forever this time."

He held me tighter. "Forever this time."

Suddenly I felt a tap on my shoulder. I broke away from John's arms and saw a smiling young man in prison blues standing next to me. His dark eyes were aglow with excitement. I knew immediately that this was our best man.

"You must be Rick!" I exclaimed, flinging my arms around him. After hearing so much about what a true friend he had been to John, I felt as if I already knew him.

"You're every bit as beautiful as I've seen in the photos John has of you." His smile was wide and contagious. "I'm so happy for all of you and thankful to be a part of your special day. All I can tell you is that you had one nervous groom this morning!"

"I'm not nervous," John corrected. "Just excited. Our whole Bible study group met with me this morning to say a prayer to bless our wedding. It really meant a lot to me that they wanted to do that. There are many people in here who are touched by our miracle. I think it gives them hope that maybe a miracle could happen for them, too."

"It can," I said, directing my gaze at Rick. John grasped my hand and led me over to Reverend Bemis, a chaplain at the prison. She had briefly prayed with our family before on one of our visits and was a special friend of John's.

"Congratulations on your special day," she said. "It's against prison regulations for me to perform marriages for the inmates, but I still wanted to be here to offer blessings and prayer. Would you all like to join hands and praise the Lord before the ceremony begins?"

Rick and the girls gathered around us to form a tight circle. Clutching each other's hands, we bowed our heads in prayer. In the distance, beyond the walls, I could hear the banging of steel doors, inmates' echoing voices, and the shuffle of the prison guards keeping watch. I wanted to tune it all out so that it had no place in our wedding and John and I could have this slot of time to forget. We could dream that after we exchanged our vows and slid on our wedding rings that we could walk out into the sunshine and begin our new life together. Knowing that our brief ceremony was all that we'd be allowed before John was led back to his cell cast a shadow on the joy of this wonderful day. My heart ached to be normal. To start over again with my husband back at home, mowing the lawn, washing the car, watching the Sunday football games on TV.

Reverend Bemis concluded the prayer, hugged the children, and then presented them with a special gift: dainty, white handkerchiefs with lace trim for them to carry. Then she turned to me and handed me a beautiful blue satin handkerchief. It also was trimmed in delicate white lace, which she had sewn by hand.

"I wanted to give you something blue in honor of the tradition. I was hoping you already had the 'something old, something new, something borrowed' part together. If not, you at least have the 'something blue'!"

Quickly, I touched the pearl earrings I wore, which my sister had loaned me from her own wedding.

"This is something borrowed," I said, whisking my hair back to show them off.

"And your dress is something new!" Mariah jumped up and down as if she were answering a game show question.

"What do you have that's old?" Vanessa asked, running her gaze over the length of my attire.

Nothing I had was old. I bought everything special just for the occasion from my ivory silk pantyhose to my bra to my satin high heels. It was the only piece of the puzzle that was missing.

Rick grinned at all of us. "What's old is the people you once were before this awesome blessing. Those hurting, lost, and broken people are now whole and joyful. This wedding symbolizes that you're letting go of the old and building a future on your newfound love and faith."

It was perfect. I reached out and hugged him. He was every bit a special friend as John had described him to be.

"Wow," he exclaimed, pulling back. "That's the first time I've smelled perfume in over ten years! It's nice."

Mayor Reid signaled that it was time for the ceremony to begin. We assembled in front of the visiting room next to the picture window that looked out over the courtyard. With our girls beside us, John and I joined hands and took our marriage vows. As Mayor Reid had us repeat the same promises we had made to each other before enduring "better or worse," the words took on new meaning after all that we had survived. Tears streamed down our faces as we vowed to stay bonded no matter what the future had to hold. She spoke of sickness and health, richer or poorer, staying faithful to each other until the end. Without hesitation, John and I said an emotional "I do" to one another.

Once we were officially pronounced husband and wife in the eyes of the law, John leaned forward and kissed me, sealing our promises to each other. Shedding tears of joy, we then embraced as a family. We felt invincible this time, that nothing would ever destroy us again. We knew that we would always be joined together, come what may. The inside of our wedding bands were inscribed with Mark 10:9 to always remind us of that: *Therefore what God has joined together, let man not separate.*

"To the bride and groom." Rick raised his ginger ale can to ours for a festive toast. "To John and Diane, who have the strongest love of any couple I know. I wish you a lifetime of peace and happiness. To Vanessa and Mariah, two beautiful and very courageous young ladies. May you both learn by your parents' example that with forgiving hearts and true love, you can conquer anything. I thank all of you for letting me be your best man today. This is a morning I will never forget."

We all clinked our soda cans and sipped our pseudo champagne. John held my hand, staring at our wedding rings. A dream had finally come true.

"Aren't you supposed to cut the cake now?" Mariah had her sights set in the center of the table on the Twinkie bar, which was serving as our wedding cake. "We don't have a knife. What are you going to use?"

With only a plastic fork at our disposal, John held it as I covered my hand over his, and we carefully cut the Twinkie into five equal pieces. He fed me my slice very neatly and respectfully, not wanting to get so much as a crumb on my elaborate dress. I wasn't as nice, however, and smashed his piece all over his face as the girls and Rick let loose gales of laughter.

"I love you," I said, looking into his astonished eyes. "I just had to. After all, this is going to be our last wedding reception."

He grinned and mopped his face with a napkin. "You're lucky that you're in such an awesome wedding gown or you'd be a mess right now, too."

"What about the bride and groom dance?" Vanessa asked. "There's no music, but you have to. It's tradition."

John and I looked at each other a little puzzled, but then he offered me his hand and led me to an open space between tables. It was an amazing feeling to have the freedom to walk and move around together. On regular visits, inmates are required to stay seated at the table at all times. Merely standing next to each other or walking together and holding hands is a rare treat. I had almost forgotten how it felt to do what so many take for granted. It made me start wanting more. Walks. Talks. Some kind of normalcy. My heart longed for my husband to come home.

"May I have this dance?" John smiled and looked into my eyes.

I pressed up against him. "Now and always."

For a few isolated minutes, as we swayed slowly in each other's arms, everything around us faded away. We were one. We were husband and wife after almost losing each other forever. How easily we could have ended up broken and bitter. What if God never spoke to me and told me to forgive? What if we never learned of John's addiction and never found that there was hope and healing for those who want it badly enough? I could only imagine the lifetime of hell we all would have lived in. Nothing would have ever compared to this moment. We would have lost the loving family that meant so much to us.

"Do you hear it?" John pulled back and stared at me, his gaze as blue and tranquil as a summer sky. He then lifted my hand to his lips and kissed my fingers tenderly.

I grinned with curious wonder. "Hear what? What are you talking about?"

"The music. It's there if we listen with our hearts and not our ears. Do you hear it, Baby?"

I closed my eyes and got lost in the movement between us. The thump of his heartbeat. The sound of our shoes moving against the tile floor. The rhythm of our breathing in unison. And in some faraway place sweet music played, more miraculous than the "Wedding March" that had blared mysteriously from that old player piano.

"Time," the guard called out. "All visitors must leave the building."

I didn't want it to end. John's arms loosened, stilling our private music. The girls scurried to throw out our soda cans and wrappers.

"And it was an honor meeting you," Rick said, giving me one last hug. "John loves you guys with all of his heart. I'm really happy for all of you and know that the future holds new hope because of today."

"Thank you." My voice was a broken whisper. "Stay strong, and we'll keep you in our prayers. You made our day so much more special by being a part of it."

John kissed the children, happy to know that we had four more glorious days to spend together. We didn't have to say good-bye with a heaviness in our hearts. We'd share many more hugs and kisses before the long trip back to Florida put miles between us again.

The guard gave John and me a few extra moments to share some final kisses. In the real world, this day would mean that my husband and I would be inseparable from now on. But this wasn't the real world. This was a place where celebrations don't belong. None of it mattered as I savored the last kiss from my groom before that massive steel door would close us off from one another once again. Our souls were one now. We were husband and wife again. I was too elated to let myself feel deprived.

"I wish we could be together on our wedding night," he said, his voice heavy with regret. "It won't feel right not even seeing you when it's supposed to be such a romantic night."

My heart ached as I held him, but then I got a wonderful idea. Maybe we couldn't consummate our new marriage like a normal couple, but we could still celebrate our blessing together.

"Can you look out your cell window tonight at nine o'clock sharp?"

He narrowed his eyes with curiosity. "Yeah. Why?"

"Which side of the prison does your window face?"

He pointed to the left of us. "I can see the Harley Davidson showroom over there across the field."

"Be at your window at exactly nine tonight. Flick the light off and on so we know which window is yours. If we can't be together, at least we can still see each other." I broke into a mischievous smile. "I think we can still make it special."

In honor of all that God had done for our family, the girls and I decided to spend the afternoon at The Living Bible wax museum. We enjoyed the amazing tour of the many recreated scenes taken from the Bible and the lifelike wax figures of Jesus and his followers. It was like actually being alive in the time when Jesus walked the earth. I felt goose bumps all over as I looked into his gentle brown eyes and touched the hem of his flowing robe. Emotions took over, and I needed a few moments to sit on a nearby bench to dry my tears. The children missed their father as much as I already did. It was awesome things like this incredible museum that made us wish he could be here with us to enjoy it.

"Pardon me," a young woman said, peering at us as if she feared she was intruding. "I couldn't help but notice that you seemed distressed. I'm the manager of the museum. I thought that perhaps you and these lovely young girls needed someone to talk to."

I lightly touched the gold band on my ring finger, feeling John's love and promise of forever like it was a part of me now. Fresh tears trailed down my face as I ached to have him near. Nothing would ever feel complete without him back with us again.

"It's been a blessed day for us," I explained, accepting a tissue from this kind woman's pocket. "My children and I drove all the way from Florida so I could marry their daddy again this morning. He's serving a long sentence in the Mansfield prison that nearly broke us apart forever, but God told us to forgive and showed us the way. Once we did, we were able to heal. That's when we discovered that our family bond was still as strong as ever. I wanted to come here today after all we've been through as a way of thanking God for the miracle he gave us. I guess looking into the lifelike eyes of Jesus kind of overwhelmed me. We're missing John and know we're very lucky to have this second chance as a family, but it's just so hard without him. It's going to be a very long road."

"God helped you before, and he'll help you again." The woman held out her arms for the children to come stand beside her. "And never stop believing that one day John will come back home, because you've come this far already. What a blessing for you. How miraculous that such a tragic situation can still have a happy ending. So many wouldn't have been able to endure the hardship of being a family separated by prison bars, but you've stood strong. Today is your victory. Don't let fears and doubts creep into your happiness. Trust God to be the judge as far as your husband's fate is concerned. He is the only one who has the power. Not the system. Not the parole board. Not a piece of paper that says you'll be separated for years. It sounds to me as if you've already received lots of blessings. Just don't lose hope that there will be many more."

"Thank you so much." I brushed tears away and saw that she was drying a few of her own. "I know that no matter how long we have to wait, at least we'll make it day by day as a family."

Her eyes met mine with a trust as strong as granite, and she took my hand in hers. "I can't imagine all you've gone through, especially with two children to take care of. But try to stay focused on where you are today and all of the strength it took for you to get here. You must have a very dedicated family to have survived this. I know you can make whatever lies ahead."

Her words stuck with me as we finished our tour and then browsed the wonderful gift shop. My spirit felt lighter, letting us get back to enjoying our wedding day. Mariah found a children's Bible with a pink leather cover, and Vanessa fell in love with a T-shirt displaying a sketch of the pierced palm of Jesus. I didn't plan on getting myself anything until a very special picture frame caught my eye. It was called "The Rings" and was meant to display four wedding photos. In the center of the frame were two gold wedding bands overlapping each other. Thanks to Reverend Bemis, we had the prison photographer take some instant photos during the ceremony. The girls and I also took a lot of pictures of us in our dresses at the hotel. It seemed the perfect frame to put a collection of pictures in from this wondrous day. We left the museum with a keepsake for each of us, but there was one more purchase I needed to make.

"Are you seriously going to do this?" Vanessa gaped at me in astonishment as I loaded up my shopping cart with fireworks and rockets. Being so close to July 4, we simply had to stop at a fireworks store. "Don't you think we might get in trouble? After all, it's a prison, you know."

I laughed, loving her protective side. "We're not going to be setting them off on prison property. We're going to be in the field right next to it where Daddy says his window faces."

"I want sparklers!" Mariah exclaimed. "They come in different colors! Can I get some to wave around so Daddy can see?"

"Absolutely. The more the merrier. You and Vanessa get whatever you think will add to our fireworks show. Let's give Daddy and Rick a wedding celebration to remember!"

It was exactly nine o'clock when a cell window in the distance began flicking its light off and on. My heart stopped short as I saw it. John was there, just as he promised. It was time to light our first rocket.

"Stand back and be careful," I cautioned the girls. I touched a lighter to the fuse and ran several yards back. With my arms around the children, we watched with anticipation as the sparks jumped, setting the rocket into the air with a high-pitched whistle. Within seconds, there was a boom and a brilliant explosion of purples and pinks rained down followed by a trail of silver squiggles.

"That was so cool!" Mariah shouted. "Light my sparklers! I want to show Daddy!"

I lit the tips so that they sprayed blue sparkles, and she marched around holding one in each hand. Vanessa also grabbed a couple, and I lit hers, as well. I then prepared another rocket. This was our celebration, and it was going to be awesome.

Another boom sounded and the sky exploded in red, white, and blue. Another and then another chased after that one. We laughed as John kept flicking his light off and on to let us know he was there and was watching.

"He sees us!" Mariah jumped up and down, waving her sparklers back and forth. "Set off more, Mom! Let him see more!"

With Vanessa's help, we lined up a series of rockets to go off at once. It was so beautiful and amazing to just stand back and watch the night sky explode with every color in the rainbow. The moment felt surreal. The prison walls, the coiled razor wire on the top of the electrical fences couldn't contain the most incredible color bursting in the sky. I swallowed an ache in my throat as I watched John's window in the distance. Just a small square to let a glimmer of the outside world in. A patch of sun. A peek at the stars. A view of the field with the tall grass blowing in the wind. Unreachable to all the guys housed behind those walls, yet overlooked by most on the other side.

"This is it," Vanessa said. "We've got the last half dozen lined up and ready to light. This is going to be the grand finale!"

With the fuses all lit, the girls and I stood back and watched as the rockets exploded. Vivid sprays of green, purple, blue, and gold blasted the clear night sky, casting a glow on the ground below that made the moment feel magical. Tears welled in my eyes as I held my daughters close, my heart filled with thanks and joy. It was our wedding day. This was our new beginning. This was the gift that came out of the storm.

Mariah kept her eyes to the sky, where the colorful bursts were still trailing down. "It's so beautiful! It's just like God is here celebrating with us. Heaven is happy and all lit up because you and Daddy got married again today."

I gazed across the field at her father's cell window, so proud of our love and all that it had survived. There'd be no looking back. We would only move ahead, counting our blessings each and every day for the miracle of a new beginning. Whatever the future held, we would make it this time. We would survive everything from now on as a family.

AFTERWORD

January 2005

It's been nearly three years since John and I exchanged vows with our daughters by our side—years that have brought joy and many blessings as well as hardship and tears. God has been at work in every one of us in so many different ways. He's teaching us patience as we continue to hold our family together despite prison walls between us. It's hard. We grow weary, and sometimes the hurt becomes almost too much to bear. Holidays are still a struggle. My bed is still too empty. The girls see other kids with their fathers and long to have theirs home. There is always an ache in our hearts because we are separated, but God keeps reminding us that our prayers for John's return won't go unanswered. We must rely on his timing and not our own. We must trust in his plan and not what we wish would happen. We must not forget how far he's brought us and believe that he'll bring us full circle. Until that day we are to keep building our faith and standing strong as a family.

Vanessa is now nineteen and such an awesome young woman. I look at her and feel my heart overflow with pride. Despite all she has gone through, she graduated from high school last May with top grades. It was difficult for her to walk that field and get her diploma without her father there to share the experience, but John found a way to be a part of it. He sent her his college ring, and she wore it on a chain around her neck during the ceremony. I know it made her feel as if he was somehow a part of her important day. Vanessa is now working for a pet store, which she truly loves. She has always been happiest when around animals. She is also going to community college, taking classes in animal sciences. Her goal is to become a veterinarian or to have a career at a zoo one day.

Mariah is nearly a teenager, but taller than her older sister! She is only twelve but stands five feet, two inches, making me wonder how tall she is going to get! Her passions are acting and modeling, although I told her to have a backup plan. For a "real job" she wants to be a fashion designer or kindergarten teacher. Mariah has gone through a very difficult time with an anxiety/panic disorder. Just as Peggy anticipated when Vanessa was in counseling so long ago, Mariah did develop problems due to all that our family endured. In third grade she developed irrational fears of dying, sleep problems, and an inability to be away from home or attend school. She began counseling and was put on medication, which helped a lot. After a year, they took her off the medication to see how she would do. Her fears and panic returned worse than ever and she became dysfunctional. She was home schooled all last year, but thanks to a new and wonderful counselor and switching to a better school, she is now thriving in fifth grade and battling her anxiety successfully without medication. She is getting excellent grades and making friends, which is an answered prayer. Her goal is to one day start her own Web site to provide friendship and support for other kids who also suffer from anxiety and panic disorder. I'm so proud of her for wanting to reach out and use her experience to help others in this situation.

John is doing well and continues to call and write us on a regular basis. He has a good support system around him with Rick's friendship, the encouragement of his prayer group, and feeding himself daily with God's Word. He is also active in a program called Nexus, which involves the prison inmates sharing their personal testimonies with troubled kids who come into the facility for a tour. The purpose is to open the kids' eyes to their wrongdoings before it is too late. John often told me that one of the hardest things about being behind bars is that it doesn't give offenders the chance to own up to what they did or to give back anything positive to society. With this program, however, he takes pride in knowing that he can make a difference in helping other young men to find the right path. When God feels the time is right and John is set free, he plans on getting actively involved in youth counseling and motivational speaking.

Over the years, Bobby and I have become friends again. We had to let some hurts heal first, since so much happened between us, but I think we both knew we were always meant to be friends. It was our pushing it further and trying to make a marriage work that put too much strain on the relationship. He now comes to our house for visits and is included in family gatherings such as birthdays and holidays. He'll often call to simply tell us he loves us and to check on the girls. We're very close, and I hope we always will be. He is truly a very special man. Although nothing has changed in his own situation and he still grieves for his daughter, I continue to pray that the two of them will be reunited one sweet day.

My parents are both well and continue to offer unconditional love and hugs whenever we need it. They visit often and share in all of our activities, accomplishments, and celebrations. They are close to John and write him often. My mother sends him puzzles from the newspaper and calendars for the new year. She writes him notes of inspiration and reminds him of happy family memories. My dad sends pictures of his oil paintings and uplifting greeting cards along with updates on all that's happening. Since my parents were the only mother and father John really knew in his life, their forgiving hearts mean the world to him.

My sister has been my cheerleader through all of this and always believed in God's plan for us. What she didn't realize was that God also had a plan for her. She is now actively involved in prison ministry and goes into Florida prisons regularly to offer hope and faith to inmates. Just like John, she sees transformations behind those walls that can only be possible with a foundation in Christ and finding purpose in new beginnings. I know with her gift, she will touch many. Her family is very close to our hearts, and they are always there to share with and to offer prayer. They also keep in contact with John by writing letters of support and love.

I am healing and growing day by day, a much different person than I used to be. I can now stand on my own as a single parent and feel a peace in my soul. There are still difficult days when I question if I can do this. The girls may go through hard times, and I use all of my energies to hold them up. Finances may get tight, and I begin to worry if I'll let us all down. I'll sit in the quiet of the house at night and wonder if my husband will ever come home. But then that voice comes to me again, that wonderful whisper of God that tells me I can do all things through him. I'm growing in my faith walk and learning to lay my fears in the Lord's hands, since I know I am not in control. I am still writing full time and hope to use the gift God has given me to continue to call attention to the power of forgiving.

The girls and I are also still involved with Prison Fellowship and Angel Tree. I'd like to become more involved with working with prison families and inspiring them to keep their bond strong despite the walls that separate them. I am proud to have written two children's storybooks that deal with the trauma young children go through when their parent is behind bars. For more information on *It Hurts to Have a Mommy in Prison* and *It Hurts to Have a Daddy in Prison*, please visit my Web site at www.dianenichols.com. These books help young children to realize that their feelings of shame, isolation, and anger are normal, and will show them how to work through those emotions. They also stress the importance of the parental bond being preserved even though a mother or father is doing time. A portion of the proceeds for these books will be donated to Angel Tree.

I pray that through reading *Prison of My Own*, you will take to heart God's message of forgiveness. It is a gift he first gives to us through the death of his Son Jesus. Once we have received it from him, we are then free to give it to others and to ourselves. Granting forgiveness helps us to move past our pain whether or not the person who hurt us remains in our lives. It is my dearest hope that broken hearts and broken families will embrace this message and find a place of healing. Only when we surrender our pain and lift our eyes toward heaven can we be truly free from our personal prisons.

Readers' Guide

For Personal Reflection

or Group Discussion

READERS' GUIDE

This is no ordinary story, just as your story is not ordinary. It's a story of hopes and fears, incredible pain and simple joys. It's also a story that demonstrates how God can work in even the worst situations—and somehow bring good out of them.

Everything doesn't all work out great in the end. Bad choices, addictions, relationships built on wrong foundations—all have consequences. Yet God remains faithful. He sometimes uses pain to draw us to himself, but he always lets us choose whether or not we will trust in him and follow his principles.

As you think about and/or discuss the following questions, be sensitive to aspects of this story that connect with your life and the lives of people you know. Pay attention to its underlying themes, which include dysfunctional relationships, using things and people in order to numb pain, marital communication, the effects of unforgiveness and forgiveness, and the hope God offers.

Some of the following questions relate specifically to the content of this book. Other questions provide you, and others who may be discussing this book with you, opportunities to explore your beliefs and responses to experiences you face. Try to be as open as you can, linking points of this story to your own story and the stories of others.

Perhaps you are wrestling with similar issues raised in this book. If so, remember you are not alone. Seek out people with whom you can discuss your feelings and thoughts. And, in the case of addictions and marital issues, you may benefit from the advice of a trained counselor.

Feel free to adapt these questions to your particular situation. Perhaps you'll think about and/or discuss one or two in great depth and spend less time on others. That's okay. Life is a journey, and where you are right now may determine which questions especially connect with you. Although your experiences may be quite different from those of Diane or other people mentioned in this book, you may be surprised by the points of connection that surface. Pain and uncertainty and issues about God and the meaning of life exist in each of our life stories. Perhaps that's why we can learn much from the journeys of other people and how they escaped prisons of their own.

Chapter One

1. What emotions did Diane feel as she entered the courtroom and began testifying?

2. When did John, Diane's husband, first become deceitful? And how did the deceit escalate?

3. Why did Diane respond the way she did when Karen first told her about the affair?

4. Were you surprised when Karen admitted that John loved Diane, not her? Why or why not?

5. If you were Diane, what might you have done to help your children deal with the unfolding situation?

6. Why, in many cases, is a spouse blindsided by infidelity? Why are "warning signs" so well hidden sometimes?

Chapter Two

1. Why do you think Diane had so much compassion for her ex-husband, despite what he had done?

2. Were you surprised by the prosecutor's questions? Why or why not?

3. How heavily did her daughters factor into Diane's thinking?

4. What "prison" did Diane feel she had been sentenced to face? Why?

5. How was Diane changing inside during the special visit she had with John before he started serving his sentence?

Chapter Three

1. What confusing emotions was Diane feeling when she met Bobby?

2. Why was Halloween a difficult day for Diane?

3. How important was it for Diane to share with the divorce support group what had happened? Why?

4. What are some ways in which people express deep pain? How did Diane's pain manifest itself?

5. Is it true that one person's pain can be much greater than another person's pain? Discuss Bobby's comment: "My problems are nothing compared to the nightmare you and those young ones are living with."

6. To what degree was Bobby in denial, avoiding his sorrow over losing Mandy by acting like a father with Vanessa and Mariah? What are the benefits and drawbacks of this type of response?

7. Why did Diane so long to be attractive to a man? How did John's affair affect her view of herself?

8. Although John didn't use the word *sin* in the letter he sent, he still described its impact. Which words stood out to you? Why?

9. What impact did Diane's anger have on herself? On her daughters? On Bobby?

10. Did Bobby have the right to say, "I'm not going to let anything ever hurt you again"? Why or why not? Is hurt always a bad thing? Explain your answer.

Chapter Four

1. How did Diane handle the good memories of John that kept coming back?

2. What symptoms of depression did Diane have?

3. Why is it important for children like Vanessa to receive professional help after family trauma?

4. What kinds of things should people live for—are solid enough to live for?

5. When someone has deep hurts, what are the benefits of confiding in someone else who hurts? What are the dangers, particularly with someone of the opposite sex?

6. What was Bobby really asking when he said, "Don't you believe in love anymore?"

7. Where might God fit in when we are faced with doing things we think are impossible?

8. What is hope? Where does it come from?

9. Why did the potential of physical closeness with Bobby scare Diane?

10. What does this phrase mean: "being able to share feelings safely"?

11. Is it possible, or even good, for someone like Diane to "forget" the pain a loved one has caused? Explain your answer.

Chapter Five

1. Why is it hard for many people, like Diane, to receive help from other people and agencies?

2. Diane wondered about the stories of other women who stood in the line for food stamps. What happens inside us when we realize we are not the only ones dealing with pain and problems?

3. How can a person know when alcohol use is dangerous?

4. To what degree do you think Bobby was trying to "rescue" Diane?

5. Why was it important for Diane's children to go through the grieving process? For her to go through it?

6. When Diane had sex with Bobby, how did she feel? Why? What do you think were the real reasons she had sex with him?

7. When John mentioned God during his phone call from prison, how did Diane react?

8. What did you notice about John's letter to Diane—what he said about himself, God, and healing?

9. As it turned out, what drew John to Karen in the first place?

10. Why do you think Diane asked John to give her relationship with Bobby his blessing?

Chapter Six

1. In what way(s) had Diane grown stronger, evidenced by her willingness to take her daughters to visit John in prison?

2. What did Diane notice about other women visiting the prison?

3. Why did Vanessa feel guilty about what her father had done?

4. Diane was using beer to ease her emotional pain, to escape a bit of reality. What kinds of things do other people use to fill up the emptiness they feel inside? Which ones are socially acceptable? Which ones are not?

5. Describe some of the feelings Diane faced during the prison visit. Do you think she was surprised at what she felt? Why or why not?

6. How was Bobby feeling during this time? Why?

Chapter Seven

1. Which words in Chaplain Smith's prayer, at the beginning of this chapter, are noteworthy?

2. If you were Diane, how would you have felt when John said, "I just won't give up on us one day being together, no matter what you decide"?

3. Why did visions of John with Karen keep coming up in Diane's mind? How did she handle them?

4. "Something significant had changed," Diane wrote, describing what happened during the prison birthday party. What changed? How did it happen?

5. What kinds of rationalizations did Diane make concerning her relationship with Bobby?

6. Despite the fact that Bobby moved in with her, why do you think Diane was still miserable?

7. As you read John's letter at the end of this chapter, what did you think? Why? In what way(s) is your view of God similar to John's views? Different from John's views?

8. As this chapter ended, what was Diane beginning to understand about John? About herself?

Chapter Eight

1. Why do you think John sent Diane the letter detailing the sex he had had with many other women?

2. According to the letter, what motivated John to do what he did during their thirteen-year marriage? And why did he write this letter?

3. What do you think was the hardest thing Diane had to face after she read the letter? Why?

4. How could Diane's time with John during their marriage have been so great? Why might some people blame Diane for what John did?

5. How can a person know when to keep hanging on to someone like John and when to go on without him?

6. In what circumstances can anger be justified? What's the difference between anger and bitterness?

7. Vanessa asked, "Did he ever love us at all? If he did, he never would have been like that." Do you agree? Why or why not?

Chapter Nine

1. Why did Diane destroy the letters and photos of John? Did her "empowered hatred" accomplish what she thought it would? Why or why not?

2. Do you think Diane was wrong in letting Vanessa communicate with her father the way they did? Why or why not? How might Diane have handled things differently?

3. What do you think motivated Bobby to do what he could to help Diane and the girls?

4. Why did Vanessa become angry at the thought of her mother being with Bobby at the beach?

5. How did drinking make Diane feel?

6. What saddened Diane about Bobby's marriage proposal? What warning signs was she picking up?

7. The counselor said, "You deserve happiness, but only you can make that happen." What did this message communicate? Do you agree with it? Why?

8. On her honeymoon, why did Diane "miss the anger" that had allowed her to function?

Chapter Ten

1. By getting married, Bobby and Diane hoped to "leave old memories behind." To what extent did their strategy work—or not work?

2. Why do you think Diane couldn't forget John, after all he had done to her?

3. To what extent do you think Diane's increased drinking was affecting her judgment? Why can things that "take the edge off" become so destructive?

4. How were the girls dealing with their pain?

5. Diane was so aware of her feelings, yet kept making marginal or even bad decisions. To what extent can we trust our feelings? What can happen when we run our lives by how we feel?

6. Is happiness a choice? Explain your answer.

7. Why do you think Diane prayed? And what happened as a result?

8. What are some of the results of unforgiveness?

Chapter Eleven

1. How did Diane's newfound hope flow out toward others?

2. Bobby stated, "I think God is something people hold on to when they've lost all faith in themselves." What do you think of this comment? Why?

3. How did Diane respond when she sensed Someone speaking absolute truth to her?

4. "Holding on to hatred and anger trapped me in a prison of my own," Diane wrote. What do you think she meant?

5. Why, according to the pastor's wife, does God allow us to suffer?

6. Do you believe God can still work miracles today? Why or why not?

7. John wrote, in a letter to Diane, "to let go and let God." What do you think he meant?

8. What did you learn about Bobby in this chapter? How do you feel about what he was experiencing?

9. Why did Diane have to keep on forgiving when bad things cropped up
    in her mind? What did she mean when she wrote, "I could see what for-
    giving really consisted of: daily choices, daily successes, one baby step
    at a time"?

10. Why was it important for Diane and John to discuss emotions during the
    prison visit rather than trying to ignore them?

11. If you had been Diane and married to Bobby, how would you have
    responded to John during the prison visit? Why?

Chapter Twelve

1. How is Diane changing, as a result of her faith in God?

2. What did Diane discover about sexual addiction?

3. What might Diane and Bobby have done to get more of their issues out on
    the table? To what degree can a person will to love someone even if some
    of the feelings aren't there?

4. Is God indeed molding and shaping us through our circumstances? If
    you feel comfortable doing so, share an illustration from your life.

5. Was it right for Diane to wish that God would restore her marriage with
    John even though she had married Bobby? Did Diane use him? Explain
    your answer.

Chapter Thirteen

1. Were you surprised by Bobby's desire to leave the marriage? Why or
    why not?

2. Which serious issues had Diane and Bobby ignored?

3. What did Diane discover as she began to do more things on her own,
    without Bobby?

4. As more people learned about Diane's story, and the stories of her chil-
    dren, how did they respond? Why? What does it reveal about God's

ability to use even our worst experiences? About how common pain is to our human condition?

5. How, in the right circumstances, can revealing one's secrets lead to healing?

6. In what ways did Diane and the girls benefit from reaching out to other people at Christmastime? Why?

7. How did you feel as you read John's marriage proposal?

Chapter Fourteen

1. Do you believe God can place thoughts in our minds, like the one Diane had in the Goodwill store? Why or why not?

2. Describe your feelings as Michelle gave Diane the wedding dress? What did this circumstance reveal about what God can do for each of us when we trust him?

3. What is your view of God? Which event(s) in your life has had the biggest part in shaping your view of God? How much do you think God cares about your wants and needs?

Chapter Fifteen

1. Diane whispered a simple prayer to God in that old Ohio farmhouse. What might the benefits be to us of praying simple prayers during the day?

2. How was God changing Diane from the inside out?

3. Why did Diane need to forgive Karen, too? What stood out to you as you read her prayer concerning Karen? Have you ever tried to do this with someone who has hurt you deeply?

4. How do you or your loved ones relate to this story? How might God want to use you and what you have experienced to help someone else? Or what might God be trying to communicate to you through this book?

5. How does the hope expressed in this story relate to you? To people you know?

6. What does it mean to "count our blessings each and every day"?

7. Why do many of our personal stories end up with loose ends and unresolved issues? How might some of what Diane learned through her journey apply to our lives? If you feel comfortable doing so, relate your answer to something you are facing in your life.

The Word at Work Around the World

A vital part of Cook Communications Ministries is our international outreach, Cook Communications Ministries International (CCMI). Your purchase of this book, and of other books and Christian-growth products from Cook, enables CCMI to provide Bibles and Christian literature to people in more than 150 languages in 65 countries.

Cook Communications Ministries is a not-for-profit, self-supporting organization. Revenues from sales of our books, Bible curricula, and other church and home products not only fund our U.S. ministry, but also fund our CCMI ministry around the world. One hundred percent of donations to CCMI go to our international literature programs.

CCMI reaches out internationally in three ways:

· Our premier International Christian Publishing Institute (ICPI) trains leaders from nationally led publishing houses around the world.

· We provide literature for pastors, evangelists, and Christian workers in their national language.

· We reach people at risk—refugees, AIDS victims, street children, and famine victims—with God's Word.

Word Power, God's Power

Faith Kidz, RiverOak, Honor, Life Journey, Victor, NexGen — every time you purchase a book produced by Cook Communications Ministries, you not only meet a vital personal need in your life or in the life of someone you love, but you're also a part of ministering to José in Colombia, Humberto in Chile, Gousa in India, or Lidiane in Brazil. You help make it possible for a pastor in China, a child in Peru, or a mother in West Africa to enjoy a life-changing book. And because you helped, children and adults around the world are learning God's Word and walking in his ways.

Thank you for your partnership in helping to disciple the world. May God bless you with the power of his Word in your life.

For more information about our international ministries, visit www.ccmi.org.